Fif

STATISTICS FOR THE TERRIFIED

John H. Kranzler
University of Florida

Prentice Hall
Boston Columbus Indianapolis New York San Francisco Upper Saddle River
Amsterdam Cape Town Dubai London Madrid Milan Munich Paris Montreal Toronto
Delhi Mexico City São Paulo Sydney Hong Kong Seoul Singapore Taipei Tokyo

Executive Editor: Susan Hartman
Associate Editor: LeAnn Doherty
Editorial Assistant: Courtney Elezovic
Marketing Manager: Nicole Kunzmann
Marketing Assistant: Shauna Fishweicher
Production Manager: Meghan DeMaio
Creative Director: Jayne Conte
Cover Designer: Suzanne Behnke
Cover Design: © Arco Images GmbH/Alamy
Full-Service Project Management/Composition Service: Munesh Kumar/Aptara®, Inc.
Printer/Binder/Cover Printer: R.R. Donnelley & Sons

Credits and acknowledgments borrowed from other sources and reproduced, with permission, in this textbook appear on appropriate page within text.

Library of Congress Cataloging-in-Publication Data
Kranzler, John H.
Statistics for the terrified/John H. Kranzler.—5th ed.
p. cm.
ISBN-13: 978-0-205-00406-5
ISBN-10: 0-205-00406-7
1. Statistics. I. Title.
QA276.12.K73 2010
519.5—dc22

2010043336

10 9 8 7 6 5 4 3 2 1

Prentice Hall
is an imprint of

PEARSON

www.pearsonhighered.com

ISBN-10: 0-205-00406-7
ISBN-13: 978-0-205-00406-5

Dedication

To the memory of my father,

Gerald D. Kranzler

CONTENTS

PREFACE

Fear of heights, fear of public speaking, fear of flying—virtually everyone is afraid of something. *Statistics for the Terrified* (5th ed.) is a user-friendly introduction to elementary statistics, intended primarily for the reluctant, math-anxious/avoidant person. Written in a personal and informal style, with healthy doses of humor and encouragement, the aim of this book is to help readers make the leap from apprehension to comprehension of elementary statistics. *Statistics for the Terrified* is intended as a supplemental text for courses in statistics and research methods, as a refresher for students who have already taken a statistics course, or as a primer for new students of elementary statistics. Millions of people have math anxiety, yet this is rarely taken into consideration in textbooks on statistics. This book also presents self-help strategies (based on the cognitive behavioral techniques of rational emotive therapy) that help people manage their math anxiety so they can relax and build confidence while learning statistics. *Statistics for the Terrified* makes statistics accessible to people by first helping them manage their emotions and by presenting them with other essential material for learning statistics before jumping into the subject. After covering the essentials required for the journey into statistics, the remainder of the book presents an introduction to elementary statistics in a personal and informal manner with a great deal of encouragement, support, step-by-step assistance, and with numerous concrete examples, without the need for lengthy theoretical discussions.

ORGANIZATION

This book is divided into five sections. Section I, Essentials for Statistics, consists of three chapters. The first chapter introduces the text and presents effective strategies for studying statistics, the second discusses effective self-help strategies for overcoming math anxiety, and the third reviews basic math concepts. Section II, Describing Univariate Data, contains chapters on frequency distributions, descriptive statistics, the normal curve, and percentiles and standard scores. Section III, Correlation and Regression, consists of chapters on correlation coefficients and linear regression. Section IV, Inferential Statistics, contains three chapters on understanding inferential statistics, the *t* Test, and analysis of variance (ANOVA). Section V, Additional Topics: Nonparametric Statistics and Using Statistical Software, introduces nonparametric statistics and the use of statistical software packages. Everything covered in this book can be done on a computer with statistical software, such as SPSS. Although most people now use computers to analyze their data, everyone still needs to know where the results of their analyses come from and what they mean. This chapter is intended to help bridge the gap between understanding how to use and interpret statistics and how to do so with the assistance of a statistical software program. The final chapter summarizes the text and congratulates the reader on a job well done.

ACKNOWLEDGMENTS

My father, Gerald D. Kranzler, was a professor of counseling psychology at the University of Oregon. His primary scholarly interest was rational emotive therapy, but he also taught an introductory statistics course. He is the principal author of this book. My father passed away in 1994, shortly after publication of the first edition of *Statistics for the Terrified.* Dr. Janet Moursund was his co-author for the first two editions of the book. I have revised a great deal of their book in the last three editions, but I tried to retain their style and approach, which are the heart and soul of the text. I would also like to thank Jeff Ditterline, a doctoral candidate in the School Psychology Program, for his careful review of the text. Any errors or omissions are mine, of course.

I would also like to thank the following reviewers for their many helpful comments for improvements to the book: Ashton Trice, Mary Siegrist, Mrinhal Sinha, and Don Hantula.

I also need to acknowledge the following Web sites, from which I borrowed many of the math and statistics cartoons, jokes, and quotes contained in this edition:

www.sciencecartoonsplus.com

www.csun.edu   www.borg.com

http://www.xs4all.nl/~jcdverha/scijokes/1_2.html

Take a look at these Web sites. I was surprised to find so many very funny things on math, science, and statistics.

Last, I would like to thank my wife, Theresa, and sons, Zach and Justin, for their understanding and patience while I worked on this book. You make every day a joy.

John H. Kranzler

SECTION I

Essentials for Statistics

If you are one of the "terrified" for whom this book is intended, the chapters in this section may be particularly helpful. Chapter 1 provides an introduction to the text. Because the nature and content of statistics courses typically differ from that of courses in many fields of study, this chapter offers study tips for students of statistics. Chapter 2 presents some general strategies and techniques for dealing with the uncomfortable feelings that many students experience when taking a course in statistics. One common problem students experience in statistics courses is not being able to demonstrate on tests what they have learned because of anxiety. If you think you might be one of these people, this chapter may help. Chapter 3 reviews basic math concepts that you may have known at one time but which have gotten rusty through disuse, or you have just plain forgotten. You need to know these concepts to learn statistics. Just as when building a house, you must have a firm foundation on which to construct statistical knowledge. Also presented in this chapter are sample problems that will allow you to practice and test your ability to use these basic math concepts.

The chapters in Section I are intended to help you get off to a running start and may well be worth your time and energy. Of course, if you are already comfortable with numbers and know all the basics, you may not get much out of these chapters. Nonetheless, "Heck, I already know all this stuff," is a great way to begin reading a book on statistics. Especially if you think it might be terrifying!

CHAPTER

1 Effective Strategies for Studying Statistics

- **Effective Strategies for Studying Statistics**

"You haven't told me yet," said Lady Nuttal, "what it is your fiancé does for a living."

"He's a statistician," replied Lamia, with an annoying sense of being on the defensive.

Lady Nuttal was obviously taken aback. It had not occurred to her that statisticians entered into normal social relationships. The species, she would have surmised, was perpetuated in some collateral manner, like mules.

"But Aunt Sara, it's a very interesting profession," said Lamia warmly. "I don't doubt it," said her aunt, who obviously doubted it very much. "To express anything important in mere figures is so plainly impossible that there must be endless scope for well-paid advice on how to do it. But don't you think that life with a statistician would be rather, shall we say, humdrum?"

Lamia was silent. She felt reluctant to discuss the surprising depth of emotional possibility which she had discovered below Edward's numerical veneer.

"It's not the figures themselves," she said finally, "it's what you do with them that matters."

—K. A. C. MANDERVILLE, *THE UNDOING OF LAMIA GURDLENECK*

Another statistics book! There are now so many statistics books on the market that it seems strange even to me that there be another one. As someone who has taken statistics courses, worked as a teaching assistant in statistics courses, and taught statistics courses, I have been dissatisfied with the available books, because they seem aimed at students who whizzed right through college algebra and considered majoring in math just for the sheer joy of it. A number of my students in social science programs are not like that. Many of them would respond with a hearty "true" to many of the following self-test statements. I invite you to test yourself, to see if you, too, fit the pattern.

1. I have never been very good at math.
2. When my teacher tried to teach me long division in the fourth grade, I seriously considered dropping out of school.
3. When we got to extracting square roots, thoughts of suicide flashed through my mind.
4. Word problems! My head felt like a solid block of wood when I was asked to solve problems such as, "If it takes Mr. Jones 3 hours to mow a lawn and Mr. Smith 2 hours to mow the same lawn, how long will it take if they mow it together?"
5. Although I never dropped out of school, I became a quantitative dropout soon after my first algebra course.
6. I avoided courses such as chemistry and physics because they required math.
7. I decided early on that there were some careers I could not pursue because I was poor in math.
8. When I take a test that includes math problems, I get so upset that my mind goes blank and I forget all the material I studied.
9. Sometimes I wonder if I am a little stupid.
10. I feel nervous just thinking about taking a statistics course.

Did you answer "true" to some of these items? If so, this book may be helpful to you. When writing it, I also made some assumptions about you:

1. You are studying statistics only because it is a requirement in your major area of study.
2. You are terrified (or at least somewhat anxious) about math and are not sure that you can pass a course in statistics.
3. It has been a long time since you studied math, and what little you knew then has been long forgotten.
4. With a little instruction, and a lot of hard work, you can learn statistics. If you can stay calm while baking a cake or reading your bank statement, there is hope for you.
5. You may never learn to love statistics, but you can change your statistics self-concept. When you finish your statistics course you will be able to say, truthfully, "I am the kind of person who can learn statistics!"

The aim of this book is to help you achieve two important objectives. The first is to deal with math anxiety and avoidance responses that interfere with learning statistics. The second is to understand and compute the most widely used elemental statistics.

EFFECTIVE STRATEGIES FOR STUDYING STATISTICS

The following is some advice on studying statistics that you will find useful as we move toward these two objectives.

Buy a Calculator

Because statistics require you to work with numbers, you should consider buying a calculator. Make sure that it has at least one memory and that it can take square roots (almost all calculators can do this). Before you buy a calculator, though, check out your personal computer or mobile phone—virtually all desktop and laptop computers, and many mobile phones, come with a calculator program that will easily handle the problems in this book. If you don't need your calculator during exams, that may be all you need. In any case, read the manual that comes with your calculator and learn how to use your calculator effectively and efficiently.

Develop a Solid Math Foundation

Most statistics courses are cumulative. New concepts are constantly added to and built upon previous concepts. Most statistics courses begin with relatively straightforward and concrete concepts and quickly become more complex and abstract. It's important to master the basic math concepts used in the computation of all statistics, because that will make success later in the course more likely. Nothing is more frustrating than understanding the statistics concept and what to do to solve a problem but not getting the right answer because of a silly computation error.

Form a Study Group

Study groups can be extremely helpful while preparing for exams, completing homework, taking notes, sharing learning strategies, and providing emotional support. The optimum size for study groups is three people. Effective groups tend to have no more than five members, however. Exchange telephone numbers and times when you can be reached. Meet regularly in a distraction-free environment. Talk about what you are studying and offer to help others (you may learn best by teaching others). When you are stuck with a problem that you can't solve, don't hesitate to ask others for their help. Very likely they will have some of the same feelings and difficulties you do. Not everyone gets stuck on the same topics, so you can help each other.

Keep Up

If you are in a statistics class, go to class every day and take complete notes. Complete all the assigned reading and homework as soon as possible and before new material is covered. This ensures that new concepts are fresh in your mind and linked to previously learned material. Students who are "terrified" of statistics are susceptible to falling behind, often because of their general dislike of the content. Playing catch-up in a statistics class is very difficult. Don't let this happen to you. The material in the next chapter on overcoming math anxiety might be helpful if you are one of these people.

http://www.glenbaxter.com/

Time Management

A widely used rule of thumb for the amount of time to spend studying for a college course is 2 hours of study time per credit hour per week. For a 3-credit class, you should plan to spend 6 hours studying outside class each week. Is this enough time for a statistics class for you? Maybe. Maybe not. For many of my students, statistics is the hardest class they will take. You should take as much time as you need to do all the assigned homework and reading and to understand the material. Regardless of the amount of time you need to learn statistics, spread the amount of time you spend studying over a number of days rather than on one or two days per week. For example, if you plan to devote 10 hours per week to the study of statistics, spend 2 hours studying at the same time for five days each week. Don't cram 10 hours of study time into one or two days each week!

Study Actively

Be actively involved in the learning process. Take responsibility for understanding the material. Recognize when you don't understand something and get help. Be an active participant in class. But if you're not comfortable asking or answering questions in class when you have difficulty grasping a new statistical concept, seek out assistance from your instructor during his or her office hours, from fellow students in your study group, or from support services or materials (e.g., resource center, peer tutors, and professional tutors). This book may be a good place to start, but find help elsewhere if you need it.

Practice, Practice, Practice

Statistics is learned best by doing, not by reading a textbook. Don't waste your time memorizing formulas! Focus instead on the concepts underlying the use and interpretation of statistics. Do the assigned homework and as many other problems and exercises as possible. In the beginning, statistics problems will be straightforward and involve only one step. Increasingly, you will be presented with problems that require you to take several steps to solve them and to make important choices at each step. Keep in mind that these problems can be broken down into a series of small steps, each of which can be solved individually before moving on to the next. Divide and conquer!

Show Your Work

When working statistics problems, resist the temptation to skip steps when solving a problem. Showing your work helps you locate logical or calculation mistakes. Sometimes partial credit is given on homework and exams for the correct portions of an answer, because it shows the instructor what you do know. Write out all numbers and variables clearly so they can be easily distinguished. Using lined or graph paper helps to organize problems on your page. If your answer is not correct, rework the problem; don't just work it out in your head and convince yourself that you could get the right answer.

CHAPTER

2 Overcoming Math Anxiety

• **How to Deal with Math Anxiety**

A statistics major was completely hung over the day of his final exam. It was a true/false test, so he decided to flip a coin for the answers. The statistics professor watched the student the entire 2 hours as he was flipping the coin . . . writing the answer . . . flipping the coin . . . writing the answer. At the end of the 2 hours, everyone else had left the final except for the one student. The professor walked up to his desk and interrupted the student, saying, "Listen, I have seen that you did not study for this statistics test, you didn't even open the exam. If you are just flipping a coin for your answer, what is taking you so long?" The student replied bitterly (as he was still flipping the coin), "Shhh! I'm checking my answers!"

If you are what might be termed a "math-anxious" or "math-avoidant" person, this chapter may be helpful to you. Most of the material in this chapter is drawn from the theory and practice of rational-emotive therapy (RET), originally developed by psychologist Albert Ellis. RET has been shown through research to be quite effective in helping people overcome problems like yours. Unfortunately, in a book devoted to statistics, I can only introduce you to some of the basic ideas and techniques. If you are interested, you can enrich your understanding by reading books such as Ellis and Harper's

A Guide to Rational Living or G. D. Kranzler's *You Can Change How You Feel.* (Notice the sneaky way of getting in a plug for my dad's book?)

Fear of math, or math anxiety, is what is called a *debilitative emotion.* Debilitative emotions such as math anxiety are problem emotions because (a) they are extremely unpleasant, and (b) they tend to lead to self-defeating behavior, such as "freezing" on a test or avoiding courses or occupations that you otherwise would enjoy.

What you do about your math anxiety (or any other problem) will depend on your theory of what is causing the problem. For example, some people believe that the cause is hereditary: "I get my fear of math from mother, who always had the same problem." Others believe that the cause lies in the environment: "Women are taught from a very young age that they are not supposed to be good in math, to avoid it, and to be afraid of it." The implication of these theories is that if the cause is hereditary, you can't do much about the problem (you can't change your genetic structure), or if the cause is the culture in which you live, by the time you can change what society does to its young, it will still be too late to help you. Although there may be some truth in both the hereditarian and environmental theories, I believe that they can, at most, set only general limits to your performance. Within these limits, your performance can fluctuate considerably. Though you have very little power to change society and no ability to change the genes you inherited, you still have enormous power to change yourself if you choose to do so, if you know how to bring about that change, and if you work hard at it.

Let's begin with the ABCs. *A* stands for Activating event or experience, such as taking a difficult math test; *C* stands for the emotional Consequence, such as extreme nervousness. Most people seem to believe that *A* causes *C*. In fact, this theory seems to be built right into our language. Consider the following examples:

Activating Event	Cause	Emotional Consequence
Something happens. . .	*that causes me. . .*	*to feel. . .*
"When you talk about math. . .	that causes me. . .	to feel. . ."
"This test. . .	makes me. . .	nervous."

The implications of this *A*-causes-*C* theory are (a) you can't help how you feel, and (b) the way to deal with the problem is to avoid or escape from activating events such as math tests.

But is the *A*-causes-*C* theory true? Respond to the following items by indicating how you would feel if you were to experience the event. Use a scale that ranges from −5, indicating very unpleasant emotions (such as rage, depression, or extreme anxiety), to +5, to indicate an emotion that is extremely positive (such as elation or ecstasy); or use a 0 if you would experience neutral, neither positive nor negative, feelings:

1. Handling snakes
2. Giving a speech in front of one of your classes
3. Seeing your eight-year-old son playing with dolls
4. The death of a loved one in an automobile accident

I have administered items like this to hundreds of people and have found that for items 1–3 the responses have ranged all the way from −5 to +5. On the item concerning the death of a loved one, most people respond with a −5, but when questioned, they have heard of cultures where even death is considered to be a positive event (in the United States everyone wants to go to heaven but nobody wants to die). Why is it that, given the same Activating event, people's emotional Consequences vary so much?

Differing responses like this suggest that maybe $A \rightarrow C$ isn't the whole story. There must be something else, something that accounts for the different ways people respond to the same stimulus. I believe that it is not *A*, the Activating event, that causes *C*, the emotional Consequence. Rather, it is *B*, your Belief about *A*, that causes you to feel as you do at point *C*. Take the example of observing your eight-year-old son playing with dolls. What does a person who experiences feelings of joy believe about what he or she sees? Perhaps something like, "Isn't that wonderful! He's learning nurturing attitudes and tenderness. I really like that!" But the person who experiences very negative feelings probably is thinking, "Isn't that awful! If he keeps that up, he'll surely turn into an effeminate man, or even be gay, and that really would be terrible!"

Ellis has identified some specific beliefs that most of us have learned and that cause us a great deal of difficulty. He calls these beliefs "irrational beliefs." A number of these beliefs have particular relevance to the phenomenon of math anxiety:

- I must be competent and adequate in all possible respects if I am to consider myself to be a worthwhile person. (If I'm not good at math, I'm not a very smart person.)
- It's catastrophic when things are not the way I'd like them to be. (It's terrible and awful to have trouble with statistics.)
- When something seems dangerous or about to go wrong, I must constantly worry about it. (I can't control my worrying and fretting about statistics.)
- My unhappiness is externally caused. I can't help feeling and acting as I do, and I can't change my feelings or actions. (Having to do math simply makes me feel awful; that's just what it does to me.)
- Given my childhood experiences and the past I have had, I can't help being as I am today, and I'll remain this way indefinitely. (I'll never change; that's just how I am.)
- I can't settle for less than the right or perfect solution to my problems. (Since I can't be a math whiz, there's no sense in trying to do math at all.)
- It is better for me to avoid life's frustrations and difficulties than to deal with them. (Since math always makes me feel bad, the only sensible thing to do is to avoid math.)

Do any of these sound familiar? If they do, chances are good that you not only learned to believe them a long time ago but also that you keep the belief going by means of self-talk. The first step in changing is to increase your awareness of the kind of self-talk that you do. When you think, you think with words, sentences, and images. If you pay attention to these cognitive events, you may notice one or more of the following types of self-talk, which may indicate your underlying irrational beliefs.

Math phobic's nightmare

Catastrophizing

This type of self-talk is characterized by the use of terms or phrases such as "It's awful!" "It's terrible!" or "I can't stand it!" Now, there are some events that most of us would agree are extremely bad, such as bombing innocent people and earthquakes that kill thousands. Chances are good that you will never be the victim of such an event. But your mind is powerful: If you believe that your misfortunes are catastrophes, then you will feel accordingly. Telling yourself how catastrophic it is to do badly on a statistics test will almost guarantee that you will feel awful about it. And that emotional response, in turn, can affect how you deal with the situation. It is appropriate to be concerned about doing well on a test, because concern motivates you to prepare and to do your best. But when you are overconcerned, you can make yourself so nervous that your performance goes down instead of up.

Do you see how all this relates to the first irrational belief on our list? Performing poorly on a statitics test would be awful, because you believe that you must be competent in all possible respects. If you were to fail at something important to you, that would make you a failure: someone who couldn't respect himself or herself. One of the oddest things about irrational beliefs such as this is the uneven way we apply them. Your friend could bomb a test, and you'd still think of him or her as a worthwhile person. But do badly yourself, and the sky falls in!

When you indoctrinate yourself with catastrophic ideas, when you tell yourself over and over again how horrible it would be if you were to perform poorly, then you defeat yourself, because you become so anxious that you help bring about the very thing you're afraid of, or you avoid the experience that could benefit you.

Overgeneralizing Self-Talk

When you overgeneralize, you take a bit of evidence and draw conclusions that go beyond the data. If you experienced difficulty with math as a child, you may have concluded, "I'll never be good at math" or "I'm stupid in math." If you failed a math course, then you tended to think of yourself as a failure who will never be able to succeed, and trying harder would be completely useless.

Rationally, though, failing once doesn't make you a "failure." Because you had difficulty in the past doesn't mean that you will never succeed. If it did, nobody would ever learn to walk!

The most pernicious form of overgeneralizing is self-evaluation. We have a tendency to tie up our feelings of self-worth with our performance. When we do well at something, we say, "Hey! I'm a pretty good [or competent or worthwhile] person!" But when we perform poorly, we tend to believe that we are now worthless as a person. This process begins in childhood. When Johnny does something we consider bad, we tend to encourage overgeneralization by saying, "Johnny, you are a bad boy" (i.e., you are worthless as a person).

If you were a worthless or stupid person, you wouldn't have gotten far enough in your education to be reading this book. True, in the past, you may have had difficulty in math, and math may be difficult for you now. But how does that prove you can't learn it? There is absolutely no evidence that your situation is hopeless or that it is useless to try. The only way to make it hopeless is to tell yourself, over and over, how hopeless it is.

Demanding Self-Talk

This type of self-talk includes the use of words such as *should, must,* and *need.* If you are math-anxious, chances are that you use these words to beat up on yourself. You make a mistake and say, "I shouldn't have made that mistake! How could I have been so stupid?" I have a tennis partner who informed me that she finds it difficult to concentrate on her work for the rest of the day after she has played poorly. She believes that she should have done better. Instead of being calmly regretful for having made some errors and thinking about how to do better next time, she bashes herself over the head psychologically for not doing perfectly well, every time.

"But," you may say, "I need to be successful" or "I have to pass this course." Have to? The first time? Or you can't survive? It would be nice to be successful given the advantages it would bring you, but lots of people do manage to function in life even after doing badly in a statistics course. To the degree that you believe you need a certain level of performance, to that degree you will experience anxiety about possible failure and thereby increase the chance of failure.

HOW TO DEAL WITH MATH ANXIETY

What can you do about a way of thinking that seems so automatic, so ingrained? Here is a series of steps that will probably help. I suggest that you try them out, in order, even though you may not expect them to work for you. You might just be surprised!

Step 1. Record Your Feelings (*C*)

When you notice that you are feeling anxious, guilty, angry, or depressed about some aspect of your statistics course, record your emotional experience. Describe your feelings as accurately as you can. You might write things such as, "I feel guilty about not having taken more math as an underclassman," or "I feel really nervous about the test we're having next week," or "I'm too shy to ask questions in class," or "I just get furious that they make us take statistics when I'll never have to use it." Write down all the unpleasant feelings you have at the time. When you have done this, you will have described *C*, the emotional Consequence part of the ABC paradigm.

Step 2. Describe the Activating Event or Experience (*A*)

Briefly write down what it was that seemed to trigger your feelings. Here are some common Activating events for math anxiety. When you write your own, record the thing that is most likely to have happened. Find the immediate trigger, the thing that happened just before your experiencing of the negative emotion. Here are some examples:

- I was assigned some difficult statistics problems, and I don't know how to do them.
- I thought about a test coming up, one that I will almost surely fail.
- I discovered that I need more information about some of the material, but I'm afraid to ask about it in class because I'll look stupid.

Step 3. Identify Your Irrational Beliefs (*B*)

As accurately as you can, record what you were saying to yourself before and during the time when you experienced the emotions you recorded in Step 1. The first few times you do this, you may have difficulty, because you don't usually pay much attention to the thoughts that seem to race through your head. Although it is difficult to become aware of your thoughts, it is not impossible. One technique you can use is to ask yourself, "What must I have been saying to myself about *A* (the Activating event) at point *B* in order to experience *C* (the emotional Consequence)?" Suppose your first three steps looked like this:

1. (Describing *C*, the emotional Consequence) I feel really nervous and miserable.
2. (The Activating event, *A*) My adviser told me I need to take a statistics class.
3. Identify *B*, the Belief that leads from *A* to *C*. Obviously, you're not saying, "Wow, I'm really going to enjoy that class!" You must have been saying something like:
   "If I fail, that'll be awful!"
   "I'll be a real loser!"
   "I'll never be any good at statistics!"

"I'm going to have a terrible term and hate every minute of it."
"What will the other students and the professor think of me when I do badly?"

Step 4. Challenge Each of the Beliefs You Have Identified

After you have written down your self-talk in Step 3, look at each statement and dispute them one by one. One question you can ask to test the rationality of any belief is, "Where's the evidence for this belief?" Let's look at each of the examples listed in Step 3 above:

1. Where's the evidence that it will be awful if I fail? True, failure would be unfortunate, but would it be catastrophic? I'd do better to remember that if I'm overconcerned with doing well, I will be even more likely to fail.

2. Where's the evidence that if I fail the test, I, as a person, will be a failure? The worst I can possibly be is an FHB (fallible human being) along with the rest of the human race.

3. Where's the evidence that I'll never be good in statistics? I may have some evidence that similar material was difficult for me in the past, but how can that prove anything about the future?

4. Where's the evidence that I will hate every single minute of the term? This statement has several irrational beliefs to be challenged: (a) that I'll hate the course (I might have a great teacher, with a wonderful sense of humor, and actually enjoy it), (b) that the discomfort will generalize to the entire term (I might dislike my statistics class but very much enjoy my other courses), and (c) that I will spend every single minute of the term feeling hateful (no help needed to challenge this one, right?).

5. This statement appears to be a rhetorical question. Chances are I'm not really wondering what others will think of me if I fail but rather telling myself all the bad things they'll think and how awful that will be. Both parts of this can be challenged: Where's the evidence that they'll think bad things about me and, even if they do, would that be catastrophic?

Step 5. Once You Have Identified and Challenged an Irrational Belief, the Next Step Is to Replace It with a Rational One

Ask yourself what you would rather believe—what your best friend might believe—what Harrison Ford or Albert Einstein or Desmond Tutu probably would believe. Then, every time you find yourself moving into that old irrational self-talk, answer it with the new alternative belief.

Step 6. Do Rational-Emotive Imagery

After you have practiced replacing your irrational beliefs a few times, you may feel better. Some people, however, report that they now understand that their beliefs cause their unpleasant emotions, and they realize that those beliefs are irrational, but they still feel much the same way as before. If this is true of you, you may benefit from doing some imagery. I will discuss both mastery and coping imagery techniques, because some of my students have reported that one approach is more effective for them than the other. Before attempting either kind of imagery, however, do spend several days practicing Steps 1–5.

MASTERY IMAGERY. In the mastery imagery approach, you are to imagine yourself mastering the situation—that is, feeling and acting in an appropriate way in the presence of the Activating event. If you are anxious about a statistics test, imagine feeling calm or at most only slightly concerned while taking the test, answering the questions as well as you can, calmly leaving the exam, and being able to look back on the experience with some satisfaction. Imagine speaking rationally to yourself during the whole experience (taken from your material in Step 5). Make the image (the daydream, if you want to call it that) as vivid and real as possible. If you feel very upset during the experience, terminate the imagery; go back and reread Step 4 and attempt the imagery again the next day. For any kind of positive imagery to be effective, you will need to work at it for at least a half hour per day for a week; don't expect immediate results.

COPING IMAGERY. Again, imagine yourself in the experience that you're having problems with—for example, taking a statistics test. This time include having difficulty and starting to experience anxiety. Then imagine dealing with the anxiety by saying to yourself, "Stop! Relax!" Try to force yourself to feel more calm. Breathe deeply a few times, remind yourself of rational self-talk, and try to change the extremely anxious feelings to ones that are more calm. Imagine coping with the problem. Again, you won't experience immediate success; it usually takes at least a week of imagery work before you begin to get results.

Step 7. Do Activity Homework

You can only live in your imagination so long if you want to attain objectives in the real world. Sooner or later you need to take a deep breath and *do something.* If you experience math anxiety, one such "something" might be to work your way through this book. As you begin to make these sort of conscious, real-world changes, be aware of your self-talk. When you notice yourself feeling anxious or emotionally upset, dispute your irrational beliefs as actively as you can. If things don't get better immediately, don't give up—keep using these techniques for at least a couple of weeks. Remember, the odds are in your favor!

CHAPTER

3 Basic Math Review

Three men are in a hot-air balloon. Soon, they find themselves lost in a canyon somewhere. One of the three men says, "I've got an idea. We can call for help in this canyon and the echo will carry our voices far." So he leans over the basket and yells out, "Hellllooooo! Where are we?" (They hear the echo several times.) Fifteen minutes later, they hear this echoing voice: "Hellllooooo! You're lost!!" One of the men says, "That must have been a statistician." Puzzled, one of the other men asks, "Why do you say that?" The reply: "For three reasons: (1) he took a long time to answer, (2) he was absolutely correct, and (3) his answer was absolutely useless."

Being terrified of math didn't just happen to you overnight. Chances are that you have been having bad experiences with math for many years. Most people who have these sorts of bad experiences have not mastered some of the basic rules for working with numbers. Because they don't know the rules, the problems don't make sense. It's sort of like trying to play chess without knowing how the pieces can be moved or what checkmate means. When the problems don't make sense, but everyone else seems to understand them, we are likely to decide that there's something wrong with us. We'll just never be able to do it and, besides, we hate math anyhow. So we tune out, turn off—and a bad situation gets worse. Given that most statistics courses are cumulative, with new concepts constantly being added to previously learned concepts, an introductory statistics course can quickly become complex and abstract. It's important to master the basic math concepts used in virtually all statistics, because that will make understanding the results of statistical analyses much easier.

This chapter is designed to help you get past that kind of thinking. The chapter you're starting now will give you a chance to review the rules that you need in order to play with numbers and come up with the same answers as everyone else. Some of the material will be very familiar to you; other parts may seem completely new. Let me make a few suggestions about how to use this chapter:

1. If, after a couple of pages or so, you're completely bored and have found nothing you don't already know, just skim through the rest of the chapter and get on with Section II.
2. If the materal seems familiar, but you still feel a little shaky, go to the sample exercises at the end of each section and work them through. That will tell you which parts you need to spend more time on.
3. If a *lot* of it feels new to you, take your time with it! Most of us "word people" absorb numerical information and ideas quite slowly and need lots of practice before it really sinks in and becomes part of our way of thinking. Give it a chance. Learning the rules now will allow you to understand the rest of the book in a way that will probably surprise you.

Learning to read statistics material is somewhat analogous to learning to read music or a foreign language: impossible at first, difficult for a while, but relatively easy after some effort. One thing to remember, though: Since symbols are a way of condensing information, a paragraph that is full of mathematical symbols has much more information in it than an ordinary paragraph in a history book or a newspaper article. Don't be surprised if it takes you three or four times longer to get through a page in a statistics book (even this one!) than to get through a page in a nonnumerical book. In fact, one of the challenges for the beginning statistics student is learning to slow down. Force yourself to adjust your reading speed to the density of the information on the page, and you'll find that things get much easier.

I've divided the basic math rules into six sections: (1) positive and negative numbers, (2) fractions and percents, (3) roots and exponents, (4) order of computation, (5) summation, and (6) equations. Each section presents a number of important rules that should be followed when using statistics. At the end of each section are sample problems that you can do for practice or to make sure you understand the material. Answers to the sample problems can be found at the end of the chapter.

POSITIVE AND NEGATIVE NUMBERS

In a perfect and orderly world, all numbers would be positive (they'd be whole, too—no fractions or decimals). But the world isn't perfect, and negative numbers have to be dealt with. Actually, they're not so bad; you just have to show them who's boss. If you're a visually oriented person, it may help to think of numbers as standing for locations on a straight line, with zero as your starting point. The number 2 is 2 steps to the right from zero; add 4 more steps and you're 6 steps out, and so on. The negative numbers are just steps in the opposite direction. If I'm 6 positive steps (6 to the right) away from zero, and I add 4 to that, I take 4 steps back toward zero; now I'm at 2. If you're not visually oriented, the last paragraph may confuse you; if so, just ignore it and follow the rules I'm about to give you.

Rule 1. If a number or an expression is written without a sign, it's positive.

$$+2 = 2 \qquad +x = x$$

Rule 2. When adding numbers of the same sign, add them up and prefix them with the same sign as the individual numbers had.

$$+3 + (+5) = +8 \qquad 2 + 7 = 9$$

Rule 3. When summing up a group of numbers with mixed signs, think of the process as having three steps:

1. Add the positive numbers; add the negative numbers as if they were positive.
2. Subtract the smaller sum from the larger sum.
3. Prefix your answer with the sign of the larger sum.

$$5 - 3 + 2 - 1 \rightarrow (5 + 2) \text{ and } (3 + 1) = (7) \text{ and } (4)$$
$$7 \text{ (larger)} - 4 \text{ (smaller)} = 3$$

The answer is +3 because the positive sum (7) was larger than the negative sum. Here's another example:

$$-2 + 6 - 14 + 3 - 4 \rightarrow (6 + 3) \text{ and } (2 + 14 + 4) = (9) \text{ and } (20)$$
$$20 \text{ (larger)} - 9 \text{ (smaller)} = 11$$

The answer is −11 because the negative sum (20) was larger than the positive sum.

Rule 4. Subtracting a positive number is the same as adding a negative number; adding a negative number is the same as subtracting a positive number. Subtracting a negative is the same as adding a positive. In other words, two negative signs make a positive sign; a positive and a negative make a negative (you visually oriented thinkers, work it out on the number line).

$$5 - (+3) = 5 + (-3) = 5 - 3 = 2$$
$$7 + (-12) = 7 - (+12) = 7 - 12 = -5$$
$$5 - (-4) = 5 + 4 = 9$$

Rule 5. When multiplying or dividing two numbers with the same sign, the answer is always positive.

$$3 \times 7 = 21 \qquad -8 \cdot -3 = 24 \qquad 12(8) = 96$$

Notice the three different ways of indicating multiplication: an × sign, a "center dot" (•) between the numbers, or no sign at all. Parentheses around an expression just means to treat what's inside as a single number; we'll talk more about that a little later.

$$15 \div 5 = 3 \qquad (-9) \div (-1) = 9 \qquad \frac{-6}{-4} = 1.5$$

Notice the two different ways of indicating division: an ÷ sign or a line in between two numbers.

Rule 6. When multiplying or dividing two numbers with different signs, the answer is always *negative.*

$$3 \times -7 = -21 \qquad -8 \cdot 3 = -24 \qquad (12)(-8) = -96$$

$$-15 \div 5 = -3 \qquad (9) \div (-1) = -9 \qquad \frac{-6}{4} = -1.5$$

Rules 5 and 6 aren't as "sensible" as some of the other rules, and the number line won't help you much with them. Just memorize.

Rule 7. With more than two numbers to be multiplied or divided, take them pairwise, in order, and follow Rules 5 and 6. (The rule for multiplication and division is that if there is an odd number of negative numbers, the answer will be negative; with an even number of negatives, the answer will be positive. If this helps, use it. If not, forget it.)

$$3 \times -2 \times -4 \times 3 = -6 \times -4 \times 3 = 24 \times 3 = 72$$

$$40 \div 2 \div 2 \div -2 = 20 \div 2 \div -2 = 10 \div -2 = -5$$

$$6 \div 3 \times -1 \div 5 = 2 \times -1 \div 5 = -2 \div 5 = -.4$$

PROBLEMS

1. $-5 + 4 = ?$

2. $6 - (-2) = ?$

3. $-6 - 4 + 2 = ?$

4. $3(-4) = ?$

5. $3 \cdot 4 = ?$

6. $(-3)(-4) = ?$

7. $(-3)(+4) = ?$

8. $(-4)(1)(2)(-3) = ?$

9. $(-a)(-b)(c)(-d) = ?$

10. $-4 \div -3 = ?$

11. $(10)(3) \div 2 = ?$

12. $(-1)(-1)(-1)(-1) \div (-1) = ?$

FRACTIONS

Rule 1. A fraction is another way of symbolizing division. A fraction means "divide the first (top) expression (the numerator) by the second (bottom) expression (the

SidneyHarris/www.sciencecartoonsplus.com

denominator)." Fractions answer the question, "If I cut the top number up into the bottom number of equal pieces, how much will be in each piece?"

$$1 \div 2 = .5 \qquad 4 \div 2 = 2 \qquad 4 \div -2 = -2$$

$$\frac{-9}{3} = -3 \qquad \frac{6}{4 - 1} = 2 \qquad \frac{(13 - 3)(7 + 3)}{-3 + 2} = \frac{(10)(10)}{-1} = -100$$

Rule 2. Dividing any number by 0 is impossible. If any problem in this book seems to be asking you to divide by 0, you've made an arithmetic mistake somewhere.

Rule 3. You can turn any expression into a fraction by making the original expression the numerator and putting a 1 into the denominator.

$$3 = \frac{3}{1} \qquad -6.2 = \frac{-6.2}{1} \qquad 3x + 4 = \frac{3x + 4}{1}$$

Rule 4. To multiply fractions, multiply their numerators together and multiply their denominators together.

$$\frac{2}{3} \cdot \frac{1}{2} = \frac{2}{6} = .33 \qquad \frac{1}{5} \cdot 10 = \frac{1}{5} \cdot \frac{10}{1} = \frac{10}{5} = 2 \qquad 3xy \cdot \frac{3}{4} = \frac{3xy}{1} \cdot \frac{3}{4} = \frac{3(3xy)}{4} = \frac{9xy}{4}$$

Rule 5. Multiplying both the numerator and the denominator of a fraction by the same number doesn't change its value.

$$\frac{1}{2} = \frac{2 \cdot 1}{2 \cdot 2} = \frac{2}{4} = \frac{100}{200} = \frac{\left(\frac{1}{200}\right) \cdot 100}{\left(\frac{1}{200}\right) \cdot 200} = \frac{.5}{1} = .5$$

Rule 6. To divide by a fraction, invert and multiply. That is, take the fraction you're dividing by (the divisor), switch the denominator and numerator, and then multiply it by the thing into which you're dividing (the dividend).

$$21 \div \frac{3}{5} = \frac{21}{1} \div \frac{3}{5} = \frac{21}{1} \cdot \frac{5}{3} = \frac{105}{3} = 35$$

(I cheated a little in that last example and used some algebra. If you don't understand it yet, come back to it after you've read the "Equations" section of this chapter.)

Rule 7. To add or subtract fractions, they must have a common denominator—that is, their denominators must be the same. For example, you can't add 2/3 and 1/5 as they are. You have to change them to equivalent fractions with a common denominator. How? By multiplying the denominators (and, of course, the numerators) by a number that will make the denominators equal. Of course, you don't have to use the same number for each fraction. Multiply each fraction by the smallest numbers that will make the denominators equal. You may have heard of the "least common denominator": That's what you're looking for. For example, 2/3 = 10/15 and 1/5 = 3/15. Then add or subtract the numerators, leaving the denominator unchanged.

$$\frac{2}{3} + \frac{1}{2} = \frac{2 \cdot 2}{2 \cdot 3} + \frac{3 \cdot 1}{3 \cdot 2} = \frac{4}{6} + \frac{3}{6} = \frac{7}{6} = 1\frac{1}{6}$$

$$\frac{1}{5} + \frac{1}{10} = \frac{2 \cdot 1}{2 \cdot 5} + \frac{1 \cdot 1}{1 \cdot 10} = \frac{2}{10} + \frac{1}{10} = \frac{3}{10}$$

$$\frac{5}{8} - \frac{1}{2} = \frac{1 \cdot 5}{1 \cdot 8} + \frac{4 \cdot 1}{4 \cdot 2} = \frac{5}{8} - \frac{4}{8} = \frac{1}{8}$$

$$\frac{1}{3} + \frac{1}{2} + \frac{3}{4} - \frac{1}{12} = \frac{4}{12} + \frac{6}{12} + \frac{9}{12} - \frac{1}{12} = \frac{18}{12} = 1\frac{6}{12} = 1\frac{1}{2}$$

PROBLEMS

1. $\frac{6}{3} = ?$
2. $-4 \div -3 = ?$
3. $\frac{3}{4}(-1) = ?$
4. $\frac{1}{2} \cdot \frac{2}{3} = ?$
5. $5 \cdot \frac{1}{2} \cdot 2 \cdot \frac{6}{3} = ?$
6. $\frac{7}{8} \div \frac{1}{2} = ?$
7. $\frac{1}{2} + \frac{5}{6} = ?$
8. $\frac{7}{3} - \frac{1}{2} = ?$
9. $5 - \frac{8}{2} = ?$
10. $7 + \frac{1}{2} - \frac{1}{3} + \frac{1}{4} - \frac{1}{5} = ?$

DECIMALS AND PERCENTS

Rule 1. Decimals indicate that the part of the number following the decimal point is a fraction with 10, 100, 1000, and so on, as the denominator. Rather than trying to find words to express the rule, let me just show you:

$$3.2 = 3\frac{2}{10} \qquad 3.25 = 3\frac{25}{100} \qquad 3.257 = 3\frac{257}{1000}$$

See how it works? Not particularly complicated, right?

Rule 2. Some fractions, divided out, produce decimals that go on and on and on. To get rid of unneeded decimal places, we can *round off* a number. Say you have the number 1.41421 and you want to express it with just two decimal places. Should your answer be 1.41 or 1.42? The first step in deciding is to create a new number from the digits left over after you take away the ones you want to keep, with a decimal point in front of it. In our example, we keep 1.41 and drop the last three digits (421). The next steps are as follows:

1. If the new decimal number is less than .5, just throw it away; you're done with the rounding-off process.

2. If the new decimal is .5 or greater, throw it away, but increase the last digit of the number you keep by 1. For example, 1.41684 would round to 1.42.

Rule 3. Percents are simply fractions of 100 (two-place decimals).

$$45\% = \frac{45}{100} = .45 \qquad 1.3\% = \frac{1.3}{100} = .013 \qquad 110\% = \frac{110}{100} = 1.1$$

PROBLEMS

1. Round off the following to two decimal places:
   a. 3.5741 **b.** 10.1111111 **c.** 90.0054
   d. 9.0009 **e.** 43.52500
2. Convert the following to percents:
   a. .75 **b.** .7532 **c.** 1.5
   d. $\frac{2}{3}$ **e.** $1 - .77$
3. 20% of 100 = ?
4. .2 of 100 = ?
5. .20(100) = ?

EXPONENTS AND ROOTS

Rule 1. An exponent is a small number placed slightly higher than and to the right of a number or expression. For example, 3^3 has an exponent of 3; $(x - y)^2$ has an exponent of 2. An exponent tells how many times a number or expression is to be multiplied by itself.

$$5^2 = 5 \cdot 5 = 25 \qquad 10^3 = 10 \cdot 10 \cdot 10 = 1000 \qquad Y^4 = Y \cdot Y \cdot Y \cdot Y$$

Rule 2. Roots are like the opposite of exponents. You can have square roots (the opposite of an exponent of 2), cube roots (opposite of an exponent of 3), and so on. In statistics, we often use square roots, and seldom any other kind, so I'm just going to talk about square roots here.

Rule 3. The square root of a number is the value that, when multiplied by itself, equals that number. For example, the square root of 9 is 3 and $3 \cdot 3 = 9$. The instruction to compute a square root (mathematicians call it "extracting" a square root, but I think that has unfortunate associations to wisdom teeth) is a "radical" sign: $\sqrt{\ }$. You take the square root of everything that's shown under the "roof" of the radical.

$$\sqrt{9} = 3 \quad \sqrt{8100} = 90 \quad \sqrt{36 + 13} = \sqrt{49} = 7 \quad \sqrt{36} + 13 = 6 + 13 = 19$$

When extracting a square root, you have three alternatives:

1. Use a calculator with a square root button.
2. Learn how to use a table of squares and square roots.
3. Find a sixth-grader who has just studied square roots in school.

I simply cannot recommend alternative (1) too strongly, given the inconvenience of using tables and the unreliability of sixth-graders.

PROBLEMS

1. $5^2 = ?$ **2.** $32^2 = ?$ **3.** $3^2 = ?$ **4.** $\sqrt{4^2} = ?$

5. $\sqrt{22{,}547} = ?$ **6.** $\sqrt{14{,}727}$ **7.** $\sqrt{71.234}$ **8.** $\sqrt{.0039}$

ORDER OF COMPUTATION

Rule 1. When an expression is enclosed in parentheses (like this), treat what's inside like a single number. Do any operations on that expression first, before going on to what's outside the parentheses. With nested parentheses, work from the inside out.

$$4(7 - 2) = 4(5)20$$

$$9 \div (-4 + 1) = 9 \div -3 = -3$$

$$12 \times (5 - (6 \times 2)) = 12 \times (5 - 12) = 12 \times -7 = -84$$

$$12 \times (5 - 6) \times 2 = 12 \times (-1) \times 2 = -12 \times 2 = -24$$

With complicated fractions, treat the numerator and the denominator as if each were enclosed in parentheses. In other words, calculate the whole numerator and the whole denominator first, then divide the numerator by the denominator:

$$\frac{3 + 2}{5 \cdot (7 - 3)} = \frac{5}{5 \cdot 4} = \frac{5}{20} = \frac{1}{4}$$

Rule 2. If you don't have parentheses to guide you, do all multiplication and division before you add or subtract.

$$5 + 3 \cdot 2 - 4 = 5 + (3 \cdot 2) - 4 = 5 + 6 - 4 = 7$$
$$8 \div 2 + 9 - 1 - (-2) \cdot (-5) - 5 = 4 + 9 - 1 - (+10) - 5 = -3$$

An algebra teacher in North Dakota taught her students a mnemonic to help them remember the correct order of operation: My Dear Aunt Sally fi Multiply, Divide, Add, Subtract.

Rule 3. Exponents and square roots are treated as if they were a single number. That means you square numbers or take square roots first of all—before adding, subtracting, multiplying, or dividing. Maybe we should treat My Dear Aunt Sally like a mean landlord and make the rule be "Roughly Evict My Dear Aunt Sally," in order to get the Roots and Exponents first in line!

Here are some examples of how the rules of the order of computation work together:

$5 - (3 \times 4) \times (8 - 2^2)(-3 + 1) \div 3$ (*exponent*)
$= 5 - (3 \times 4) \times (8 - 4)(-3 + 1) \div 3$ (*things inside parentheses*)
$= 5 - (12) \times (4) \times (-2) \div 3$ (*multiply*)
$= 5 - 48 \times -2 \div 3$ (*multiply again*)
$= 5 - -96 \div 3$ (*divide*)
$= 5 - (-32)$ (*and the addition comes last*)
$= 37$

Did you remember that subtracting a negative number is the same as adding a positive number?

$$2x - 3^2 \div (3 + 2) - \sqrt{25} \cdot 10 + (8 - (3 + 4))$$
$$= 2x - 9 \div (3 + 2) - 5 \cdot 10 + (8 - (3 + 4))$$
$$= 2x - 9 \div 5 - 5 \cdot 10 + (8 - 7)$$
$$= 2x - 9 \div 5 - 5 \cdot 10 + 1$$
$$= 2x - 1.8 - 50 + 1$$
$$= 2x - 50.8$$

PROBLEMS

1. $3 + 2 \cdot 4 \div 5 = ?$

2. $3 + 2 \cdot (4 \div 5) = ?$

3. $(3 \div 2) \cdot 4 \div 5 = ?$

4. $(3 + 2 \cdot 4) \div 5 = ?$

5. $\dfrac{\frac{1}{2} + \frac{7}{4}}{2 + \frac{1}{2}} = ?$

6. $(1 \div 2 + 7 \div 4) \div (2 + 1 \div 2) = ?$

SUMMATION

A summation sign looks like a goat's footprint: $\sum$. Its meaning is pretty simple: Add up what comes next. Most of the time, "what comes next" is obvious from the context. If you have a variable designated as x, with individual values x_1, x_2, x_3, and so on, then $\sum x$ refers to the sum of all those individual values.

Actually, $\sum x$ is a shorthand version of $\sum_{i=1}^{N} x$, which means that there are N individual x's. Each x is called x_i, and the values of i run from 1 to N. When $i = 10$ and $N = 50$, x_i would be the 10th in a set of 50 values; $\sum_{i=1}^{N} x$ would mean to find the sum of all 50 of them. For our purposes, a simple $\sum^{i=1} x$ says the same thing, and we'll just use that.

There are a few rules that you should know about doing summation, however. Let's look at an example. Five people take a pop quiz, and their scores are 10, 10, 8, 12, and 10. In other words, $x_1 = 10$, $x_2 = 10$, $x_3 = 8$, $x_4 = 12$, and $x_5 = 10$. $\sum x = 50$. What about $\sum x^2$? Well, that would be $100 + 100 + 64 + 144 + 100$. $\sum x^2 = 508$.

Now, does it make sense to you that $\sum x^2 \neq (\sum x)^2$? This is a key idea, and it has to do with the order of computation. $(\sum x)^2$ is read "sum of x, quantity squared," and the parentheses mean that you add up all the x's first, and square the sum: $(\sum x)^2 = (50)^2 = 2500$.

Now, just to make things interesting, we'll throw in another variable. Let y stand for scores on another quiz: $y_1 = 4, y_2 = 5, y_3 = 6, y_4 = 5, y_5 = 4$. $\sum y = 24$, $\sum y^2 = 118$, and $(\sum y)^2 = 576$. And we have some new possibilities:

$$\sum x + \sum y \quad \sum x^2 + \sum y^2 \quad \sum(x + y) \quad \sum(x^2 + y^2) \quad \sum(x + y)^2 \quad (\sum(x + y))^2$$

See if you can figure out these values on your own, and then we'll go through each one.

$\sum x + \sum y$	Add up the x values, add up the y values, and add them together: 74.
$\sum x^2 + \sum y^2$	Add up the squared x values, add up the squared y values, and add them together: 626.
$\sum(x + y)$	Add each x, y pair together, and add up the sums: $14 + 15 + 14 + 17 + 14 = 74$. Yup, $\sum x + \sum y = \sum(x + y)$. Every time.
$\sum(x^2 + y^2)$	Square an x and add it to its squared y partner; then add up the sums: $116 + 125 + 100 + 169 + 116 = 626$. $\sum(x^2 + y^2) = \sum x^2 + \sum y^2$.
$\sum(x + y)^2$	Add each x, y pair together, square the sums, and add them up: 1102.
$(\sum(x + y))^2$	Did those double parentheses throw you? Use them like a road map, to tell you where to go first. Starting from the inside, you add each x, y pair together. Find the sum of the pairs, and last of all square that sum: 5476.

PROBLEMS

Use these values to solve the following problems:

x	y
1	5
2	4
3	3
4	2
5	1

1. $\sum x + \sum y$
2. $\sum x^2 + \sum y^2$
3. $\sum(x + y)$
4. $\sum(x^2 + y^2)$
5. $\sum(x + y)^2$
6. $(\sum(x + y))^2$

EQUATIONS

An equation is two expressions joined by an equal sign. Not surprisingly, the value of the part in front of the equal sign is exactly equal to the value of the part after the equal sign.

Rule 1. Adding or subtracting the same number from each side of an equation is acceptable; the two sides will still be equivalent.

$$5 + 3 = 9 - 1 \qquad 5 + 3 + 5 = 9 - 1 + 5 \qquad 5 + 3 - 5 = 9 - 1 - 5$$
$$8 = 8 \qquad 13 = 13 \qquad 3 = 3$$

$$6 \div 4 + 1 \div 2 = 2 \qquad 6 \div 4 + 1 \div 2 + 5 = 2 + 5 \qquad 6 \div 4 + 1 \div 2 - 5 = 2 - 5$$
$$2 = 2 \qquad 7 = 7 \qquad -3 = -3$$

$$12 - 2 = (2)(5) \qquad 12 - 2 + 5 = (2)(5) + 5 \qquad 12 - 2 - 5 = (2)(5) - 5$$
$$10 = 10 \qquad 15 = 15 \qquad 5 = 5$$

Rule 2. If you add or subtract a number from one side of an equation, you must add or subtract it from the other side as well if the equation is to balance—that is, if both sides are to remain equal.

$$8 - 2 = 3 + 3 \qquad 8 - 2 + 2 = 3 + 3 + 2 \qquad 8 = 8$$
$$2x + 7 = 35 \qquad 2x + 7 - 7 = 35 - 7 \qquad 2x = 28$$

Rule 3. If you multiply or divide one side of an equation by some number, you must multiply or divide the other side by the same number. You can't multiply or divide just one part of each side; you have to multiply or divide the whole thing.

$$3 + 2 - 1 = 7 - 5 + 2$$

Multiply both sides by 6:

$$6 \cdot (3 + 2 - 1) = 6 \cdot (7 - 5 + 2)$$
$$6 \cdot (4) = 6 \cdot (4)$$
$$24 = 24$$

Look what would happen if you multiplied just one of the numbers on each side by 6:

$$6 \cdot (3) + 2 - 1 = 6 \cdot (7) - 5 + 2$$
$$18 + 2 - 1 = 42 - 5 + 2$$
$$19 = 39$$

Writing out these kinds of rules is a lot like eating hot buttered popcorn: It's hard to know when to quit. And, as with popcorn, it's a lot better to quit too soon than to quit too late; the former leaves you ready for more tomorrow, while the latter can make you swear off the stuff for months.

We could go on and on here, and end up with the outline for a freshman math course, but that's not our purpose. These rules will allow you to do all the math in this book and a great deal of the math in more advanced statistics courses. So let's get going on the fun part!

Problems

1. Use the equation $2 \cdot 3 + 4 = 10$ to answer the following:
   - **a.** Demonstrate that you can add the same number to each side of the equation without changing its balance.
   - **b.** Show the same thing using subtraction.
   - **c.** Multiply both sides of the equation by 2.
   - **d.** Divide both sides of the equation by 2.
2. Use addition and/or subtraction to solve these equations:
   - **a.** $5 + x = 3 - 7$
   - **b.** $x - 3 = 10$
   - **c.** $x - 3 + 2 = 8 \div 4$
3. Use multiplication and/or division to solve these equations:
   - **a.** $3x = 12$
   - **b.** $x \div 4 = 3$
   - **c.** $2x - 7 = 8$

Answers to Example Problems

POSITIVE AND NEGATIVE NUMBERS

1. −1 **2.** 8 **3.** −8 **4.** −12 **5.** 12
6. 12 **7.** −12 **8.** 24 **9.** $-(abcd)$

10. $\frac{4}{3}$ or 1.33 **11.** 15 **12.** −1

FRACTIONS

1. 2 **2.** $1\frac{1}{3}$ **3.** $-\frac{3}{4}$ **4.** $\frac{2}{6} = \frac{1}{3}$

5. $\frac{5}{1} \cdot \frac{1}{2} \cdot \frac{2}{1} \cdot \frac{6}{3} = \frac{60}{6} = 10$

6. $\frac{7}{8} \cdot \frac{2}{1} = \frac{14}{8} = 1\frac{3}{4}$

7. $\frac{3}{6} + \frac{5}{6} = \frac{8}{6} = 1\frac{2}{6} = 1\frac{1}{3}$

8. $\frac{14}{6} - \frac{3}{6} = \frac{11}{6} = 1\frac{5}{6}$

9. $\frac{10}{2} - \frac{8}{2} = \frac{2}{2} = 1$

10. $7 + \frac{30}{60} - \frac{20}{60} + \frac{15}{60} - \frac{12}{60} = 7\frac{13}{60}$

DECIMALS AND PERCENTS

1. a. 3.57 **b.** 10.11 **c.** 90.01 **d.** 9.00 **e.** 43.53
2. a. 75% **b.** 75.32% **c.** 150% **d.** 67% **e.** 23%
3. 20 **4.** 20 **5.** 20

EXPONENTS AND ROOTS

1. 25 **2.** 1024 **3.** 9 **4.** 4 **5.** 150.16
6. 121.35 **7.** 8.44 **8.** .06

ORDER OF COMPUTATION

1. 4.6 **2.** 4.6 **3.** 1.2 **4.** 2.2
5. $\frac{9}{4} \div \frac{5}{2} = \frac{9}{4} \cdot \frac{2}{5} = \frac{18}{20} = \frac{9}{10}$
6. Exactly the same answer as #5.

SUMMATION

1. 30 **2.** 110 **3.** 30 **4.** 110 **5.** 180
6. 900

EQUATIONS

1. a. $2 \cdot 3 + 4 = 10$
$2 \cdot 3 + 4 + 100 = 10 + 100$
$110 = 110$

b. $2 \cdot 3 + 4 = 10$
$2 \cdot 3 + 4 - 100 = 10 - 100$
$-90 = -90$

c. $2 \cdot 3 + 4 = 10$
$2(2 \cdot 3 + 4) = 2(10)$
$20 = 20$

d. $2 \cdot 3 + 4 = 10$
$\frac{2 \cdot 3 + 4}{2} = \frac{10}{2}$
$5 = 5$

2. a. $5 + x = 3 - 7$
$5 - 5 + x = 3 - 7 - 5$
$x = -9$

b. $x - 3 = 10$
$x - 3 + 3 = 10 + 3$
$x = 13$

c. $x - 3 + 2 = 8 \div 4$
$x - 1 = 2$
$x = 3$

3. a. $3x = 12$
$\frac{3x}{3} = \frac{12}{3}$
$x = 4$

b. $\frac{x}{4} = 3$
$4 \cdot \frac{x}{4} = 4 \cdot 3$
$x = 12$

c. $2x - 7 = 8$
$\frac{2x - 7}{2} = \frac{8}{2}$
$\frac{2x}{2} - \frac{7}{2} = 4$
$x - 3.5 = 4$
$x - 3.5 + 3.5 = 4 + 3.5$
$x = 7.5$

SECTION II

Describing Univariate Data

Isn't this a great statistics book? Here we are on Chapter 4 and we haven't even begun covering statistics yet! Well, I hate to spoil the fun, but the time has come. If you apply what you learned in Section I, however, you're ready for the challenge. The purpose of this section is to teach you how to describe univariate data—that is, information gathered on a single variable. Chapter 4 describes some straight forward techniques for summarizing data in the form of frequency distributions and displaying that information graphically. Chapter 5 shows how to calculate and interpret descriptive statistics to summarize the level and variability of data. Chapter 6 presents a discussion of the characteristics of one particularly important frequency distribution for statistics called the *normal distribution*. Finally, Chapter 7 explains how to interpret percentiles and standard scores.

CHAPTER

4 Frequency Distributions

- Variables
- Scales of Measurement
- Frequency Distributions
- Graphing Data
- The Normal Curve
- Problems
- Answers to Problems

Two statisticians were traveling in an airplane from L.A. to New York. About an hour into the flight, the pilot announced that they had lost an engine. "But don't worry," he said, "there are three left." However, instead of 5 hours it would take 7 hours to get to New York. A little later, he announced that a second engine failed, and they still had two left, but it would take 10 hours to get to New York. Somewhat later, the pilot again came on the intercom and announced that a third engine had died. "Never fear," he announced, "because the plane can fly on a single engine." However, it would now take 18 hours to get to New York. At this point, one statistician turned to the other and said, "Gee, I hope we don't lose that last engine, or we'll be up here forever!"

What are statistics? Statistics are a broad range of techniques and procedures for gathering, organizing, analyzing, and displaying quantitative data. *Data* means information: Any collection of information is a collection of data. For statisticians, *data* generally refers to quantitative information—that is, something that can be expressed in numbers (e.g., quantity or amount). There are two main kinds of statistics: descriptive and inferential. *Descriptive statistics* are used to describe a set of quantitative data. *Inferential statistics* are used to make inferences about large groups of people (i.e., populations) by analyzing data gathered on a smaller subset of the larger group (i.e., samples). Results of these analyses are used to make inferences about the larger group.

VARIABLES

For those of us interested in the social sciences (e.g., education, psychology), the data we gather often involve the characteristics of people. When observing people, what's one of the first things you notice? That's right: We differ, sometimes a little and sometimes a lot. In fact, people differ on virtually every biological and psychological characteristic that can be measured. Familiar examples of physical characteristics on which people differ include height and weight, blood type and pressure, body temperature, visual acuity, and eye color. But we also differ on intelligence, academic achievement, temperament, personality, values, and interests, among many others. In statistics, characteristics on which people differ are called *variables.* Variables can be either *discrete* or *continuous.* Discrete variables can only take on certain values. For example, the number of people in a household is a discrete variable. You can have 1, 2, 3, or 4 people in a household, for example, but not 1.5. Continuous variables are characteristics that can take on any value (e.g., height, weight).

In research, variables can also be categorized as *dependent* or *independent.* An independent variable is a variable that is manipulated to determine its effect on another variable. A dependent variable is the focus of most statistical analyses, because it is the variable that is measured in response to manipulation of the independent variable.

SCALES OF MEASUREMENT

Measurement refers to the assignment of numbers to the characteristics on which people differ (variables). Different kinds of variables require different rules for assigning numbers that accurately reflect how people differ on those variables. Not all variables can be assigned numbers according to the same rules. It depends on what you are trying to measure. Variables can be measured on one of four different *scales* of measurement: nominal, ordinal, interval, and ratio. Each scale has a particular set of rules that defines how numbers are assigned to variables and what you can do with those numbers with statistics.

NOMINAL SCALE. Variables that are measured on a nominal scale are often referred to as qualitative or categorical variables. Measurement on a nominal scale involves the assignment of people or objects to categories that describe the ways in which they differ on a variable. Examples include gender (Male, Female), marital status (Single, Married), eye color (Blue, Green, Brown), and race/ethnicity (Caucasian, African American, Hispanic, Asian, Other). All people or objects within the same category are assumed to be equal. On a nominal scale of measurement, numbers are often used to stand for the names or labels of each category (e.g., Male = 1, Female = 2). The number assigned to each category is completely arbitrary, however, and no rank ordering or relative size is implied.

ORDINAL SCALE. On an ordinal scale of measurement, it is possible to rank persons or objects according to magnitude. Numbers on this scale are used to rank order persons or objects on a continuum. The continuum used depends on the variable. Variables measured on an ordinal scale include class rank (Frosh–Senior), socioeconomic status (Poor–Rich), and Olympic marathon results (First–Last). For example, on an ordinal scale the first-place finisher in the Olympic marathon would be assigned a rank of 1, the second place finisher a rank of 2, and so on. On an ordinal scale, these numbers (ranks) express a "greater than" relationship, but they do not indicate "how

Bizapro (New) © 1997 Dan Piraro. King Features Syndicate

much greater." Although we know that first place is better than second place, we do not know anything about how close the race was. We don't know whether the top two finishers differed by a tenth of a second, 10 seconds, or 10 minutes; nor can we assume that the difference between first and second place is the same as that between second and third, and so on. This is an important point about ordinal scales of measurement—while the numbers assigned on an ordinal scale do reflect relative merit, the units of measurement are not equal (e.g., $3 - 2 \neq 2 - 1$.)

INTERVAL SCALE. On an interval scale, numbers that are assigned to variables reflect relative merit and have equal units of measurement. When a variable has equal units of measurement it means that the same difference between two points on a scale means the same thing in terms of whatever you are measuring. An example of a variable assumed to be measured on an interval scale is intelligence. On tests of intelligence, we can say that a person with an IQ of 120 is more intelligent than a person with an IQ of 100. We also know that the 20-point difference between IQ scores of 120 and 100 means the same thing in terms of intelligence as the 20-point difference between scores of 90 and 70. However, variables measured on an interval scale lack an *absolute zero point*, or the absence of the characteristic being measured. For example, there is no absolute zero point of intelligence, or no intelligence at all, although in an election year one is tempted to argue otherwise. Because it is impossible to establish a true zero point, it is not possible to speak meaningfully about the *ratio* between scores. For example, we cannot say that a person with an IQ of 140 is twice as smart as someone with an IQ of 70.

RATIO SCALE. Variables measured on an ratio scale have a true zero point and equal units of measurement. Many physical characteristics such as height, weight, and reaction time are measured on a ratio scale. The true zero point not only indicates the absence of the thing being measured (e.g., no height at all), but it also designates where measurement begins. Equal units of measurement provide consistent meaning from one situation to the next and across different parts of the scale. For example, 12 inches in Eugene, Oregon, is the same as 12 inches in Gainesville, Florida. Further, the difference between 12 and 24 inches is identical to the difference between 100 and 112 inches. We can also determine ratios on a ratio scale. For example, we can say that 12 inches is half as long as 24 inches or that it took somebody twice as long to run a marathon as somebody else.

FREQUENCY DISTRIBUTIONS

Whenever you gather data, the initial result is some unordered set of scores. A common first step in the examination of data is to create a frequency distribution. Frequency distributions organize and summarize data by displaying in a table how often specific scores were obtained. Imagine that you have administered a test of emotional intelligence to 100 college students. Emotional intelligence refers to one's ability to understand, perceive, and regulate emotions. On this test, higher scores reflect more emotional intelligence and lower scores reflect less emotional intelligence. The scores these 100 college students earned are as follows (in no particular order):

Emotional Intelligence Test Scores

46	50	48	47	48	47	49	43	47	46	50	48	49
46	46	45	46	46	47	46	46	46	48	47	46	47
44	49	47	48	49	48	48	49	45	48	46	46	51
48	44	45	44	46	49	50	48	43	48	46	48	46
48	46	47	47	47	47	49	49	46	47	47	44	45
45	48	50	48	47	47	49	47	45	48	49	45	47
47	44	48	47	47	51	47	46	47	46	45	47	45
45	47	48	48	46	48	45	50	47				

What can we say about these data? Not much. About all we can say is that most of the scores appear to be in the 40s and a few are in the 50s. Suppose you obtained a score of 48 on this test. What would that tell you? Are you more emotionally intelligent than the average college student or less? Just from perusing this table you can see that a 48 is not the highest score; nor is it the lowest. But it's hard to know more. Are you above average, average, or below average? As you can see, when scores are unordered, it's difficult to get a feel for the data. Making a frequency distribution can help. To create one, follow these steps:

1. Locate the highest and lowest score values. In our example, by looking over the data we find that the highest score is 51 and the lowest score is 43.
2. Record all *possible* scores from the highest to lowest score, even if it's not an actual obtained value. For our example, it would look like this:

Emotional Intelligence Test Scores

51	50	49	48	47	46	45	44	43

3. Go through the list of scores, score by score, and tally each time a score occurs. At the end of this process, our data look like this:

Score	Tally
51	||
50	|||||
49	||||||||||
48	||||||||||||||||||||
47	|||||||||||||||||||||||||
46	||||||||||||||||||||
45	|||||||||||
44	|||||
43	||

4. Now count the number of tallies to find the frequency (f) with which each score was earned. Your completed frequency distribution would look like this:

Score	Tally	f
51	||	2
50	|||||	5
49	||||||||||	10
48	||||||||||||||||||||	20
47	|||||||||||||||||||||||||	25
46	||||||||||||||||||||	20
45	|||||||||||	11
44	|||||	5
43	||	2

From the frequency distribution, we can see that scores on the test of emotional intelligence ranged from 43 to 51. We can also see the frequency of each score—that is, the number of individuals who obtained each score—in the next column. As you can see, two students obtained a score of 51, five students a score of 50, and so on. The score obtained most often was 47, with a frequency count of 25. We can also see that most of the scores tend to be clustered around the middle of the distribution, with relatively few scores at the extremes. In fact, 65 of the 100 scores are between 46 and 48. Further, we can see that there are no large gaps between emotional intelligence test scores. Now what can we say about a hypothetical score of 48? As we can see from the frequency distribution, a score of 48 is slightly above average compared to the other students in the class. That's a lot more than we knew before.

Grouped Frequency Distributions

When scores vary more widely than they did in our example, it is often difficult to see patterns in the data with a frequency distribution. By collapsing the possible score values into a smaller number of groups of scores, however, it may be easier to display the data and get a better sense of how people differed on the attribute measured. For example, let's suppose the following scores were obtained by university frosh on a midterm history examination:

Midterm Examination Scores

44	35	20	40	38	52	29	36	38	38
38	38	41	35	42	50	31	43	30	37
32	47	43	41	47	32	38	29	41	26
41	51	48	49	37	26	34	48	23	29
38	47	41	33	39	48	38	20	48	34
29	44	29	33	35	50	41	38	35	35
32	26	24	38	38	56	56	48	41	29
26	26	38	37	44	24	44	47	32	41

To create a grouped frequency distribution, there are a few principles you should follow: (a) class intervals should be created so that each score can be assigned to only one class interval; (b) all class intervals should be the same width; (c) place the class interval with the highest score at the top of the distribution; (d) class intervals should be continuous throughout the entire distribution even if the frequency in some intervals is zero; and (e) try to use between ten and twenty class intervals for most distributions. Here is a list of steps to follow when constructing a grouped frequency distribution:

1. Find the highest and lowest score. For these data, the highest score is 56 and lowest is 20.
2. Subtract the lowest score from the highest score to determine the range of scores. For our example: $56 - 20 = 36$.
3. Determine the width of the class intervals so that you end up with ten to twenty intervals. This is often done by inspection of the data so that you use a convenient whole number for an interval width (e.g., 2 or 3). For our example, let's use an interval width of 3.
4. Determine the starting point of the lowest interval. For an interval width of 3, the score limits for our lowest interval could be: 18–20, 19–21, or 20–22.
5. Record the score limits for all *possible* class intervals from the highest to lowest.
6. Go through the list of scores, score by score, and make a check each time a score occurs.
7. Convert the number of checks made for each interval into a frequency. If we chose an interval width of 3 and a starting point of 20, our grouped frequency distribution would look like this:

Score Limits	Tally	*f*
56–58	||	2
53–55		0
50–52	||||	4
47–49	||||||||||	10
44–46	||||	4
41–43	|||||||||||	11
38–40	||||||||||||||	14
35–37	|||||||||	9
32–34	||||||||	8
29–31	||||||||	8
26–28	|||||	5
23–25	|||	3
20–22	||	2

From this distribution, you can see that two people scored between 56 and 58, none between 53 and 55, and so on. There are a couple things to keep in mind when creating or viewing frequency distributions. First, once scores have been placed in an interval, you lose information about the specific scores that were obtained. In other words, some information is lost. Second, a number of different grouped frequency distributions can be created from the same set of data. Decisions about the number of class intervals to use, their width, and the starting point will alter the distribution in some way. Keep this in mind when both creating your own and examining the grouped frequency distributions of others.

GRAPHING DATA

Frequency distributions can also be displayed graphically as a histogram (bar graph) or as a frequency polygon (smooth-line curve). Let's talk in some detail about one of the most important kinds of graphs to understand in the study of statistics: the frequency polygon.

Frequency Polygon

Graphs have a horizontal axis (known as the *X*-axis) and a vertical axis (known as the *Y*-axis). It is conventional in statistics to place scores along the *X*-axis and frequencies on the *Y*-axis. The frequency distribution of emotional intelligence scores in our earlier example in graph form would look like that in Figure 4-1. Just in case you haven't worked much with graphs, I'll go through this one slowly. First, look at the *X*s along the humped line that makes up the shape of the graph. Specifically, look at the *X* directly above the score of 44. Notice that the *X* is directly across from the frequency of 5, which indicates that 5 persons earned a score of 44. Similarly, the graph indicates that 20 persons earned a score of 46. Got it? Good!

Second, look at the lines connecting the *X*s. When constructing a frequency polygon, connect all the *X*s with a line (you haven't had this much fun since you were a kid). Since the scores 42 and 52 each had zero frequency, we complete the graph by bringing our line down to the baseline at these points, indicating that neither of them had anybody scoring there. Now we have constructed a frequency polygon—a many-sided figure—describing the shape of a distribution.

Cumulative Frequency Polygon

Occasionally, a researcher may want to display data in cumulative form. Instead of building a graph that shows the number of scores occurring at each possible score, a cumulative

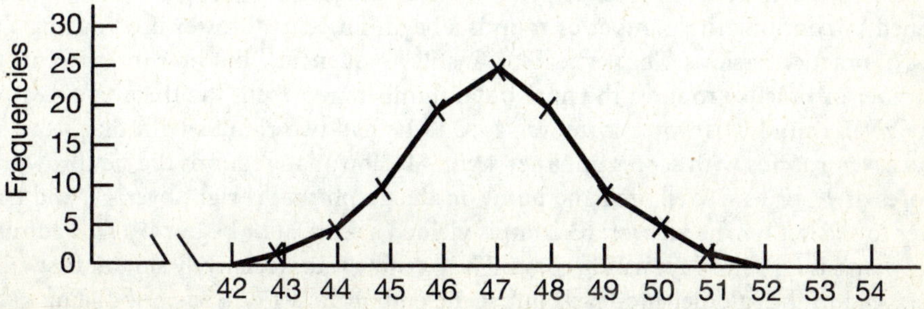

FIGURE 4-1 A frequency polygon.

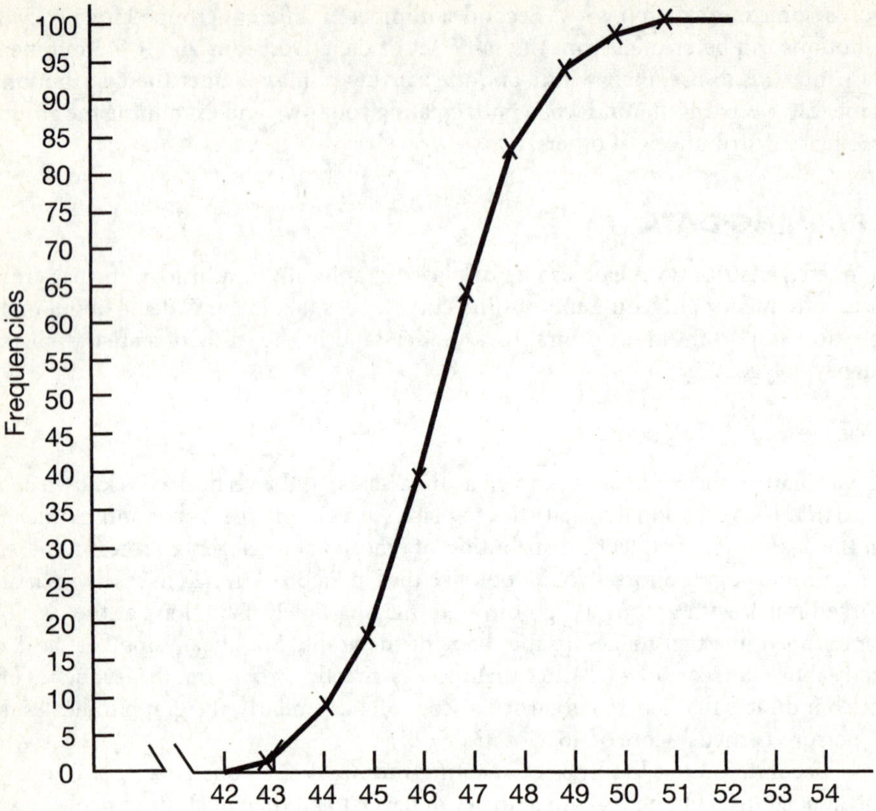

FIGURE 4-2 A cumulative frequency polygon.

frequency polygon shows the number of scores occurring at or below each point. The cumulative frequency polygon for the emotional intelligence test score data is shown in Figure 4-2. By finding the point on the line that is exactly above any number on the horizontal axis, and then reading across to the left, we can see how many students scored at or below that point. For example, 38 students had anxiety test scores at or below 46.

A cumulative frequency polygon is particularly useful in illustrating learning curves, when a researcher might be interested in knowing how many trials it took for a subject to reach a certain level of performance. Imagine that the graph here was obtained by counting the number of rounds a beginning dart thrower used during a series of practice sessions. The vertical axis is still "frequencies," but now it represents the number of practice rounds; the horizontal numbers represent the thrower's score on any given round. His worst score was 43, and he had two rounds with that score. He had seven rounds with scores of either 43 or 44. How many rounds did he throw with scores of 47 or less? Well, find the point on the graph that is right over 47, and trace over to the left for the answer: 63 rounds yielded a score at or below 47. This cumulative graph is typical of a learning curve: The learning rate is relatively slow at first, picks up speed in the middle, and levels out at the end of the set of trials, producing a flattened S shape.

THE NORMAL CURVE

Around 1870, Adolphe Quetelet, a Belgian mathematician, and Sir Francis Galton, an English scientist, made a discovery about individual differences that impressed them greatly. Their method was to select a characteristic, such as weight or acuteness of vision, obtain measurements on large numbers of individuals, and then arrange the results in frequency distributions. They found the same pattern of results over and over again, for all sorts of different measurements. Figure 4-3 is an example that depicts the results of measuring chest size of over 5,000 soldiers.

The rectangles in this graph are called bars (it's a bar graph, or histogram), and the bars represent the number of folks who fell into each respective range. About 50 soldiers had chest sizes between 33.5 and 34.4 inches. If we were to put a mark at the top of

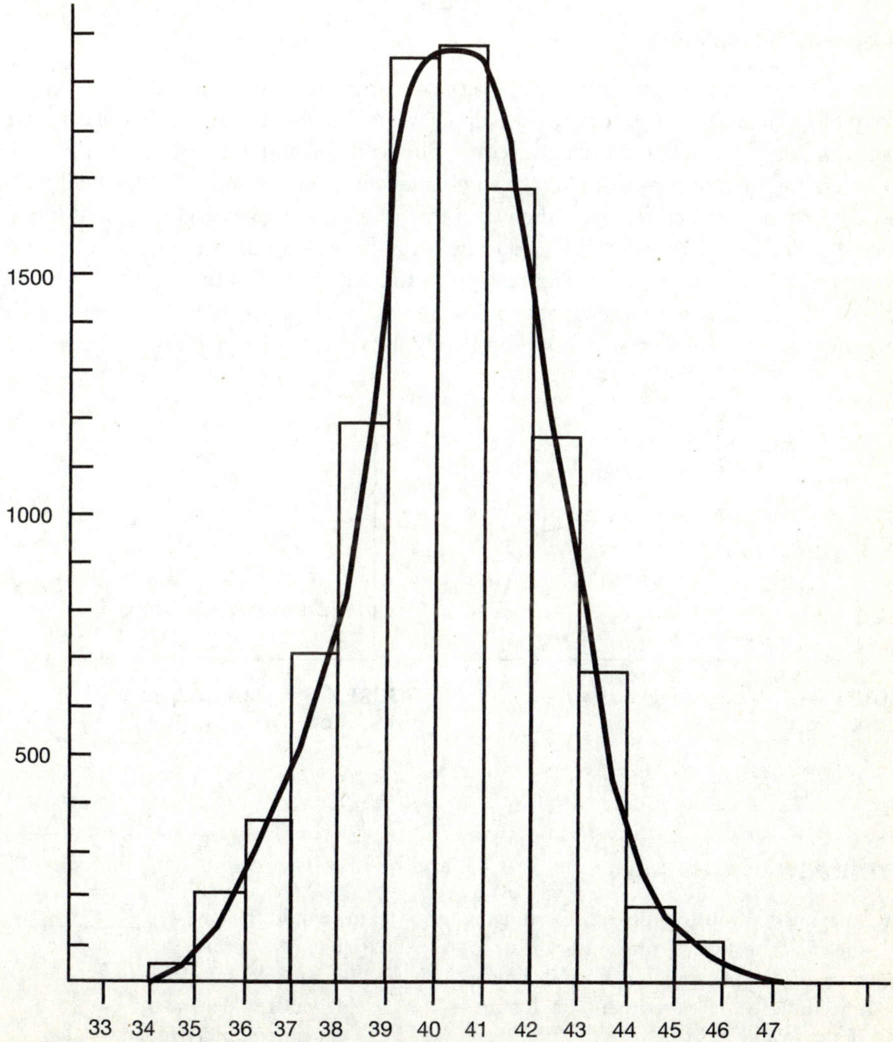

FIGURE 4-3 Chest sizes of 5,738 soldiers.

each bar and draw straight lines between the marks, we'd have a frequency polygon of the sort we drew earlier. The curve that's drawn over the bars doesn't follow that polygon shape exactly; however, it's what we'd get if we measured thousands and thousands more soldiers and plotted the bar graph or frequency polygon for all of them, using narrower measurement intervals—maybe tenths or even hundredths of an inch—instead of whole inches.

The symmetrical, bell-shaped curve that results from plotting human characteristics on frequency polygons closely resembles a curve, familiar to mathematicians, known as the normal probability curve. The normal curve is bell shaped and perfectly symmetrical and has a certain degree of "peakedness," but not all frequency distributions have this shape. Because of the importance of the normal curve to statistics, we will discuss it in further detail in Chapter 6.

Skewed Distributions

Skewed curves are not symmetrical. If a very easy arithmetic test were administered to a group of graduate students, for example, chances are that most students would earn high scores and only a few would earn low scores. The scores would tend to "bunch up" at the upper end of the graph, as if you'd taken a normal curve and pulled its bottom tail out to the left. When scores cluster near the upper end of a frequency polygon, so that the left side is "pulled down," the graph is said to be "negatively skewed." An example of a negatively skewed curve is shown in Figure 4-4. On the other hand, if the test were too difficult for the class, most people would get low scores. When graphed as a frequency polygon, these scores would be said to be "positively skewed," as shown in Figure 4-5.

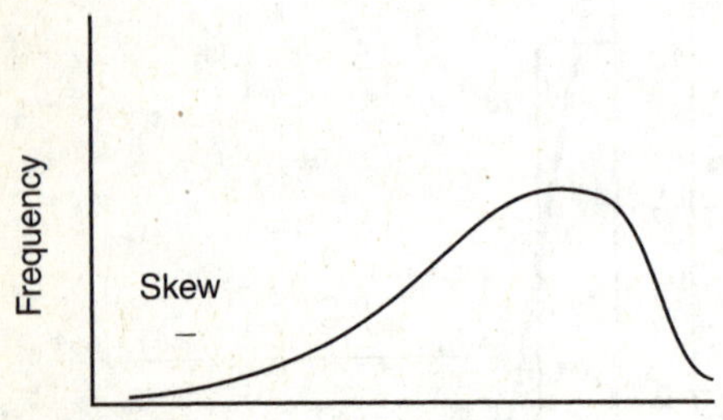

FIGURE 4-4 A negatively skewed distribution.

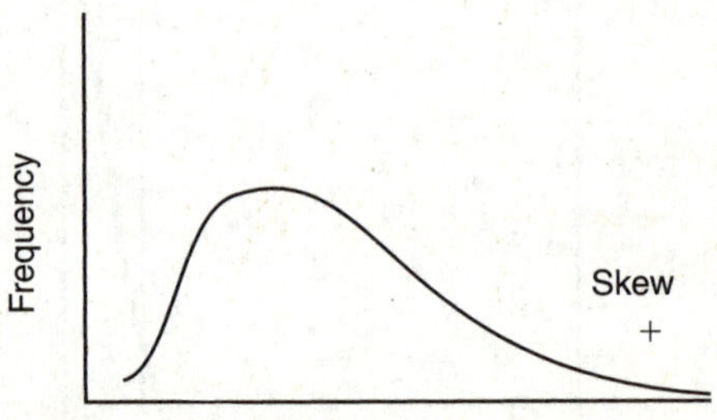

FIGURE 4-5 A positively skewed distribution.

Problems

1. Imagine that you are interested in studying the effects of type of preparatory instructions on the perception of pain during an injection. In this experiment, the instructions would be the ______________ variable and the amount of perceived pain would be the ______________ variable.
   a. independent; dependent
   b. dependent; dependent
   c. dependent; independent
   d. independent; independent

2. On a test of verbal ability, Mary obtained a score of 30, Bill a score of 45, and Sam a score of 60. If the difference between Mary's score and Bill's score is equivalent to the difference between Bill's score and Sam's score, then the level of measurement for these scores must be at least:
   - **a.** nominal
   - **b.** ordinal
   - **c.** interval
   - **d.** ratio
3. Instructor, assistant professor, associate professor, and full professor form what kind of scale?
4. Suppose an exam was very easy and all but a few students obtained a high grade on it. The frequency distribution of these scores would be _______________.
   - **a.** negatively skewed
   - **b.** positively skewed
   - **c.** symmetrical
   - **d.** bimodal
5. The normal distribution:
   - **a.** is a theoretical distribution.
   - **b.** can be described completely by knowing its mean and standard deviation.
   - **c.** is symmetrical.
   - **d.** all of the above
6. The following scores were obtained by third graders on a weekly spelling test (10 points possible):

Scores									
4	3	10	3	3	2	9	3	8	3
2	3	1	5	4	0	1	4	0	3
2	4	3	1	4	2	8	2	1	2
1	5	2	9	3	6	4	4	3	2
1	4	1	3	3	2	2	2	8	3
9	4	9	3	3	10	1	3	5	3
2	2	4	3	3	6	6	4	1	2
6	2	3	7	4	4	4	4	2	4

   - **a.** Construct a frequency distribution for these test scores.
   - **b.** Graph the data using a bar graph. How would you characterize the resulting distribution of scores? Normal? Positively skewed? Negatively skewed?

Answers to Problems

1. (a)
2. (c)
3. Ordinal scale
4. (a)
5. (d)
6. (a)

<table>
<tr><th>Score</th><th>Tally</th><th>f</th></tr>
<tr><td>10</td><td>||</td><td>2</td></tr>
<tr><td>9</td><td>||||</td><td>4</td></tr>
<tr><td>8</td><td>|||||||||||</td><td>11</td></tr>
<tr><td>7</td><td>|</td><td>1</td></tr>
<tr><td>6</td><td>||||</td><td>4</td></tr>
<tr><td>5</td><td>|||</td><td>3</td></tr>
<tr><td>4</td><td>||||||||||||||||</td><td>16</td></tr>
<tr><td>3</td><td>|||||||||||||||||</td><td>17</td></tr>
<tr><td>2</td><td>||||||||||||</td><td>12</td></tr>
<tr><td>1</td><td>||||||||</td><td>8</td></tr>
<tr><td>0</td><td>||</td><td>2</td></tr>
</table>

(b) Positively skewed

CHAPTER

5 Descriptive Statistics

- **Measures of Central Tendency**
- **Selecting a Measure of Central Tendency**
- **Measures of Variability**
- **Problems**
- **Answers to Problems**

There was this statistics student who, when driving his car, would always accelerate hard before coming to any intersection, whiz straight through it, and then slow down again. One day, he took a passenger, who was understandably unnerved by his driving style, and asked him why he went so fast over junctions. The statistics student replied, "Well, statistically speaking, you are far more likely to have an accident at an intersection, so I just make sure that I spend less time there."

Frequency distributions are very useful for providing a pictorial view of a set of data. While helpful, they often do not provide us with enough or the right kind of information. We often ask questions such as, "What is the average GRE score of this class?" or "How much money does the average football player make?" When we ask such questions, we are really asking for a single number that will represent all of the different GRE scores, or player salaries, or whatever, rather than for the shape of a distribution. In such instances, measures of central tendency and variability—descriptive statistics—can be calculated to quantify certain important characteristics of a distribution. Many people are not aware that there is more than one "average." In this chapter, we will discuss three methods for computing an average: the mean, the median, and the mode. Just one number, though, can be misleading. Two very different sets of data can have the same average, yet differ greatly in terms of how much the scores vary within every dataset. The second kind of summarizing technique is finding a number that describes that variability. Variability in a distribution can be described in terms of the range, variance (SD^2), or standard deviation (SD).

MEASURES OF CENTRAL TENDENCY

Measures of central tendency provide an average or typical score that describes the level (from high to low) of a set of scores. Measures of central tendency are useful when comparing the level of performance for a group of individuals with that of another group (e.g., boys vs. girls) or with some standard (e.g., national average), or when comparing the performance of the same group over time (e.g., before and after an intervention or treatment). The three main measures of central tendency are the mean, median, and mode.

Mean

The *mean* is the most often used measure of *central tendency* (central tendency is a fancy statistical term that means, roughly, "middleness"). The mean is an old acquaintance of yours: the arithmetic average. You obtain the mean by adding up all the scores and dividing by the number of scores. Remember? Different statistics texts use different symbols to designate the mean. The most widely used method is to use a bar over the letter symbolizing the variable. For example, a group's mean score on variable X would be symbolized $\overline{X}$; the mean on variable Y would be $\overline{Y}$, and so on. By convention, the $\overline{X}$ and $\overline{Y}$ are used to designate the mean of a sample—that is, a finite set of something: test scores, heights, reaction times, what have you.

Sometimes we want to refer to the mean of a less definite, often infinite set: All the fifth-graders in the United States, for example, or the scores that all those fifth-graders would get if they all were given the same achievement test. A large, inclusive group like this is called a population; and the Greek letter μ (pronounced "mew," like the sound a kitten makes) symbolizes its mean. Values having to do with populations are called *parameters* and are usually symbolized using lowercase Greek letters; for sample values (called statistics), we use the normal English-language alphabet. To be technically correct, we would have to define a population as the collection of all the things that fit the population definition and a sample as some specified number of things selected from that population. You'll see why that's important when we talk about *inferential statistics* in Chapter 10. For now, though, just assume that we are working with samples—relatively small groups of things in which each individual member can be measured or categorized in some way.

The formula for the mean for variable X, or $\overline{X}$, is:

$$\overline{X} = \frac{\Sigma X}{N}$$

where $\sum$ means "the sum of," X refers to each obtained score, and N refers to the total number of scores. For example, here are scores for five students on a test of math computation and a test of reading comprehension. For each test, therefore, $N = 5$. The sum of the scores on the math test is 68 and for reading comprehension is 127. To find the mean of each test, we simply divide each number by 5. The mean for math computation is 13.6, and the mean for reading comprehension is somewhat higher at 25.4.

Math Computation Scores (*X*)	Reading Comprehension Scores (*Y*)
14	25
19	37
13	26
9	20
13	19
$\sum X = 68$	$\sum Y = 127$
$\overline{X} = \frac{68}{5} = 13.6$	$\overline{Y} = \frac{127}{5} = 25.4$

Have you noticed how complicated it was to describe the mean in words, compared with that short, little formula? Formulas, and mathematical relationships in general, often don't easily translate into words. Mathematicians are trained to think in terms of relationships and formulas and often don't have to translate; we do. That's one reason why social science folks can have problems with statistics: We don't realize that we need to translate, and that the translating takes time. We expect to read and understand a page in a statistics book as quickly as a page in any other sort of book. Not so! As I said earlier, symbols simply take longer to read, and we need to remember to slow ourselves down. So don't beat yourself up for being slow—you're supposed to be that way!

Median

When scores are arranged in order, from highest to lowest (or lowest to highest), the *median* (Mdn) is the middle score. In other words, the median is the score that divides the frequency distribution in half. Fifty percent of the total number of obtained scores fall above the median and 50% below. Suppose you administered a test to five persons who scored as follows:

113, 133, 95, 112, 94

To find the median, you would first arrange all scores in numerical order and then find the score that falls in the middle. Arranged from highest to lowest, these scores are:

133, 113, 112, 95, 94

Here, the Mdn = 112, because two scores are higher than 112 and two scores are lower than 112. Finding the Mdn is easy when you have an odd number of scores. But what do you do when you have an even number? Suppose you have the following six scores:

105, 102, 101, 92, 91, 80

In this example, the number 101 can't be the Mdn, because there are two scores above it and three below. Nor can the number 92 be the Mdn, because there are three scores above and two below. With an even number of scores, the Mdn is defined as the point half the distance between the two scores in the middle. In this example, the two middle scores are 101 and 92. You find the point halfway between by adding the two middle scores and dividing by 2: 101 + 92 = 193, divided by 2 = 96.5 = Mdn. (Did you notice that this is the same as finding the mean of the two middle scores? Good for you!) The Mdn of our six scores is 96.5. As you can see, now there are three scores that are higher than 96.5 and three that are lower.

Mode

The *mode* (Mo) is simply the most frequently occurring score in a set of scores. For example, suppose we are given the following scores:

110, 105, 100, 100, 100, 100, 99, 98

Because the number 100 occurs more frequently than any of the other scores, Mo = 100. Simple enough?

But what about the following set of scores?

110, 105, 105, 105, 100, 95, 95, 95, 90

In this example, both 105 and 95 occur three times. Here, we have a distribution with two modes—that is, a bimodal distribution. If there were more than two modes, it would be called a multimodal distribution.

SELECTING A MEASURE OF CENTRAL TENDENCY

Mark Twain once said, "There are three kinds of lies: lies, damned lies, and statistics." Actually, statistics don't lie. But they can be employed to enhance communication—or to deceive those who do not understand their properties. (Although we wouldn't want to do that, would we?) For example, consider the University of Football, a university so small that its entire staff consists of five persons, four professors and a football coach. Their annual incomes are as follows:

Professors' Salary	Coach's Salary
Professor 1 $60,000	$1,000,000
Professor 2 $55,000	
Professor 3 $55,000	
Professor 4 $50,000	

The coach boasts that the university is a fantastic university with an "average" annual salary of $244,000. Before rushing off to join the faculty, you would be wise to find out what measure of central tendency he is using! True, the mean is $244,000, so the coach is not lying. But is that the typical salary of all employees at the University of Football? Of course not. The coach's income is quite extreme in comparison to that of his fellow employees, so the story he is telling is not very accurate. In this case, either the median or the mode would be a more representative value of the typical salary of employees. For both, the "average" income is $55,000. The point made here is that your selection of a measure of central tendency will be determined by your objectives in communication as well as by mathematical considerations.

The mean is the only measure of central tendency that reflects the position of each score in a distribution. Because the mean is the "balance point" of the distribution, the mean is affected most by extreme scores. The mean is often the best choice for the average when the distribution of scores is symmetrical. The Mdn, in contrast, responds to how many scores lie above and below it, not how far above and below. It doesn't matter whether the coach's income in the example above is $61,000 or $1,000,000 when determining the Mdn. Because the Mdn is less affected by extreme scores, the Mdn is often the best choice of the average when the distribution in skewed. The mode, although easy to obtain, is really only suitable when you want to know the "most likely" value in a distribution. The mode is also the only measure of central tendency that can be used with scores obtained on a nominal scale of measurement.

When a distribution is skewed, the mean is the most strongly affected. A few scores far out in the tail of a distribution will "pull" the mean in that direction. The median is somewhat "pulled" in the direction of the tail, and the mode is not "pulled" at all (see Figure 5-1). To see what I mean, look at the three distributions shown in Figure 5-2. The first distribution (X) is perfectly symmetrical. Its mode, mean, and median are equal. In unimodal, symmetrical distributions, $\overline{X} = Mdn = Mo$, always. Distribution Y has been skewed by changing the largest score, 5, to 12. Skewing it to the right like this shifted the mean from 3 to 4, but it didn't change either the mode or the median. Finally, in distribution Z, we have not only shifted the 5 out to 12, but we have further skewed the distribution to the right by adding scores of 20, 30, and 40. The mean is again most sensitive to these changes. And this time, the Mdn shifts too, just a bit, from 3 to 3.5. But the mode remains unchanged.

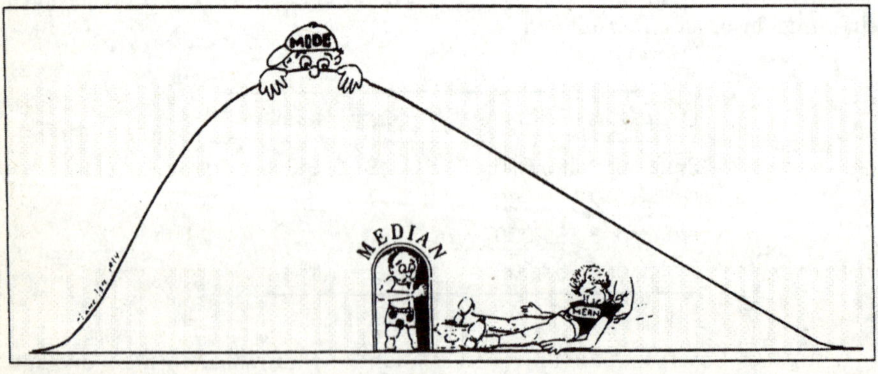

FIGURE 5-1 Relationship between the mean, median, and mode in a positively skewed distribution.

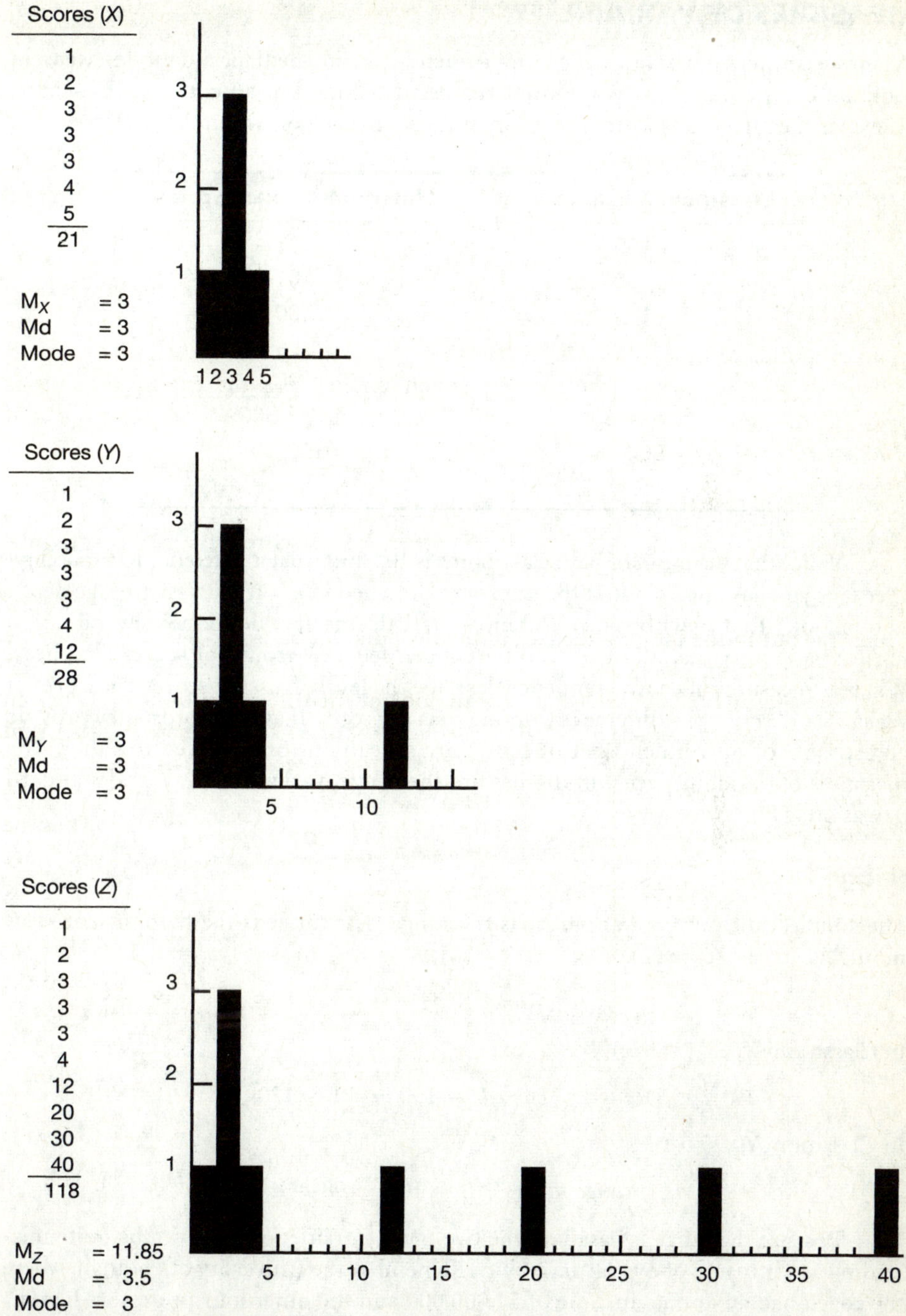

FIGURE 5-2 Symmetrical and skewed distributions.

MEASURES OF VARIABILITY

When we computed measures of central tendency (mean, median, and mode), we were looking for one score that would best represent the level of an entire set of scores. Consider the final exam scores earned by students in each of two statistics classes:

Classroom *X* Exam Scores	Classroom *Y* Exam Scores
160	102
130	101
100	100
70	99
40	98
$\Sigma X = 500$	$\Sigma Y = 500$
$\overline{X} = \frac{500}{5} = 100$	$\overline{Y} = \frac{500}{5} = 100$

Notice that the mean of both classrooms is 100. But what a difference in variability! (Perhaps you have heard about the man who drowned in a lake with an average depth of one foot.) To deal with such differences, statisticians have developed several measures of variability that allow us to differentiate between groups of scores like these. Whereas measures of central tendency describe the level of a set of scores, measures of variability describe the differences among a set of scores. In other words, they provide an estimate of how much a set of scores are spread out or clustered together. The measures of variability we will discuss are the range, variance (SD^2), and standard deviation (SD).

Range

The simplest measure of variability is the range. The range is the highest score (H) minus the lowest score (L).

$$Range = H - L$$

In Classroom X,

$$Range = H - L = 160 - 40 = 120$$

In Classroom Y,

$$Range = H - L = 102 - 98 = 4$$

Because the range is based on the two most extreme scores, it can be quite misleading as a measure of overall variability. Remember the University of Football, where the coach had an annual income of \$1,000,000 and the other four professors had incomes of \$60,000, \$55,000, \$55,000, and \$50,000? The range of this distribution is \$950,000, even though all but one of the people in the sample are clustered within \$10,000 of each other. In this distribution, the range is not as useful a measure as the variance and standard deviation, which are based on all the scores. That's where we go next. First, let's talk about the variance.

Variance (SD^2)

The variance (SD^2) is the most frequently used measure of variability and is defined as the mean of the squares of deviation scores. The formula for the variance may seem a little bit intimidating at first, but you can handle it if you follow the procedures outlined in what follows:

$$SD^2 = \frac{\Sigma(X - \overline{X})^2}{N - 1}$$

Where: Σ means "the sum of,"

X refers to each obtained score,

$\overline{X}$ is the mean of X, and

N refers to the total number of scores.

Before learning how to compute the variance, let's discuss the concept of deviations from the mean, or deviation scores.

Deviation Scores

We can tell how far each score deviates from the mean by subtracting the mean from it, using the formula $\chi = (X - \overline{X})$. Positive deviation scores indicate positions that are above the mean, and negative deviation scores indicate positions below the mean. Notice that for the following scores, we have subtracted the mean of 5.0 from each score:

Scores (X)	($X - \overline{X}$)	χ
9	9 − 5	+4
7	7 − 5	+2
5	5 − 5	0
3	3 − 5	−2
1	1 − 5	−4
$\Sigma X = 25$	$\Sigma(X - \overline{X}) = \chi = 0$	

$$\overline{X} = \frac{\Sigma X}{N} = \frac{25}{5} = 5.0$$

All we have to do to find how much these scores differ from the mean on average is to calculate the mean deviation score, right? Unfortunately, it's not that easy. As you can see, when we add up the column headed "$X - \overline{X}$," the sum of that column equals zero. Because the mean is the "balance point" of a set of scores, the sum of deviations about their mean is always zero, except when you make rounding errors. In fact, another definition of the mean is the score around which the sum of the deviations equals zero. The mean deviation score is not a very good measure of variability, therefore, because it is the same for every distribution, even when there is wide variability among distributions. In our example, we can easily see that they do in fact differ.

So how do we estimate variability? This is where the variance comes to the rescue. If we square each deviation score, the minus signs cancel each other out. In the following distribution, look carefully at the column headed "$(X - \overline{X})^2$." Notice that by squaring the deviation scores we get rid of the negative values.

Scores (*X*)	$(X - \overline{X})$	x	$(X - \overline{X})^2$
9	9 − 5	+4	16
7	7 − 5	+2	4
5	5 − 5	0	0
3	3 − 5	−2	4
1	1 − 5		16
$\Sigma X = 25$	$(X - \overline{X}) = x = 0$		$\Sigma(X - \overline{X})^2 = 40$

Now, for the sum of the squared deviations, we have $\Sigma(X - \overline{X})^2 = 40$, the numerator of the formula for the variance. To complete the computation for the variance, just divide by $N - 1$:

$$SD_x^2 = \frac{\Sigma(X - \overline{X})^2}{N - 1} = \frac{40}{5 - 1} = 10$$

The variance is defined as the mean of the *squared* deviation scores. In other words, the variance is a kind of average of how much scores deviate from the mean after they are squared. The difference between this formula and other formulas for "average" values is, of course, that here we divide by $N - 1$ rather than simply by the number of scores. The reason? It's fairly complicated, and it has to do with how we will use the variance later on, when we get to *inferential statistics.* I think it would be confusing to explain it now, so let's wait to talk about this until we get to Chapter 10.

Many students complete the computation of their first variance and then ask, "What does it mean? What good are squared deviation scores?" Perhaps you have a similar question. To statisticians, the variance reflects the "amount of information" in a distribution.

In any case, let's go back to Classrooms X and Y (from the beginning of the chapter) and find the variance for each classroom. The variance for Classroom X is

$$SD_x^2 = \frac{\Sigma(X - \overline{X})^2}{N - 1} = \frac{9000}{5 - 1} = 2250$$

And the variance for classroom Y is

$$SD_y^2 = \frac{\Sigma(Y - \overline{Y})^2}{N - 1} = \frac{10}{5 - 1} = 2.5$$

Notice that the values for the variances of Classrooms X and Y reflect the fact that there is quite a bit of difference between the variabilities of the classrooms. That's what the variance is supposed to do—provide a measure of the variability. The more variability in a group, the higher the value of the variance; the more homogeneous the group, the lower the variance.

Another way to understand the variance is to notice that, in order to find it, you need to add all the squared deviations and divide by *N*. Sound familiar? Very similar to the definition of the mean, don't you think? So one way to understand the variance is to think of it as an average deviation squared, or maybe a mean squared deviation.

COMPUTATIONAL VARIANCE FORMULA. The preceding formula given for the variance is a definitional formula. It is both accurate and adequate for small sets of numbers in which the mean turns out to be a whole number, but it is inconvenient for general use. For most purposes, it will be better for you to use a mathematically equivalent computational formula. It's not only easier to use, but it minimizes roundoff error. The computational formula for the variance is

$$SD_x^2 = \frac{\Sigma X^2 - \frac{(\Sigma X)^2}{N}}{N - 1}$$

Just take a few deep breaths and try to relax. Calmly analyze what you see. Notice that you know quite a bit already: You know that N is the total number of scores, and ΣX is the sum of all the scores. There are two terms you haven't seen before: $(\Sigma X)^2$ and ΣX^2. Let's look at each one in turn. First, $(\Sigma X)^2$: This term directs you to find the sum of all obtained scores on X and then square that sum. It's an example of the parentheses rule we talked about earlier: Work from the inside out.

***X* Scores**
10
9
8
7
6
$\Sigma X = 40$
$(\Sigma X)^2 = (40)^2 = 1600$

ΣX^2: This term directs you to square each X score and then sum the squares.

Scores (*X*)	**Scores Squared $(X)^2$**
10	100
9	81
8	64
7	49
6	36
$\Sigma X = 40$	$\Sigma X^2 = 330$

Note that ΣX^2 is not the same as $(X)^2$. It is very important that you make this distinction! Here are two rules that may help you to read statistical formulas:

Rule 1. Whenever you see parentheses around a term, as in $(X)^2$, do what's indicated inside the parentheses before doing what's indicated outside the parentheses. In the last example, you would find ΣX first and then square it: $(\Sigma X)^2 = (40)^2 = 1600$.

Rule 2. When there are no parentheses, a symbol and its exponent are treated as a unit. When you see ΣX^2, first square and then add the squared numbers. In the preceding example, square each number first and then get the sum of the squares: $\Sigma X^2 = 330$.

Another example:

Scores (X)	Scores Squared $(X)^2$
140	19,600
120	14,400
100	10,000
80	6,400
60	3,600
$\Sigma X = 500$	$\Sigma X^2 = 54{,}000$
$(\Sigma X)^2 = 500^2 = 250{,}000$	

If you have many numbers with which to work, the process of finding the square of each number first, then recording it, and then adding them is tedious. Here's where you can use your calculator's memory. Follow these steps to find ΣX^2 for the scores in the last example:

1. Clear your calculator's memory.

2. Find the square of 140 and enter it into M+. Do the same for each of your X scores without writing any of the squares on paper.

3. After you have entered the squares of all scores into M+, push your memory recall button (usually MR) and you should get the correct answer, which is 54,000 in this example. This is the value of ΣX^2.

Meanwhile, back at the computational variance formula, we still have:

$$SD_x^2 = \frac{\Sigma X^2 - \frac{(\Sigma X)^2}{N}}{N - 1}$$

Let's apply the formula to the following example:

Math Anxiety Scores				
11	9	8	8	6

Just follow these steps:

1. Look at the numerator first (it's as easy as a, b, c).

   a. Find ΣX^2. To find ΣX^2, remember to square each score first; then sum the squares: $\Sigma X^2 = 351$. Did you get that? Good. If you didn't, try again.

   b. Find $(\Sigma X)^2$. (Remember, find ΣX first and then square the result.) $(\Sigma X)^2 = (41)^2 = 1{,}681$.

   c. Find N. That's the easy part. In our example, $N = 5$.

2. Now just plug the numbers for ΣX^2, $(\Sigma X)^2$, and N into formula and calculate the variance. Remember, it really pays to go slowly and show all your work.

$$SD_x^2 = \frac{\Sigma X^2 - \frac{(\Sigma X)^2}{N}}{N-1} = \frac{351 - \frac{1681}{5}}{5-1} = \frac{351 - 336.2}{4} = \frac{14.8}{4} = 3.70$$

Now let's go back and compute the variances for Classrooms X and Y (from the beginning of the chapter) just to compare our two formulas for the variance:

Variance of Scores in Classroom *X*

1. Remember, it's as easy as a, b, c.
   a. $\Sigma X^2 = 59{,}000$
   b. $(\Sigma X^2 = (500)^2 = 250{,}000$
   c. $N = 5$
2. Compute the variance:

$$SD_x^2 = \frac{\Sigma X^2 - \frac{(\Sigma X^2}{N}}{N-1} = \frac{59{,}000 - \frac{250{,}000}{5}}{5-1} = \frac{59{,}000 - 50{,}000}{4} = \frac{9{,}000}{4} = 2{,}250$$

That is, the variance of Classroom X is 2250. Notice that this is the same value we got by using the definitional formula. Because the mean was a whole number, there was no roundoff error with the definitional formula.

Variance of Scores in Classroom *Y*

1. Remember, its as easy as a, b, c.
   a. $\Sigma Y^2 = 50{,}010$
   b. $(\Sigma Y)^2 = (500)^2 = 250{,}000$
   c. $N = 5$
2. Compute the variance:

$$SD_Y^2 = \frac{\Sigma Y^2 - \frac{(\Sigma Y)^2}{N}}{N-1} = \frac{50{,}010 - \frac{250{,}000}{5}}{5-1} = \frac{50{,}010 - 50{,}000}{4} = \frac{10}{4} = 2.5$$

Again, notice that this is the same value you found for the variance of Classroom Y when you used the definitional formula.

If there is a lesson to be learned here, it is that statistical formulas aren't so much *difficult* as they are *compressed.* There's nothing really hard about following the steps. But we are so used to reading things quickly that we tend to look once at a long formula and then give up, without taking the time to break it into chunks that we can understand. A good rule of thumb is that any line of formula should take about as long to read as a page of text.

Standard Deviation (SD)

When you read educational and psychological research, you will often come across the term *standard deviation.* Once you have found the variance of a sample, finding the standard deviation is easy: Just take the square root of the variance. If the variance is 25, the standard deviation will be 5; if the variance is 100, the standard deviation will be 10. To find the standard deviations of the exam scores from Classrooms X and Y, take the square root of the variances.

SD of Classroom X	SD of Classroom Y
$SD_x = \sqrt{SD_x^2} = \sqrt{2250} = 47.4$	$SD_Y = \sqrt{SD_Y^2} = \sqrt{2.5} = 1.6$

But what do the numbers mean? Again, as was true with the variance, the values of computed standard deviations indicate the relative variability within a group. From our descriptive statistics we know that the variability among students in Classroom X is much greater than that among students in Classroom Y. What does this mean? Why

"Yes, yes, I *know* that, Sidney—*every*body knows *that!* ... But look: Four wrongs *squared*, minus two wrongs to the fourth power, divided by this formula, *do* make a right."

are there such differences? These are interesting questions that statistics cannot answer for you. Such differences in variability could be due to differences among students across classes in prior knowledge of math and statistics, or they could be due to differences in teaching practices, or they could be due to something else.

We'll find more uses for the standard deviation in later chapters, so you'll learn more about its meaning at that time. Meanwhile, take time to practice computing some of the statistics you've learned so far.

Problems

1. Find the mean ($\overline{X}$), range (R), variance (SD^2), and standard deviation (SD) for each of the following groups of scores. Carry out all calculations to three decimal places and round them correct to two places.

Aptitude Test Scores	GPAs	Math Anxiety Scores
160	4.0	27
100	3.6	29
80	3.4	27
70	3.0	20
69	2.5	10

2. Find the range, variance, and standard deviation for the following sets of values.
   - **a.** 1, 2, 3, 4, 5, 6, 7, 8, 9
   - **b.** 10, 20, 30, 40, 50, 60, 70, 80, 90
   - **c.** .1, .2, .3, .4, .5, .6, .7, .8, .9

Answers to Problems

1.

Aptitude Test Scores	GPAs	Math Anxiety Scores
$\overline{X}$ = 95.80	3.30	22.60
R = 91.00	1.50	19.00
SD^2 = 1,443.2	.33	61.3
SD = 37.989	.57	7.83

2.
   - **a.** $R = 8$, $SD^2 = 7.5$, $SD = 2.74$
   - **b.** $R = 80$, $SD^2 = 750.0$, $SD = 27.4$
   - **c.** $R = .8$, $SD^2 = .075$, $SD = .274$

CHAPTER

6 The Normal Curve

- **What Is the Normal Curve?**
- **Proportions of Scores Under the Normal Curve**
- **Problems**
- **Answers to Problems**

A famous statistician would never travel by airplane, because he had studied air travel and estimated the probability of there being a bomb on any given flight was 1 in a million, and he was not prepared to accept these odds. One day a colleague met him at a conference far from home. "How did you get here, by train?" "No, I flew." "What about the possibility of a bomb?" "Well, I began thinking that if the odds of one bomb are 1 in a million, then the odds of TWO bombs are (1/1,000,000) × (1/1,000,000). *This is a very, very small probability, which I can accept. So, now I bring my own bomb along!"*

The normal curve is a mathematical idealization of a particular type of symmetric distribution. It is not a fact of nature. Since many actual distributions in the social and behavioral sciences approximate the normal curve, we can use what mathematicians know about it to help us interpret test results and other data. When a set of scores is distributed approximately like the normal curve, mathematicians can provide us with a great deal of information about those scores, especially about the proportions of scores that fall in different areas of the curve. Before discussing how to use the normal curve to find certain proportions of scores, let's talk a little bit more about the characteristics of the normal curve.

WHAT IS THE NORMAL CURVE?

The normal distribution describes a family of normal curves, just like a circle describes a family of circles—some are big, some are small, but they all have certain characteristics in common. What are the common features of normal curves?

1. All normal curves are symmetric around the mean of the distribution. In other words, the left half of the normal curve is a mirror image of the right half.
2. All normal curves are unimodal. Because normal curves are symmetric, the most frequently observed score in a normal distribution—the mode—is the same as the mean.
3. Since the normal curves are unimodal and symmetric, the mean, median, and mode of all normal distributions are equal.
4. All normal curves are asymptotic to the horizontal axis of the distribution. Scores in a normal distribution descend rapidly as one moves along the horizontal axis from the center of the distribution toward the extreme ends of the distribution, but they never actually touch it. This is because scores on the normal curve are continuous and held to describe an infinity of observations.
5. All normal curves have the same proportions of scores under the curve relative to particular locations on the horizontal axis when the scores are expressed in a similar basis (i.e., in standard scores).

All normal curves have these features in common, but they can differ in terms of their mean and standard deviation.

The Normal Curve as a Model

As mentioned above, the normal curve is a good description of the distribution of many variables in the social and behavioral sciences. The distribution of scores on standardized tests of intelligence, or "IQ" tests, for example, is roughly normal. Not all variables are normally distributed, however. The distribution of reaction time, for example, is positively skewed. This is because there is a physiological lower limit to time in which a person can respond to a stimulus, but no upper limit.

In addition to the fact that the normal curve provides a good description for many variables, it also functions as a model for distributions of statistics. Imagine that you randomly selected a sample of people from a population, calculated the mean of that sample, and then put them back into the population. Now imagine doing that again and again, an infinite number of times. If you created a frequency distribution of the means for those samples, the distribution of those statistics would approximate the normal curve. This is known as a sampling distribution. Knowing the shape of distributions of statistics is crucial for inferential statistics, as we'll see in later chapters in Section IV.

SidneyHarris/www.sciencecartoonsplus.com

PROPORTIONS OF SCORES UNDER THE NORMAL CURVE

In the next few paragraphs, I am going to show you how the mean, median, mode, standard deviation, and the normal probability curve all are related to each other. Consider the following example:

Test Scores (*X*)	Frequency
110	1
105	2
100	3
95	2
90	1

If you were to calculate the mean, median, and mode from the data in this example, you would find that $\overline{X} = Mdn = Mo = 100$. Go ahead and do it, just for practice. The three measures of central tendency always coincide in any group of scores that is symmetrical and unimodal.

Recall that the median is the middle score, the score that divides a group of scores exactly in half. For any distribution, you know that 50% of the remaining scores are below the median and 50% above. In a normal distribution, the median equals the mean, so you know that 50% of the scores also are higher than the mean and 50% are lower. Thus, if you know that the mean of a group of test scores is 70, and if you know that the distribution is normal, then you know that 50% of the persons who took the test (and who didn't get a score of exactly 70) scored higher than 70 and 50% scored lower.

Now let's see how the standard deviation fits in. Suppose again that you had administered a test to a very large sample, that the scores earned by that sample were distributed like the normal probability curve, and that the $\overline{X} = 70$ and the $SD_x = 15$. Mathematicians can show that in a normal distribution, exactly 68.26% of the scores lie between the mean and one standard deviation away from the mean. (You don't need to know why it works out that way; just take it on faith.) In our example, therefore, about 34.13% of the scores would be between 70 and 85 (85 is one standard deviation above the mean: $\overline{X} + SD_x = 70 + 15 = 85$). We know that the normal curve is symmetrical, so we know that about 34.13% of the scores will also be between 70 and 55 ($\overline{X} - SD_x = 70 - 15 = 55$). Thus, if we administered our test to 100 persons, approximately 34 would have scores between 70 and 85, and about 68 would have scores between 55 and 85 (34.13% + 34.13%). Most students find it helpful (necessary?) to see a picture of how all of this works; use the graph in Figure 6-1 to check it out.

To take another example, suppose that grade-point averages (GPAs) were calculated for 1,000 students and that for GPA the $\overline{X} = 2.5$ and $SD_x = 0.60$. If our sample of GPAs was drawn from a normal distribution, you would know that approximately 500 students had GPAs higher and 500 had GPAs lower than 2.5 You would also know that approximately 683 of them (34.13% + 34.13% = 68.26%; 68.26% of 1,000 is approximately 683) had GPAs somewhere between 1.90 and 3.10 (the mean ± one standard deviation). Figure 6-2 shows what the graph would look like.

Mathematicians can tell us the proportion of the population between any two points under the normal curve, because the area under the normal curve is proportional

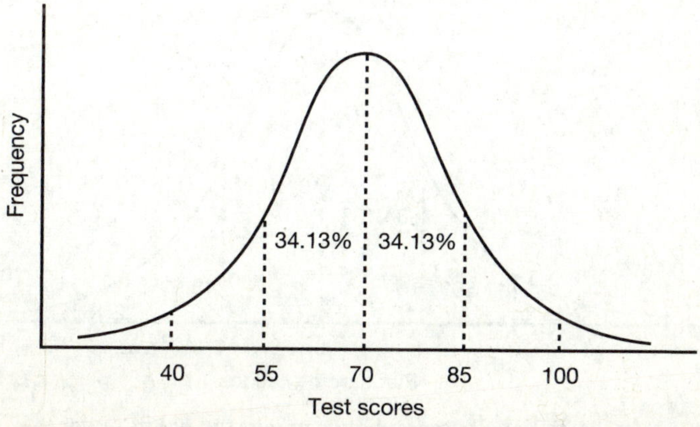

FIGURE 6-1 A distribution of IQ scores ($\overline{X} = 70$, $SD_x = 15$).

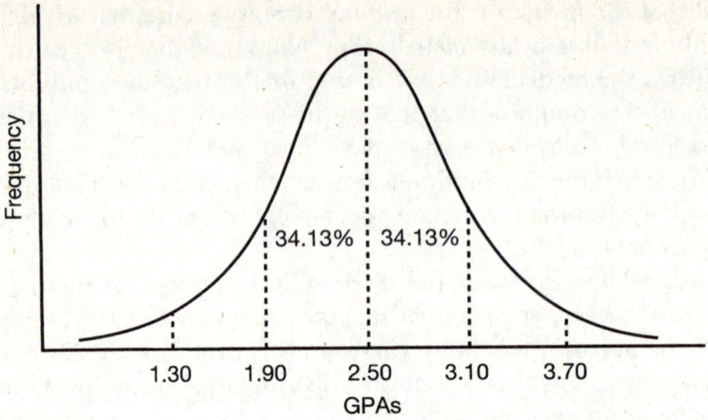

FIGURE 6-2 A distribution of GPAs ($\overline{X} = 2.50$, $SD_x = 0.60$).

to the frequency of scores in the distribution. Figure 6-3 presents information about some selected points.

The numbers on the baseline of the figure represent standard deviations (*SD*), where −1 represents one standard deviation below the mean, +2 represents two standard deviations above the mean, and so on.

Given the information in the graph, you can answer some interesting questions. For example, suppose again that you administered a test to 100 people, that the scores were distributed approximately normally, and that $\overline{X} = 70$ and $SD_x = 15$. You know from the preceding discussion that about half of the 100 people scored lower than 70 and 50 scored higher; and you know that approximately 68 scored between 55 and 85. The graph also tells you the following:

1. About 13.59% of the scores are between −1*SD* and −2*SD*. In our example, therefore, around 14 people scored between 40 (two standard deviations below the

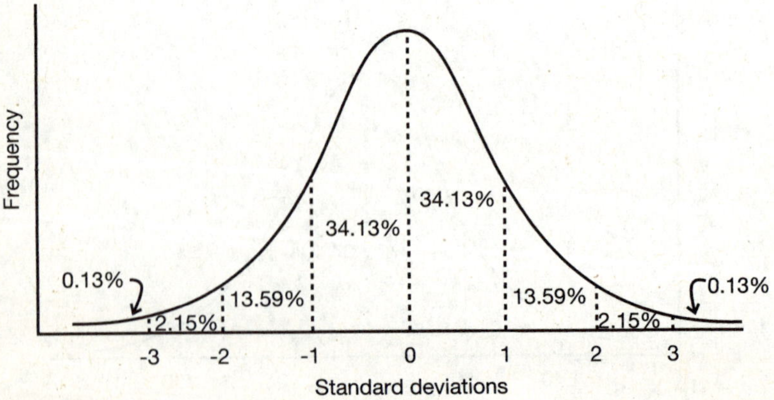

FIGURE 6-3 Percentage of scores between selected points under the normal curve.

mean) and 55 (one standard deviation below the mean). Of course, 13.59% (approximately) of the cases also are between $+1SD$ (85) and $+2SD$ (100).

2. About 95.44% of the cases fall between $-2SD$ and $+2SD$ (13.59% + 34.14% + 34.13% + 13.59%), so we know that approximately 95 out of 100 people scored between 40 ($-2SD$) and 100 ($+2SD$).

3. About 99.74% of the cases fall between $-3SD$ and $+3SD$. Nearly all persons in our example scored between 25 ($-3SD$) and 115 ($+3SD$).

4. About 84.13% had scores lower than 85. How do we know this? Fifty percent of the persons scored below 70 (the mean and median, remember?), and another 34.13% scored between 70 and 85. Adding the 50% and the 34.13%, you find that 84.13% of the scores are predicted to fall below 85.

The following problems will test your understanding of the relationships among the mean, median, mode, standard deviation, and the normal probability curve. Remember that these relationships hold only if the data you are working with are distributed normally. When you have a skewed distribution or one that is more or less peaked than normal, what you have just learned does not hold true.

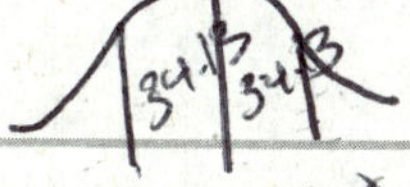

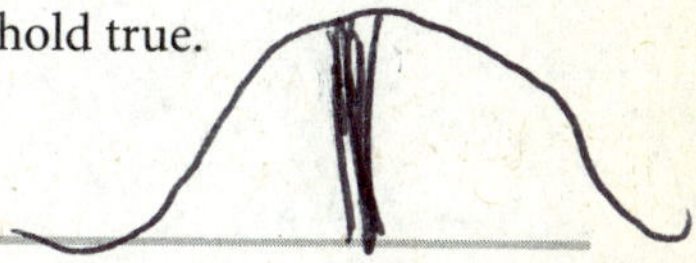

Problems

1. Suppose that a test of math anxiety was given to a large group of persons, the scores are assumed to be from a normally distributed population, and that $\overline{X} = 50$ and $SD_X = 10$. Approximately what percentage of persons earned scores:
   - **a.** below 50?
   - **b.** above 60?
   - **c.** between 40 and 60?
2. A major pharmaceutical company has published data on effective dosages for their new product, FeelWell. It recommends that patients be given the minimum effective dose of FeelWell and reports that the mean effective minimum dose is 250 mg, with a standard deviation of 75 mg (dosage effectiveness is reported to be normally distributed). What dose level will be effective for all but 2% of the total population? What dose level can be expected to be too low for all but 2%?
3. New American cars cost an average of \$17,500, with $SD = \$2,000$. (That's not really true; I just made it up for this problem.) If I'm only willing to spend up to \$15,500, and if car prices are normally distributed, what percentage of the total number of new cars will fall within my budget?

Answers to Problems

1. **a.** 50%
   b. 15.87%
   c. 68.26%
2. 400 mg; 100 mg
3. 15.87%

CHAPTER

7 Percentiles and Standard Scores

- **Percentiles**
- **Standard Scores**
- **Other Standard Scores**
- **Converting Standard Scores to Percentiles**
- **A Word of Caution**
- **Problems**
- **Answers to Problems**

A musician drove his statistician friend to a symphony concert one evening in his brand new midsized Chevy. When they arrived at the hall, all the parking spots were taken except one in a remote, dark corner of the lot. The musician quickly maneuvered his midsized Chevy into the space and they jumped out and walked toward the hall. They had only taken about ten steps when the musician suddenly realized he had lost his car key. The statistician was unconcerned because he knew the key had to be within one standard deviation of the car. They both retraced their steps and began searching the shadowed ground close to the driver's door. After groping on his hands and knees for about a minute, the musician bounced to his feet and bolted several hundred yards toward a large street light near the back of the concert hall. He quickly got down on all fours and resumed his search in the brightly lit area. The statistician remained by the car dumbfounded, knowing that the musician had absolutely zero probability of finding the key under the street light. Finally, after 15 minutes, the statistician's keen sense of logic got the best of him. He walked across the lot to the musician and asked, "Why in the world are you looking for your key under the streetlight? You lost it back in the far corner of the lot by your car!" The musician, in his rumpled and stained suit, slowly got to his feet and muttered angrily, "I KNOW, BUT THE LIGHT IS MUCH BETTER OVER HERE!!"

If you work as a teacher or a member of one of the other helping professions (e.g., school psychologist, psychologist, counselor), you frequently will be required to interpret material in student or client folders. Material in the folders typically will include several types of test scores. This chapter will introduce you to two common types of scores—percentiles and standard scores—as well as their major variations. Some of the material may appear complicated at first, but it's just a logical extension of what you've learned so far. You may not even find it particularly difficult!

Before discussing percentiles and standard scores, I want to point out some of the disadvantages of three types of scores with which you may be familiar from your school days: the raw score, the percentage correct score, and rank in class. Consider the following dialog:

BOY: Mom! I got 98 on my math test today!

MOTHER: That's very good, son. You must be very happy!

BOY: Yes, but there were 200 points on the test.

MOTHER: Oh! I'm sorry. I guess you didn't do too well.

BOY: Yes, but I got the second highest score in class.

MOTHER: Very good!

BOY: Yes, but there are only two of us in the class.

As you can see, the number of points the boy obtained on the math test—his raw score—didn't communicate much information. But neither did his percentage correct score, because it didn't tell us whether the test was extremely difficult or very easy. Nor was his rank in class very helpful unless we knew how large the class was, and even when we found that out, we didn't know a whole lot, because the class was small and our knowledge of the one person with whom he was being compared is nonexistent. When interpreting someone's test score, we would like to know, at a minimum, something about the group of persons with whom he or she is being compared (the norm group) and how he or she did in comparison with that group.

The norm group of a test usually will include a large sample of people. For a standardized aptitude test, for example, test publishers often attempt to get a large representative sample of people in general. In their sample, they often include a sample of persons in the various age, gender, racial/ethnic, and socioeconomic groups likely to be measured by that test, in proportions reflecting the United States Census data. Test manuals often contain detailed descriptions of normative samples and the way in which they were obtained; a good textbook on tests and measurement can also give you that kind of information. Obviously, a test's usefulness to you is strongly influenced by the group(s) on which it was normed. For instance, if you intend to use a test with preschoolers, but it was normed on adults, you would have no way of meaningfully interpreting your clients' scores.

PERCENTILES

Percentiles are one of the most frequent types of measures used to report the results of standardized tests, and for good reason: They are the easiest kind of score to understand. An individual whose score is at the 75th percentile of a group scored higher than about 75% of the persons in the norm group, someone whose score is at the 50th percentile scored higher than about 50% of the persons in the norm group, someone whose score is at the 37th percentile scored higher than about 37% of the persons in the norm group, and so on.

The percentile rank of a score in a distribution is the percentage of the whole distribution falling below that score, plus half the percentage of the distribution falling exactly on that score. Consider the following two distributions:

Distribution A	Distribution B
1	4
2	5
3	5
4	5
5	5
5	5
6	5
7	5
8	5
9	10

In both distributions, a score of 5 is at the 50th percentile; it has a percentile rank of 50. In Distribution A, 40% of the scores are below 5, and 20% are at 5. In Distribution B, 10% of the scores are below 5, and 80% are at 5. Fortunately, most scores are normed on very large groups in which the scores form an approximately normal distribution, so you can take a person's percentile rank as a very close estimate of how many folks could be expected to score lower than that person. It is important to note that, if the percentile rank is based on a small group, or on one that isn't normally distributed, you will need to be more cautious in interpreting it.

No matter how large or small the group, though, or what the shape of the distribution, computing a score's percentile rank is always the same: the percentage of scores below the one in question, plus half the percentage right at that score.

STANDARD SCORES

On many published psychological tests, raw scores are converted to what are called *standard scores.* Standard scores are very useful, because they convert raw scores to scores that are meaningfully interpreted. This makes it possible to compare scores or measurements from very different kinds of distributions. The most basic standard score is known as the *Z* score. *Z* scores state the position of a score in relation to the mean in standard deviation units. Let's see how it works.

The *Z* score formula is as follows:

$$Z = \frac{X - \overline{X}}{SD_x}$$

Where: X is an individual's raw score,

$\overline{X}$ is the mean of the group with which the individual is being compared (usually a norm group of some kind), and SD_x is the standard deviation of that group.

With *Z* scores you can compare all scores, from any distribution, on a single, comparable basis. The *Z* score has the following properties:

1. The mean of any set of *Z* scores is always equal to 0.
2. The standard deviation of any set of *Z* scores is always equal to 1.
3. The distribution of *Z* scores has the same shape as the distribution of raw scores from which they were derived.

Suppose you administered a test to a large number of persons and computed the mean and standard deviation of the raw scores with the following results:

$$\overline{X} = 42$$

$$SD_x = 3$$

Suppose also that four of the individuals tested had these scores:

Person	Score (*X*)
Jim	45
Sue	48
George	39
Jane	36

What would be the *Z* score equivalent of each of these raw scores? Let's find Jim's *Z* score first:

$$Z_{Jim} = \frac{Jim's\ Score - \overline{X}}{SD_x} = \frac{45 - 42}{3} = \frac{3}{3} = +1$$

Notice that (a) we substituted Jim's raw score ($X = 45$) into the formula, and (b) we used the group mean ($\overline{X} = 42$) and the group standard deviation ($SD_x = 3$) to find Jim's Z score. Because lots of Z scores turn out to have negative values, we use the + sign to call attention to the fact that this one is positive.

Now for George's Z score:

$$Z_{George} = \frac{George's\ Score - \overline{X}}{SD_x} = \frac{39 - 42}{3} = \frac{-3}{3} = -1$$

Your turn—you figure out Sue's and Jane's Z scores. Did you get $Z_{Sue} = +2$, and $Z_{Jane} = -2$? You did? Very good!

Here is some more practice. Suppose you administered a test to 16 persons who earned the following scores:

20, 19, 19, 18, 18, 18, 17, 17, 17, 17, 16, 16, 16, 15, 15, 14

Start by finding the mean and the standard deviation. I'll give you the answers, but check yourself to see if you can get the same ones:

$$N = 16$$
$$\overline{X} = 17$$
$$SD_x = 1.63$$

Fred was one of the two persons who scored 19; so for Fred, $X = 19$. To find Fred's Z score,

$$Z_{Fred} = \frac{Fred's\ Score - \overline{X}}{SD_x} = \frac{19 - 17}{1.63} = \frac{2}{1.63} = 1.23$$

Sarah's raw score (X) was 14. Her Z score is—what? You figure it out. That's right, −1.84.

Notice that the sign in front of the Z score tells you whether the individual's score was above (+) or below (−) the mean.

Here's another example. Suppose a test was given to a large number of persons with the following results: $\overline{X} = 47$, $SD_x = 5$. Check your computation of Z scores.

Raw Score (X)	Z Score
57	+2.0
55	+1.6
52	+1.0
50	+0.6
47	0.0
45	−0.4
42	−1.0
40	−1.4
37	−2.0

What does a Z score of -1.40 tell us? First, the minus sign tells us that the score was below the mean. Second, the number 1.4 tells us that the score was 1.4 standard deviations below the mean.

What about a Z score of $+2.00$? The plus indicates that the score is above the mean, and the 2.00, again, tells us that the score is 2 standard deviations above the mean.

Notice that whenever a person's raw score is equal to the mean, his or her Z score equals 0. Take the person whose raw score (X) was 47, for example. That person's Z score $= 0$. If the score had been 1 standard deviation above the mean, the Z score would have been $+1.00$; had it been 1 standard deviation below the mean, the Z score would have been -1.00.

To summarize, the Z score tells you if the raw score was above the mean (the Z score is positive) or if the raw score was below the mean (the Z score is negative), and it tells you how many standard deviations the raw score was above or below the mean.

OTHER STANDARD SCORES

Many people are uncomfortable with negative numbers; others don't like using decimals. Some don't like negatives or decimals! Since Z scores often involve both, these folks would rather not have to deal with them. Our mathematical friends have developed several ways to transform Zs into other measures that are always positive and usually can be rounded to whole numbers without distorting things too much. The most common of these scores is the T score, which always has a mean of 50 and a standard deviation of 10. We'll discuss T scores next, because they are one of the most commonly used standard scores.

T Scores

A number of published personality inventories report test results in a manner similar to that employed by the California Psychological Inventory (CPI). An example of a CPI profile is shown in Figure 7-1. Along the top of the profile, you can see a number of scales designated with letters naming the psychological characteristics measured by the CPI, such as Sc (self-control) and To (tolerance). Under each scale name is a column of numbers. These are raw scores. More interesting to us are the numbers on the left- and right-hand edges. These are the standard score equivalents of the raw scores.

The standard score utilized by the CPI is a T score. The formula for T scores is

$$T = 10(Z) + 50$$

The Z in this formula is the Z you've just learned to compute. Remember that the formula for computing Z scores is

$$Z = \frac{X - \overline{X}}{SD_x}$$

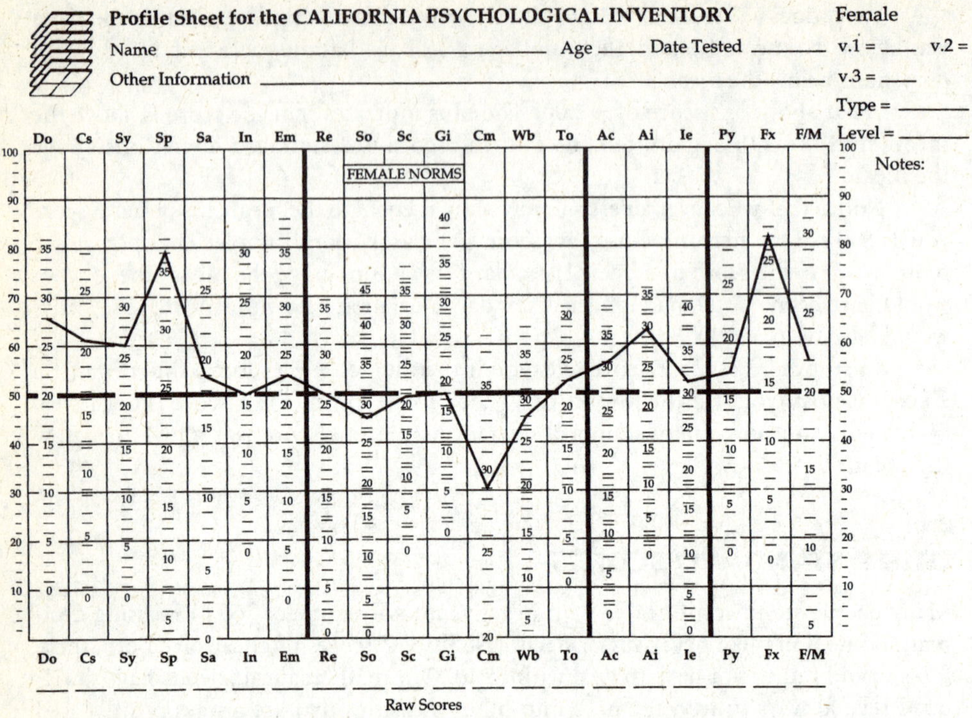

FIGURE 7-1 Example profile sheet for the California Psychological Inventory.

To convert raw scores to *T* scores, you must do the following:

1. Calculate the $\overline{X}$ and SD_x of the raw scores.
2. Find the *Z* score equivalent of each raw score.
3. Convert the *Z* scores to *T* scores by means of the formula $T = 10(Z) + 50$.

Imagine that you visited a large number of high school gym classes and counted the number of sit-ups that each student could do in 3 minutes. You computed the mean and standard deviation of these scores and found that $\overline{X} = 40$, $SD_x = 13$. Matt, one of the students you tested, had a raw score of 46. What was his *T* score?

1. Step 1 has been done for you; we have found that $\overline{X} = 40$ and $SD_x = 13$.
2. Matt's *Z* score is

$$Z_{Matt} = \frac{Matt's\ Score - \overline{X}}{SD_x} = \frac{46 - 40}{13} = \frac{6}{13} = +0.46$$

3. Matt's *T* score is

$$T = 10(Z) + 50 = 10(0.46) + 50 = 4.6 + 50 = 54.6$$

Here are the *Z* and *T* score equivalents of seven more persons. See if you can get the same answers as I did.

Person	Raw Score	*Z* Score	*T* Score
Frank	49	+0.69	56.9
Sam	40	0	50.0
Sharon	58	+1.38	63.8
George	35	−0.38	46.2
Herman	20	−1.54	34.6
Fred	27	−1.00	40.0
Katie	67	+2.08	70.8

Notice that if a person's raw score is exactly at the mean of the group (see Sam's score), then his or her *T* score is 50; if the raw score is one standard deviation below the mean (see Fred's score), then his or her *T* score is 40, and so on.

Let's look at the sample CPI profile again. Notice that the score on the Sc scale has a *T* score equivalent of almost exactly 50. This *T* score lets you know that, relative to the norm group, this person's score was at or near the mean. On the other hand, look at the Sp (social presence) score. The *T* score is 80, so we know that it is three standard deviations above the mean. Very few people in the norm group score that high—the graph in Chapter 6 indicates that well under 1% are up there—so we can conclude that this person had an extremely elevated Sp score. Finally, imagine that someone had a score of 20 on both Sp and Py. Even though their raw scores are the same, they are well below the mean on Sp (their *T* score would be just under 40) and well above the mean on Py ($T = 61$).

Converting scores to *T* scores makes it possible to compare them meaningfully. But it doesn't end there—we can do lots more!

CONVERTING STANDARD SCORES TO PERCENTILES

The choice of what kind of test score will be used by a test publisher is somewhat arbitrary. Some types of scores are relatively easy for anyone to understand, whereas others can be really understood only by those who are sophisticated statistically (like you). My own preference of test-score type is the percentile. Percentile rank tells us exactly where a person stands relative to their norm group, without any need for further translation. A percentile rank of 50 corresponds to a score that is exactly in the middle of the norm group—at the median; a percentile rank of 30, in contrast, corresponds to a score that is at the point where 30% of the remaining scores are below it and 70% above it; and a percentile rank of 95 means that 95% of the remaining scores are below it and only 5% of the norm group scores are above it.

Figure 7-2 will help you to see the relationship between standard scores (*Ts*, *Zs*, IQ scores), percentiles, and the normal curve. If all those numbers look a little threatening to you, don't worry; just take it slowly, and it will make perfect sense. With a ruler or other straightedge to guide you, you can use the figure to make a rough conversion

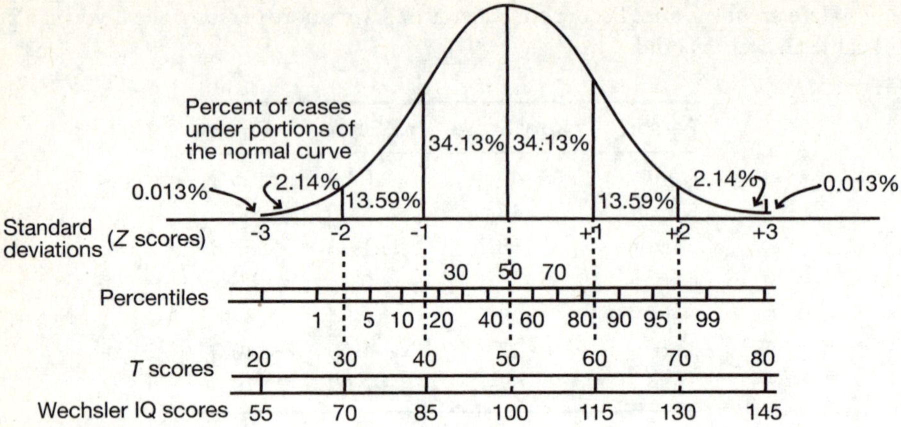

FIGURE 7-2 Relationship among areas under the normal curve, standard deviations, percentiles, and *Z* and *T* scores.

from one kind of score to another. For now, though, let's just look at the figure. As you can see, this figure displays several different kinds of standard scores, including *Z* scores, percentiles, *T* scores, and Wechsler IQ scores.

To use Figure 7-2 to move among different kinds of scores, you first need to convert a raw score to a *Z* score. Having done that, you can easily go to any of the other scores. For example, say a score was 1 standard deviation below the mean. This is equivalent to the following:

Z score of −1
T score of 40
Percentile rank of about 16 (15.87)
Wechsler IQ of 85

Similarly, a raw score that is 2 standard deviations above the mean is equivalent to the following:

Z score of +2
T score of 70
Percentile rank of about 98 (97.72)
Wechsler IQ of 130

Make sense? Not complicated stuff once you get the hang of it.

Chances are that it will be helpful at some time in your work to translate standard scores into approximate percentiles. For example, if you know that a person's MMPI Depression score is 70, and if you know that MMPI scores are *T* scores, then you also know that he or she scored higher than almost 98% of the norm group on that scale. Similarly, if he or she earned an IQ of 85, you will know that the score is below average and at approximately the 16th percentile.

What is the percentile equivalent of someone with a *Z* score of +0.5? You can answer that question by looking down from the *Z* score scale to the percentile score on Figure 7-2 and making a rough approximation (a *Z* score of +0.5 is about the 69th percentile). A more precise answer can be obtained by consulting Appendix A, which presents proportions of area under the standard normal curve.

Don't be nervous; I'll tell you how to use Appendix A. First, though, remember what you already know: If scores are distributed normally, the mean equals the median. Therefore, the mean is equal to the 50th percentile. Recall also (you can check it on Figure 7-2) that a raw score equal to the mean has a *Z* score equal to 0. Putting these facts together, you can see that $Z = 0 = $ 50th percentile.

You may also recall from Chapter 6 that a score that is 1 standard deviation above the mean is higher than 84.13% of the norm group, which is another way of saying that a *Z* score of +1 is at the 84th percentile.

Now let's see how to use Appendix A. Look at the following example. Suppose you gave a statistics test to a large group of people, scored their tests, and computed the mean and standard deviation of the raw scores. Assume that the population of scores was distributed normally and that $\overline{X} = 45$, $SD_x = 10$. Justin had a raw score of 58, which corresponds to a *Z* score of +1.3. What is his percentile rank?

At this point, I always draw a picture of a normal (approximately) curve, mark in one and two standard deviations above and below the mean, and put a check mark where I think the score I'm working with should go, as shown in Figure 7-3.

As you can see, it doesn't have to be a perfect figure, but it does give me an idea of what the answer is going to be. In this case, I know from my picture that the percentile is more than 84 and less than 98. Do you know why? One standard deviation above the mean (in a normal distribution, of course) is at the 84th percentile; two above the mean is at the 98th percentile. Our score is in between those two benchmarks, probably somewhere in the high 80s. Knowing that helps me to avoid dumb mistakes like reading from the wrong column of the table. If this step helps you, too, do it. If not, don't.

Now look in the *Z* columns of Appendix A until you find the *Z* score you just obtained ($Z = +1.3$), and write the first number to the right (in our example, 0.4032).

This number indicates that between the mean and a *Z* score of +1.3, you will find a proportion of 0.4032, or 40.32% of the whole distribution (to convert proportions to percents, move the decimal two places to the right). You know that 50% of the

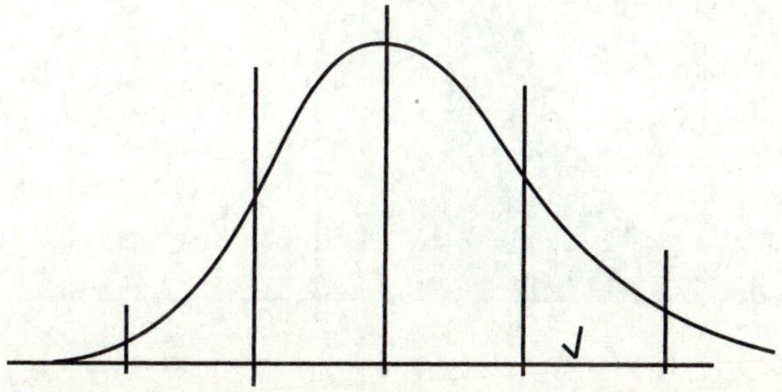

FIGURE 7-3 Example picture of an approximately normal curve.

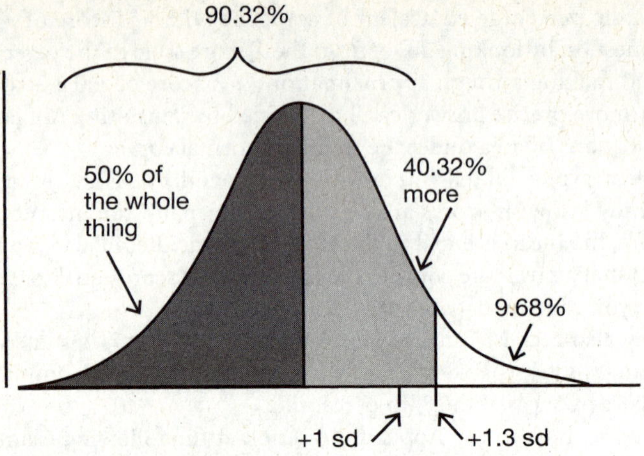

FIGURE 7-4 Relationship between a raw score of 58, the corresponding *Z* score of +1.30, and the percentile rank of 90.32.

cases in a normal curve fall below the mean, so a *Z* score of +1.3 is as high or higher than 0.50 + 40.32% = 0.9032, or 90.32% of the cases. Justin's raw score of 58, therefore, corresponds to a percentile rank of 90.32. That's pretty close to my guess of "high 80s"! A more accurate picture of what we just did is shown in Figure 7-4.

Another example: In Appendix A, locate a *Z* score of +0.89. The table indicates that 31.33% of the cases fall between the mean ($Z = 0$) and $Z = +.89$, and that 18.67% of the cases fall above +0.89. As in the previous problem, the percentile equivalent of $Z = +0.89$ is 50% + 31.33% = 81.33%, a percentile rank of approximately 81. See Figure 7-5.

Remember that the standard normal curve is symmetrical. Thus, even though Appendix A shows areas above the mean, the areas below the mean are identical. For

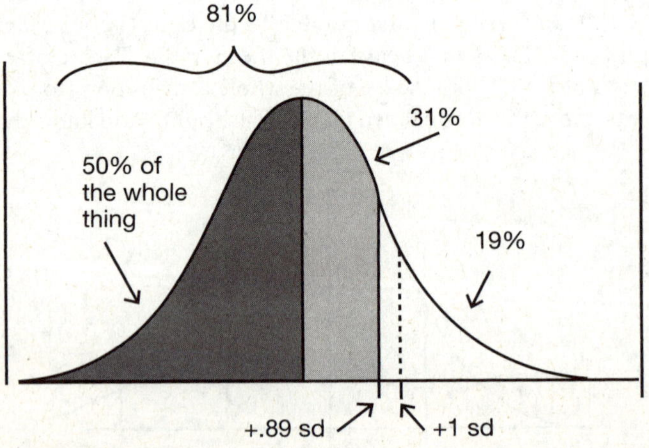

FIGURE 7-5 Relationship between a *Z* score of 0.89 and the corresponding percentile rank of 81.

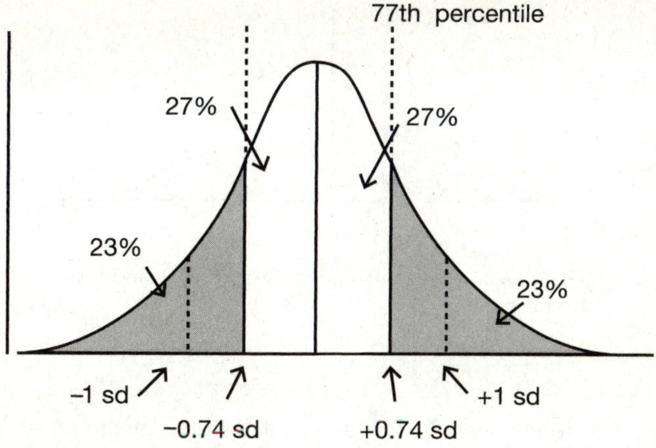

FIGURE 7-6 Relationship between a *Z* score of −.74 and the corresponding percentile rank of 23.

example, the percentage of cases between the mean ($Z = 0$) and $Z = -0.74$ is about 27%. What is the corresponding percentile rank? Appendix A indicates that beyond $Z = 0.74$, there are 23% of the cases (third column). Therefore, the percentile rank is 23. See Figure 7-6.

I find that when I sketch a distribution, and use it to get the sense of what I'm looking for, problems like this are easy. When I don't make a sketch, I very often get confused. That's why I recommend that, unless you're very good at this indeed, you always draw a picture. Enough advice now—back to business!

What percent of cases fall between $Z = +1$ and $Z = -1$? Appendix A indicates that 34.13% fall between the mean and $Z = +1$. Again, since the standard normal curve is symmetrical, there is also 34.13% between the mean and $Z = -1$. Therefore, between $Z = -1$ and $Z = +1$, there will be 34.13% + 34.13% = 68.26% of the cases.

Verify for yourself that 95% of the cases fall between $Z = \pm1.96$ (i.e., between $Z = +1.96$ and $Z = -1.96$) and that 99% of the cases lie between $Z = \pm2.58$.

You can use Appendix A to go backwards to find out what *Z* score corresponds to a given percentile. What *Z* score marks the point where two-thirds of the scores are below and one-third above? Well, that would be at the 66.67th percentile. Before you go to Appendix A and look in the second column for 66.67, and get all frustrated because you can't find it, draw a picture, as shown in Figure 7-7.

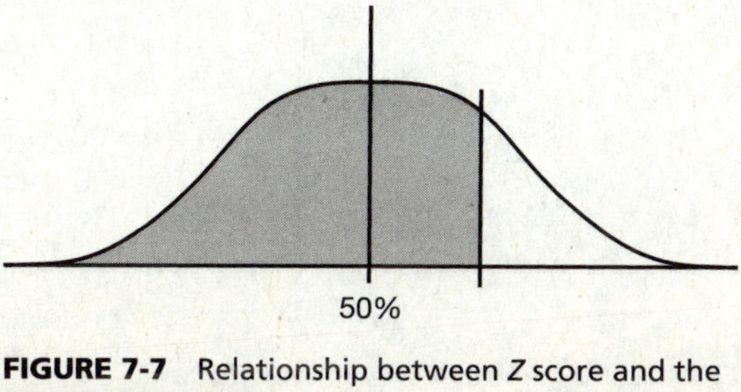

FIGURE 7-7 Relationship between *Z* score and the 66.67th percentile.

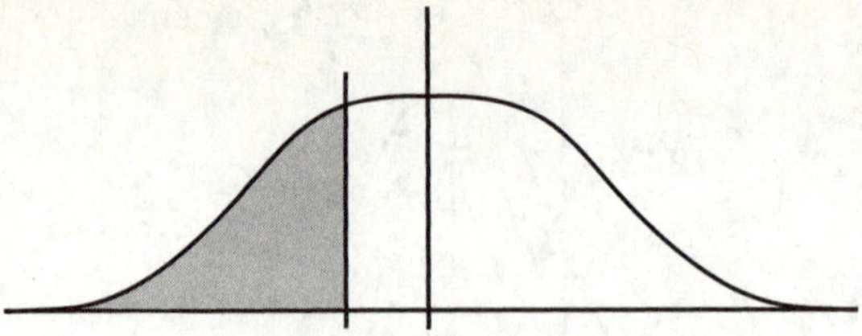

FIGURE 7-8 Relationship between *Z* score and the 30th percentile.

I've shaded in about two-thirds of this distribution, just to see what's going on. Below the mean is 50%; the lighter shaded area above the mean is 16.7%, because the whole shaded part is 66.67%. That's the number I have to find in the table, in the middle column. (The little diagrams at the top of the columns in Appendix A show you what part of the curve is being described in that column.) In this case, we find the number closest to 0.1667 (0.1664) in the far-right column of the first page of Appendix A; reading over to the left, we see that this value corresponds to a *Z* score of +0.43.

Working in the lower half of the distribution is just a bit more complicated, but using a sketch makes it easy. What *Z* score corresponds to a percentile rank of 30? Picture first: See Figure 7-8.

Since the curve is symmetrical (or it would be if I could draw), you can flip it over and work with its mirror image: See Figure 7-9.

Thirty percent of the distribution was in the shaded tail of the first picture, so 30% is in the upper unshaded tail of the second, leaving 20% in the lower part of the top half. Looking up that 20%, we find that it corresponds to a *Z* score of 0.52—that is, +0.52 standard deviation above the mean. What we want is the *Z* score that is 0.52 standard deviation below the mean—hey, we know how to do that; that's just $Z = -0.52$!

If you draw the picture, and use common sense to figure out what you're looking for, you should zip right through these kinds of problems.

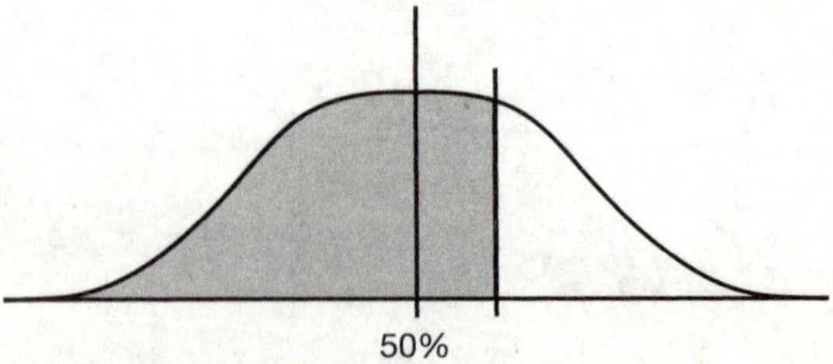

FIGURE 7-9 Another way to look at the *Z* score–30th percentile relationship.

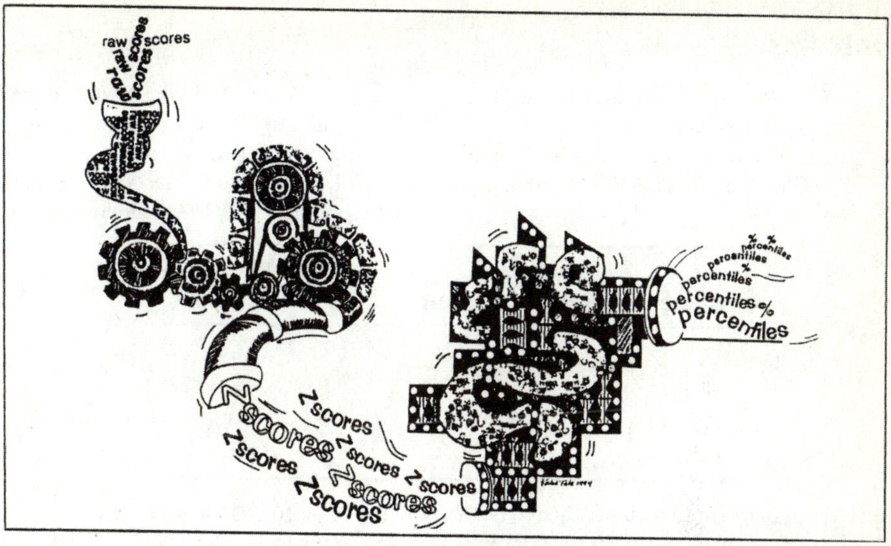

FIGURE 7-10 Pictorial transformation of raw scores into standard scores.

A WORD OF CAUTION

Remember that all the material in this chapter assumes that the scores you are interpreting are from normal (or nearly normal) distributions. If the distribution is skewed, then conversions from standard scores to percentiles using the normal curve will not be accurate. However, you can always convert raw scores to standard scores. If you feel really ambitious, find a friend and explain why this is so.

SidneyHarris/www.sciencecartoonsplus.com

Problems

1. SAT scores are normally distributed, with a mean of 500 and SD_x of 100. Find the *Z*, *T*, and percentile equivalents of the following scores: 500, 510, 450, and 460.

2. Jack, Jill, James, and John all took a math aptitude test. The test was normed on a group that had a mean score of 70, $SD_x = 15$; the scores were normally distributed. Complete the following table:

Name	Raw Score	*Z* Score	*T* Score	Percentile Rank
Jack	73			
Jill		−1.2		
James			60	
John				23

3. Draw a diagram that shows the relationship of a raw score of 20 to *Z*, *T*, and percentile in a distribution with the following:

   a. $\overline{X} = 20$, $SD_x = 5$
   b. $\overline{X} = 40$, $SD_x = 7$
   c. $\overline{X} = 15$, $SD_x = 4$

Answers to Problems

1. 500 (raw score) = 0 (*Z* score) = 50 (*T* score) = 50th percentile
   510 (raw score) = 0.1 (*Z* score) = 51 (*T* score) = 54th percentile
   450 (raw score) = −0.5 (*Z* score) = 45 (*T* score) = 31st percentile
   460 (raw score) = −0.4 (*Z* score) = 46 (*T* score) = 34th percentile

2.

Name	Raw Score	*Z* Score	*T* Score	Percentile Rank
Jack	73	+.2	52	58
Jill	52	−1.2	38	11.5
James	85	+1.0	60	84
John	59	−0.7	42	23

3. a.

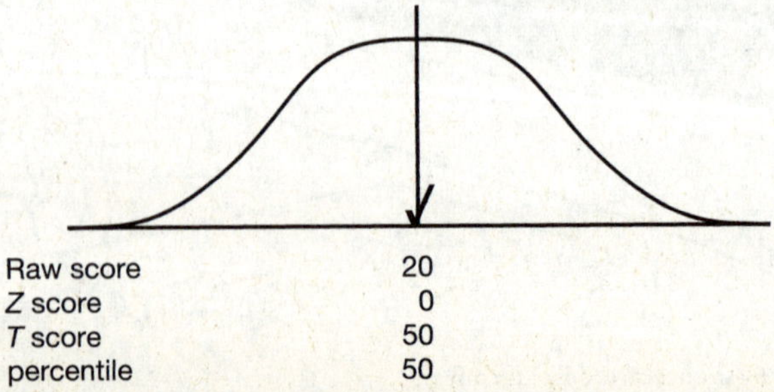

b.

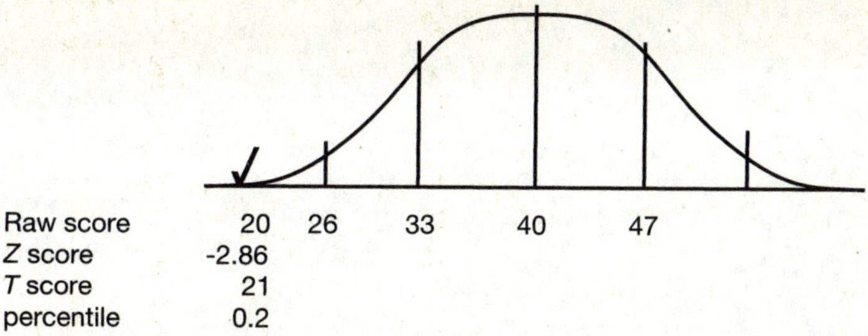

Raw score 20 26 33 40 47
Z score -2.86
T score 21
percentile 0.2

c.

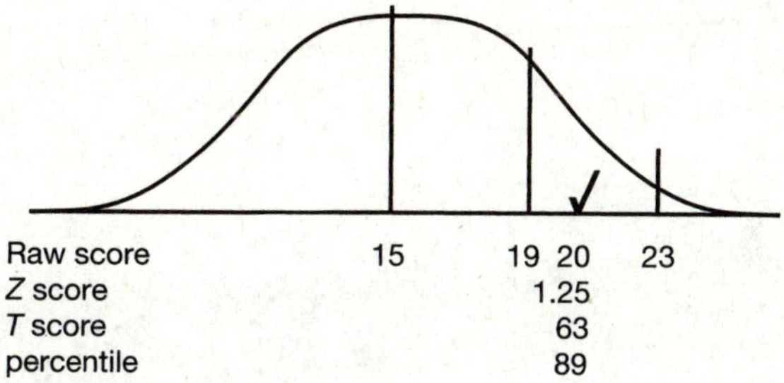

Raw score 15 19 20 23
Z score 1.25
T score 63
percentile 89

SECTION III

Correlation Coefficients and Linear Regression

Right now, I imagine you're feeling pretty good. And you should feel good! We've come a long way. Up to this point, we've focused on describing single variables one at a time. In the preceding chapters you've learned how to summarize data in the form of frequency distributions and display them graphically. You've learned how to use descriptive statistics to describe the level and spread of a set of scores. And you've learned all about the normal curve and how to use standard scores and percentiles to describe the proportions of scores in different areas of the normal curve. That's a lot! Good job. In this section, you learn to determine whether two variables are related and, if so, how. You also find out how to make predictions from one variable to another. In Chapter 8, we discuss the methods of correlation that describe the empirical relationship between two variables. In Chapter 9, we cover how to make predictions with regression equations and how to get an idea of how much error to expect when making those predictions. Let the fun begin!

CHAPTER

8 Correlation Coefficients

- Correlation Coefficients
- Pearson Product-Moment Correlation Coefficient
- Interpreting Correlation Coefficients
- Other Methods of Correlation
- Spearman Rank Correlation Coefficient
- Problems
- Answers to Problems

"In God we trust; all others must have data."

—ANONYMOUS

"A judicious man uses statistics, not to get knowledge, but to save himself from having ignorance foisted upon him."

—THOMAS CARLYLE

"The invalid assumption that correlation implies cause is probably among the two or three most serious and common errors of human reasoning."

—STEPHEN JAY GOULD

Up to now, we've been dealing with one variable at a time. In this chapter, we will discuss how to examine the relationship between two variables. Using the methods of correlation, we will be able to answer important questions such as, Are achievement test scores related to grade-point averages? Is counselor empathy related to counseling outcome? Is student toenail length related to success in graduate school? Hey, inquiring minds want to know.

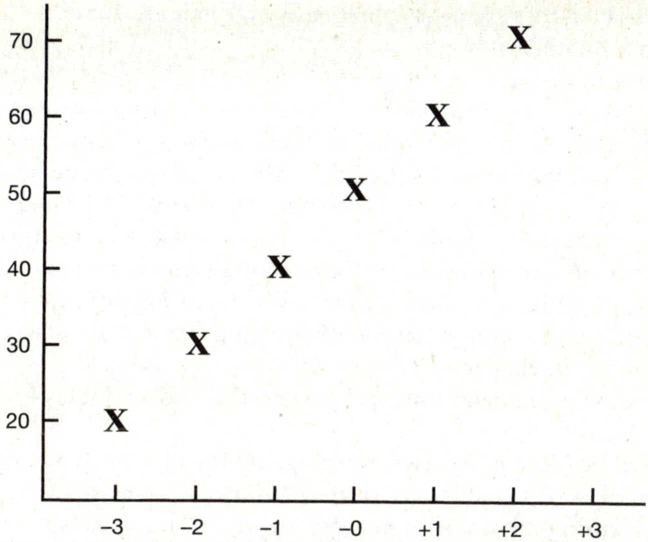

FIGURE 8-1 Relationship between *Z* and *T* scores.

The relationship between two variables can be depicted graphically by means of a scatter diagram. Suppose a group of students took an aptitude test. We'll use a scatter diagram to look at the relationship between *Z* scores and *T* scores on this test. We designate their *Z* scores as the *X* variable (the *X* variable is always plotted on the horizontal axis, or "*X*-axis" of a scattergram) and their *T* scores will be the *Y* variable (plotted on the vertical, or "*Y*-axis"). Each student has two scores. We find a given student's position on the graph by drawing an invisible line out into the center of the graph from the vertical-axis value (the *Y* value, in this case, the student's *T* score) and drawing another invisible line up into the graph from the *X*-axis value (the student's *Z* score). Put an *X* where the two lines cross, and you've plotted that student's location.

As you can see in Figure 8-1, all the *X*s representing the relationship between *Z* scores and *T* scores fall on a straight line. When two variables have this kind of relationship, we say that they are perfectly correlated. This means that if we know the value of something on one of the variables, we can figure out exactly what its value is on the other. If we know that someone has a *T* score of 50, her or his *Z* score has to be 0. Every time.

CORRELATION COEFFICIENTS

Graphs that show relationships such as this in picture form are useful, but often we need a numerical way of expressing the relationship between two variables. In the next few pages, you'll learn how to compute a correlation coefficient. Here are some facts about correlation coefficients:

1. The methods of correlation describe the relationship between two variables. Most methods of correlation were designed to measure the degree to which two variables are linearly related—that is, how closely the relationship resembles a straight line.

2. The correlation coefficient—symbolized by r_{xy}—indicates the degree of association between two variables.
3. The values of r_{xy} can range from -1.00 to $+1.00$.
4. The *sign* of the correlation indicates how two variables are related. Positive values of r_{xy} indicate that low values on one variable are related to low values on the other, and vice-versa. For example, height and weight are positively correlated. Taller people tend to be heavier than shorter people, on average. Negative values of r_{xy} indicate an inverse relationship between two variables; low values on one variable are related to high values on the other, and vice-versa. Intelligence and reaction time, for instance, are negatively related. More intelligent people tend to have lower reaction times, on average, than people who aren't as intelligent.
5. When $r_{xy} = 0$, no relationship between the two variables exist. They are uncorrelated.
6. The absolute value of r_{xy}. (when you ignore the plus or minus sign) indicates how closely two variables are related. Values of r_{xy}. close to -1.00 or $+1.00$ reflect a strong relationship between two variables; values near 0 indicate a weak relationship.

Scatterplots and correlation coefficients are related. Figure 8-2 shows example scatterplots depicting various correlation coefficients. As you can see here, correlation coefficients are a quick and easy way to express how and how well two variables are related or go together. The greater the correlation coefficient is, the smaller the scatter around a hypothetical straight line drawn through the middle of the scatterplot. Perfect correlations of -1.00 and $+1.00$ fall on a straight line. High correlations, such as those around $+0.90$ or -0.80, tend to have minimal scatter, whereas lower correlations, such as those around $+0.30$, tend to have much more scatter. Also shown in this figure are three ways in which the relationship between two variables can be zero. For each, the values of one variable are totally unrelated to values of the other variable. Keep in mind that a correlation of zero means no *linear* relationship at all. Two variables could be related in a *curvilinear* manner and still have a correlation of zero (as you can see in the lower-left scatterplot in Figure 8-2).

PEARSON PRODUCT-MOMENT CORRELATION COEFFICIENT (r_{xy})

Many measures of correlation have been developed by statisticians for different purposes. The most commonly used measure of correlation is the Pearson product-moment correlation coefficient, designated by lowercase r_{xy}. The Pearson r_{xy} is used to describe the linear relationship between two quantitative variables. Try to relax as much as you can before you look at the next formula, because it may look horrendous. Smile. We'll do it together, following the indicated steps, one at a time. It isn't as bad as it looks. I'm going to show you two different ways to calculate the Pearson r_{xy} to find the correlation between two variables (X and Y)—the deviation score formula and the computing formula. Both formulas will give you the same r_{xy}, as we'll see.

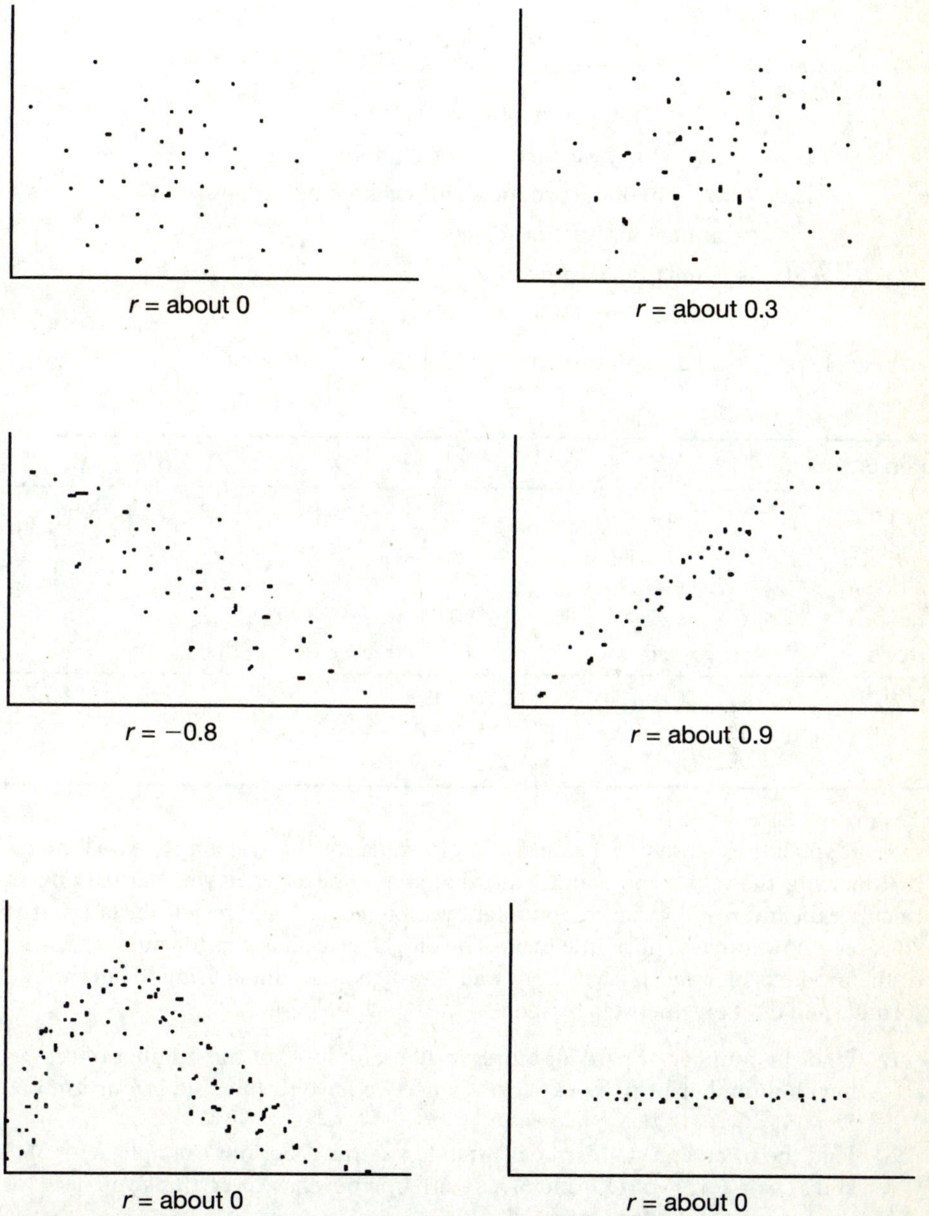

FIGURE 8-2 Sample graphs depicting various degrees of correlation.

Deviation Score Formula:

$$r_{xy} = \frac{Cov_{xy}}{SD_x SD_y}$$

Where: $Cov_{xy} = \frac{\Sigma(X - \overline{X})(Y - \overline{Y})}{N - 1}$ or $\frac{\Sigma xy}{N - 1}$

$x = (X - \overline{X})$, the deviation scores for X

$y = (Y - \overline{Y})$, the deviation scores for Y

Σxy = the sum of the products of the paired deviation scores

N = number of pairs of scores

SD_x = standard deviation of X

SD_y = standard deviation of Y

Here are hypothetical data on variables *X* and *Y* for five individuals:

Persons	***X***	***Y***	***x***	***y***	***xy***
Justin	37	75	−1.8	−4.8	8.64
Theresa	41	78	2.2	−1.8	−3.96
Zachary	48	88	9.2	8.2	75.44
Koko	32	80	−6.8	0.2	−1.36
David	36	78	−2.8	−1.8	5.04
$N = 5$	$\Sigma X = 194$	$\Sigma Y = 399$			$\Sigma xy = 83.8$
	$\overline{X} = 38.8$	$\overline{Y} = 79.8$			
	$SD_x = 6.1$	$SD_y = 4.9$			

If you'll look closely at the derivation formula for the Pearson r_{xy}, you'll notice that many of the values and computations are the same as when you learned how to calculate the mean and variance. You might want to go back and review the last part of Chapter 5 now if that's still a little fuzzy. The only new term in this formula is the sum of the products of x and $y(\Sigma xy)$. Let's walk through an example using the derivation formula and do it together step by step:

1. Find the number of pairs of scores in the sample—not the number of scores, but the number of pairs of scores. Since we have five people in our sample, $N = 5$
2. Find the mean and standard deviation for X and Y. For our example, $\overline{X} = 38.8$ and $SD_x = 6.1$; $\overline{Y} = 79.8$ and $SD_y = 6.1$. You now have everything you need for the denominator of the formula!
3. Find x by subtracting $\overline{X} = 38.8$ from each score on X.
4. Find y by subtracting $\overline{Y} = 4.9$ from each score on Y.
5. Multiply each value of x with each value of y

6. To find the Cov_{xy}, first find Σxy by finding the sum of the products of x and y. Here, $\Sigma xy = 83.8$. Now complete the formula:

$$Cov_{xy} = \frac{\Sigma(X - \overline{X})(Y - \overline{Y})}{N - 1} = \frac{\Sigma xy}{N - 1} = \frac{83.8}{5 - 1} = 20.95$$

7. The final step is to calculate r_{xy}:

$$r_{xy} = \frac{Cov_{xy}}{SD_x SD_y} = \frac{20.95}{(6.1)(4.9)} = \frac{20.95}{29.89} = +.70$$

Now let's work the same dataset using the computing formula.

Computing Formula:

$$r_{xy} = \frac{N(\Sigma XY) - (\Sigma X)(\Sigma Y)}{\sqrt{[N\Sigma X^2 - (\Sigma X)^2][N\Sigma Y^2 - (\Sigma Y)^2]}}$$

If you'll look closely at the computing formula for the Pearson r_{xy}, only one term in this formula is new: the $N(\Sigma XY)$ term found in the numerator. N is, of course, the number of pairs of measurements. In our example, $N = 5$. The rest of the term, (ΣXY), directs you, first, to multiply each person's X score by his or her Y score and then to sum the products. Here are the same data used in the aforementioned example, but with the values needed for the computing formula:

Persons	X	Y	X^2	Y^2	XY
Justin	37	75	1,369	5,625	2,775
Theresa	41	78	1,681	6,084	3,198
Zachary	48	88	2,304	7,744	4,224
Koko	32	80	1,024	6,400	2,560
David	36	78	1,296	6,084	2,808
$N = 5$	$\Sigma X = 194$	$\Sigma Y = 399$	$\Sigma X^2 = 7674$	$\Sigma Y^2 = 31{,}937$	$\Sigma XY = 15{,}565$

Now you have everything you need to complete the computing formula for r_{xy}:

1. Look at the numerator of the formula for r_{xy} first:
   (a) Find $N(\Sigma XY)$. In our example, $N = 5$ and $\Sigma XY = 15{,}565$.

$$N(\Sigma XY) = (5)(15{,}565) = 77{,}825$$

   (b) Find $(\Sigma X)(\Sigma Y)$. For our data, $\Sigma X = 194$ and $\Sigma Y = 399$. So we get

$$(\Sigma X)(\Sigma Y) = (194)(399) = 77{,}406$$

   (c) Find $N(\Sigma XY) - (\Sigma X)(\Sigma Y)$.

$$N(\Sigma XY) - (\Sigma X)(\Sigma Y) = 77{,}825 - 77{,}406 = 419$$

2. OK. We're almost done. Now let's look at the denominator:

$$\sqrt{[N\Sigma X^2 - (\Sigma X)^2][N\Sigma Y^2 - (\Sigma Y)^2]}$$

(a) Look inside the square-root sign at the left-hand side of the denominator first. Find $[N\Sigma X^2 - (\Sigma X)^2]$. For our example, $N = 5$, $\Sigma X^2 = 7674$, and $\Sigma X = 194$. So for the left side of the denominator we have

$$\left[N\Sigma X^2 - (\Sigma X)^2\right] = (5)(7674) - (194)^2$$
$$= 38{,}370 - 37{,}636 = 734$$

(b) Now look inside the square-root sign at the right-hand side of the denominator. Find $[N\Sigma Y^2 - (\Sigma Y)^2]$. For our example, $N = 5$, $\Sigma Y^2 = 31{,}937$, and $\Sigma Y = 399$. So for the right side of the denominator we have

$$\left[N\Sigma Y^2 - (\Sigma Y)^2\right] = (5)(31{,}937) - (399)^2$$
$$= 159{,}685 - 159{,}201 = 484$$

(c) All that remains to be done to find the denominator is to take the square root of the product of $[N\Sigma X^2 - (\Sigma X)^2]$ and $[N\Sigma Y^2 - (\Sigma Y)^2]$.

$$\sqrt{[N\Sigma X^2 - (\Sigma X)^2][N\Sigma Y^2 - (\Sigma Y)^2]}$$
$$= \sqrt{(734)(484)} = \sqrt{355{,}256} = 596$$

3. You're (finally) ready to calculate r_{xy}! All you have to do is divide the numerator, the value you found in Step 1(c), by the denominator, the value you found in Step 2(c):

$$r_{xy} = \frac{419}{596} = +.70$$

So, as you can see, the derivation and computing formulas both provide the same r_{xy} for this dataset. Most people think the computation formula is faster and easier to compute. My advice to you is to use the one that you feel most comfortable using.

INTERPRETING CORRELATION COEFFICIENTS

In our example, we obtained a correlation of +.70 between X and Y. What does this mean? There are a number of possible interpretations. You will recall that a perfect correlation between two variables would result in $r_{xy} = +1.00$ or -1.00, whereas if there were no correlation at all between X and Y, then $r_{xy} = 0$. Since the correlation of +0.70 is positive and greater than 0, we can say that variables X and Y are related but that the relationship is not perfect. This means that, on average, high scores on X are related to high scores on Y, and vice-versa.

Another common way to interpret r_{xy} is to calculate what is known as the *coefficient of determination*. The coefficient of determination is simply the square of the correlation coefficient, r_{xy}, or r_{xy}^2. The coefficient of determination is interpreted as the percent of variance in one variable that is "accounted for" or "explained" by knowing the value of the other variable. In other words, when two variables are correlated, the r^2_{xy}. tells us the proportion of variability in one variable that is accounted for by knowing another variable. In our example, the obtained $r_{xy} = +.70$ and $r^2_{xy} = 0.49$. The percentage of variance in Y explained by X is equal to $r^2_{xy} \times 100$. Thus, we could say that 49% of the differences in Y are related to differences in X. If we obtained a r_{xy} of -0.60 measures of self-esteem and bullying—meaning that on average high self-esteem is related to less bullying and vice-versa—squaring that value would give you 0.36. (I know that it seems wrong when you see that the square of a number is smaller than the number being squared, but it's true. Try it.) The obtained square of the correlation coefficient (in our example, 0.36) indicates that 36% of the variability in bullying is "accounted for" by the variability in self-esteem. "Why is it that some people achieve more in school than others?" some might ask. If intelligence is related to academic achievement, and if the r_{xy} between intelligence and academic achievement is $r_{xy} = 0.50$, then 25% (squaring 0.50 and converting it to a percentage) of the variability in achievement among people would be "accounted for" by intelligence, the other 75% being independent of intelligence. Another way of saying the same thing is that variables X and Y have 25% of their variability "in common."

It is important not to confuse correlation with causation. In our example above, $r_{xy} = 0.70$, the two variables are related. But that doesn't prove that X causes Y, any more than it proves that Y causes X. The correlation between the number of counselors and the number of alcoholics in a state may be positive, for example, but that does not mean that one causes the other. Two variables may be correlated with each other due to the common influence of a third variable. On the other hand, if two variables do not correlate with each other, one variable cannot be the cause of the other. If there is no difference in counseling outcome between, for example, "warm" and "cold" counselors, then "warmth" cannot be a factor determining counseling outcome. Thus, the correlational approach to research can also help us to rule out variables that are not important for our theory or practice. This point is so important that it bears repeating: If two variables are correlated, it does not mean that one causes the other. However, if they are not correlated, one cannot be the cause of the other.

OTHER METHODS OF CORRELATION

The Pearson r_{xy} is a measure of the linear relationship between two variables, but some variables are related to each other in a curvilinear fashion. For example, the relationship between anxiety and some kinds of performance is such that moderate levels of anxiety facilitate performance, whereas extremely high and low levels of anxiety interfere with it. A scatterplot showing the relationship between the two variables would show the dots distributing themselves along a curved line resembling an inverted U (curvilinear), rather than a straight line (linear). The Pearson r_{xy} is not an appropriate measure of relationship between two variables that are related to each other in a curvilinear fashion. If you are interested in the relationship between two variables measured on a large number of participants, it's a good idea to construct a scatterplot for twenty or so participants before calculating r_{xy}, just to get a general idea of whether the relationship (if any) might be curvilinear. There are a number of other correlational techniques in addition to the Pearson r_{xy}. One of these, the Spearman correlation for ranked data, is presented here.

SPEARMAN RANK CORRELATION COEFFICIENT

The Spearman rank correlation (r_s), also called Spearman's rho, can be used with variables that are *monotonically* related. A monotonic relationship is one in which the values of one variable tend to increase when the values of the other variable increase, and vice-versa, but not necessarily linearly. In addition, the r_s can be used with ranked data. When scores on variables X and Y are ranked, the following formula may be used:

$$r_s = \frac{Cov_{xy}}{SD_x SD_y}$$

Where: X, Y are ranks

Here are some example data for six people:

Persons	X	X_r	Y	X_r	X	Y	XY
Linda	30	1	100	6	−2.5	2.5	−6.25
Griff	40	2.5	80	3	−1.0	− 0.5	0.5
Max	40	2.5	70	2	−1.0	−1.5	1.5
Carolyn	50	4	90	5	0.5	1.5	0.75
Lynn	60	5	88	4	1.5	0.5	0.75
Jasper	70	6	60	1	2.5	−2.5	−6.25
$N = 6$		$\Sigma X_r = 21$		$\Sigma Y_r = 21$			$\Sigma xy = -9.0$
		$\overline{X}_r = 3.5$		$\overline{Y}_r = 3.5$			
		$SD_{xr} = 1.8$		$SD_{y_r} = 1.9$			

Let's walk through one example of the Spearman r_s step by step:

1. First set up the table as you see it above.
2. Then set up the values for X and Y for each subject. List the scores on X from smallest to largest.
3. Convert the values for X to ranks, 1 = lowest rank and so on. If two or more values of X are tied at a particular rank, average the rank and assign the same rank to all of those values.
4. Find $N, \overline{X}_r, \overline{Y}_r, SD_{xr}, SD_{yr}$, and Σxy, using the ranks instead of scores.
5. Calculate r_s using the formula:

$$r_s = \frac{Cov_{xy}}{SD_x SD_y} = \frac{\frac{\Sigma xy}{N-1}}{SD_x SD_y} = \frac{\frac{-9.0}{6-1}}{(1.8)(1.9)} = \frac{\frac{-9.0}{5}}{3.42} = \frac{-1.8}{3.42} = -0.53$$

This correlation reflects a moderate, negative correlation between scores on X and Y. The coefficient of determination, $r_s^2 = 0.28$. This indicates that 28% of the variance in variable X is explained by Y.

Problems

1. Given the following data, what are the correlation and the coefficient of determination between
   a. Scores on tests of intelligence (IQ) and emotional intelligence (EQ)?
   b. IQ scores and exam scores?
   c. EQ test scores and exam scores?

Student	IQ (X)	EQ (Y)	Exam Scores (Z)
1	140	14	42
2	130	20	44
3	120	29	35
4	119	6	30
5	115	20	23
6	114	27	27
7	114	29	25
8	113	30	20
9	112	35	16
10	111	40	12

2. A researcher is interested in determining the relationship between the popularity of high school students and academic rank in class. Using these ranked data, calculate Spearman r_s and the coefficient of determination.

Class	Popular
8	1
4	2
6	3
10	4
7	5
2	6
1	7
8	8
3	9
5	10

Answers to Problems

1. $r_{xy} = -0.61$ coefficient of determination $= 0.37$
   $r_{xz} = 0.85$; coefficient of determination $= 0.73$
   $r_{yz} = -0.66$; coefficient of determination $= 0.44$
2. $r_s = -0.353$; $r_s^2 = 0.125$, or 12.5%.

CHAPTER

9 Linear Regression

- **Regression Equations**
- **Standard Error of the Estimate**
- **Problems**
- **Answers to Problems**

Statistical Analysis: Mysterious, sometimes bizarre, manipulations performed upon the collected data of an experiment in order to obscure the fact that the results have no generalizable meaning for humanity. Commonly, computers are used, lending an additional aura of unreality to the proceedings.

Statisticians and researchers and teachers and weather forecasters and all sorts of other folks are interested in making predictions. A prediction, in this sense, is simply a best guess as to the value of something. We try to make our predictions so that, over the long run, the difference between the value we predict and the actual value (what the thing really turns out to be) is as small as possible.

If we have no additional information, the best guess that we can make about a value is to predict that it will equal the mean of the distribution it comes from. If I want to predict John's score on a test, and I know that the average score students like John have received on that test is 50, my best prediction of John's score is 50. Over time, across lots and lots of predictions, always predicting that somebody's score will equal the mean of the distribution will give me the best chance of coming close to a correct answer. Making predictions with no extra information is not very useful, however. If the weatherperson always made exactly the same forecast (variable clouds, possibility of showers) day after day, people would quickly stop paying attention. Most often, though, we do have additional information, and we use that information to improve the accuracy of our prediction.

You know from Chapter 8 that when there is a positive correlation between two variables, X and Y, those persons who score high on the X variable also tend to score high on the Y variable, and those who score low on X tend to score low on Y.[1] For example, suppose you know that there is a positive correlation between shoe size and weight. Given a person's shoe size, you can improve your guess about his weight. If you knew that John's shoe size is 12, you would predict that he weighs more than Jim, whose shoe size is 7. You can increase the accuracy of predictions of this sort considerably if you use what statisticians call a regression equation. If two variables are correlated, it is possible to predict with greater than chance accuracy the score on one variable from another with the use of a regression equation. The higher the correlation is between two variables, the better the prediction. If the r_{xy} is $+1.00$ or -1.00, then prediction is perfect. In this case, knowledge of a person's standing on variable X tells us exactly where he or she stands on variable Y. If the r_{xy} is zero, then prediction is no better than chance.

REGRESSION EQUATIONS

The following is an intuitive form of the regression equation:

$$\hat{Y} = \overline{Y} + b(X - \overline{X})$$

The predicted value of $Y(\hat{Y})$ is equal to the mean of the Y distribution $(\overline{Y})$—no surprise here—plus something that has to do with the value of X. Part of that "something" is easy—it's how far X is from its own mean $(\overline{X})$. That makes sense: Having a shoe size that is way above the mean would lead us to predict that weight would also be above the mean, and vice versa. That takes care of the $(X - \overline{X})$ part. But what's the b stand for? Well, b is a term that adjusts our prediction so that we take into account differences in the means and the standard deviations of the two distributions with which we're working, as well as the fact that they aren't perfectly correlated. In our example, if IQ scores and achievement test scores had a correlation of $+1.00$, and if they had the same mean and the same standard deviation, the value of b would turn out to be 1 and we could just ignore it.

It isn't necessary to go into the details of where b comes from or why it works to make our predictions; all we need to know for now is how to calculate it. Fortunately, it's fairly easy to calculate:

$$b = r_{xy}\left(\frac{SD_y}{SD_x}\right)$$

So, to make a prediction about Y, based on knowing the corresponding value of X, all you need to know is the correlation between X and Y (that's the Pearson r_{xy} we computed in Chapter 8), the means and standard deviations of both distributions, and the value of *X*. And you already know how to get those values, right?

Let's work it out with an example. A researcher has been collecting information about teenage school achievement and family life. She discovered that the average high-schooler in her community spends an average of 5.3 hours per week on homework, with $SD = 1.4$; she also learned that the parents of these students pay an average of \$1.32 for each grade of A their kids earn, with $SD = 0.35$. Finally, she calculated that there is a $r_{xy} = +0.43$ between money paid for grades of A and time spent on homework. Putting all that in table form, we have

Payment per grade of A (*X*):	$\overline{X} = 1.32, SD_x = 0.35$
Hours of homework per week (*Y*):	$\overline{Y} = 5.30, SD_Y = 1.40$
	$r_{xy} = +.43$

This researcher happens to have a teenage son, Marty, whom she pays a dollar and a half for every A he brings home. Can you predict how many hours per week Marty will study next term? To find the answer to this question, first find the value of *b*:

$$b = r_{xy}\left(\frac{SD_y}{SD_x}\right) = 0.43\left(\frac{1.40}{0.35}\right) = 0.43(4.00) = 1.72$$

Now we can plug all the values into the basic regression equation:

$$\begin{aligned}\hat{Y} &= \overline{Y} + b(X - \overline{X})\\ &= 5.30 + 1.72(1.50 - 1.32)\\ &= 5.30 + 1.72(0.18)\\ &= 5.30 + 0.31\\ &= 5.61\end{aligned}$$

Based on this regression equation, we predict that Marty will spend approximately one-third of an hour (0.31 to be exact), which is about 19 minutes, more time studying than the 5.30 hours the average kid does, and his mom was paying him a little more than the average kid was paid.

How about Kindra, who doesn't get any money at all (that is $X = 0$) for the As she earns?

$$\begin{aligned}\hat{Y} &= \overline{Y} + b(X - \overline{X})\\ &= 5.30 + 1.72(0 - 1.32)\\ &= 5.30 + 1.72(-1.32)\\ &= 5.30 + (-2.27)\\ &= 3.03\end{aligned}$$

Based on our regression results, we predict that Kindra will spend a lot less time studying than most of her classmates, only about 3.03 hours per week.

Once you've calculated the value of *b*, everything is easy. The basic formula is always the same. The only thing that changes is the *X* value for each person.

Now, do these numbers mean that Marty will study exactly 5.61 hours every week, and Kindra will always put in only 3.03 hours of book time? Well, no. For one thing, I cheated a little when I made up that example. The regression calculation is based on some mathematical assumptions that may or may not be true for these data. But even if the assumptions were met, our predictions wouldn't be perfectly accurate. We will overestimate the amount that some kids study per week and underestimate the amount for others. On the average, we'll be right, but there will be errors when we look at individuals. Is there any way to know ahead of time just how much error we can expect? Well, yes, there is. Unfortunately, though, this isn't a simple problem; it will require some explanation.

CLOSE TO HOME JOHN McPHERSON

Unfortunately, Brad had neglected to stretch his brain before taking the big algebra midterm.

STANDARD ERROR OF THE ESTIMATE

Schools and employers use a variety of measures to predict how well people will do in their settings. Although such predictions usually are more accurate than those made by nonmathematical methods (guesstimation), there is some danger in using the results of predictions in a mechanical way. Suppose, for example, that the University of Michifornia uses an admissions test to predict the expected GPA of incoming students. Over the years, it has been established that the mean score on the Test of Admissions (X) is 50.00 ($SD = 10$) and the mean Frosh GPA (Y) is 2.40 ($SD = 0.60$). The correlation between these two variables is +0.70. After conducting a linear regression analysis, they found a regression or prediction equation of

$$\hat{Y} = (0.042)X + (0.302)$$

Denny, a twelfth-grader, took the admissions test and got a score of 34. To predict his GPA using linear regression, we calculate

$$\hat{Y} = (0.042)X + (0.302) = (0.042 \times 34) + 0.302 = 1.73$$

Since his predicted GPA of 1.73 is less than a C average, it might be tempting to conclude that Denny is not "college material." Before jumping to that conclusion, however, it is wise to remember that predictions about individual performance aren't perfectly accurate. Not everyone who has a predicted GPA of 1.73 achieves exactly that: Some do better than predicted (overachievers?), and others do worse (underachievers?).

In fact, if you took 100 persons, all of whom had a predicted GPA of 1.73, their actual GPAs would vary considerably—they would form a distribution. If you could look into a possible future and actually see how well these students did, you could compute a mean and standard deviation of the distribution of their GPAs. Theoretically, the scores would be distributed normally, would have a mean equal to the predicted GPA of 1.73, and would have a standard deviation of the predicted GPA of

$$\sigma_{est} = \left(SD_y\sqrt{1 - r_{xy}^2}\right)\sqrt{\frac{N-1}{N-2}}$$

Where: σ_{est} is the standard error of the estimate
N is the number of pairs of observations
r_{xy}^2 is squared correlation between the X and Y variables

Now this is a very important idea. We're talking about a group of people, selected out of probably thousands who took the college admissions test—selected because that test predicted that they would get a 1.73 GPA. But they don't all get a GPA of 1.73: Some do better than predicted and some not so well. Their GPAs will tend to cluster around the predicted value, however. If there were enough of them (it would probably take more than 100 in order to smooth out the curve), the distribution would be normal in form, would have a mean equal to the predicted value, and would have a standard deviation of

$$\sigma_{est} = \left(SD_y\sqrt{1 - r_{xy}^2}\right)\sqrt{\frac{N-1}{N-2}}$$

$$= 0.60\sqrt{1 - 0.70^2} = 0.60\sqrt{1 - 0.49} = 0.60\sqrt{0.51} = 0.60(0.71) = 0.43$$

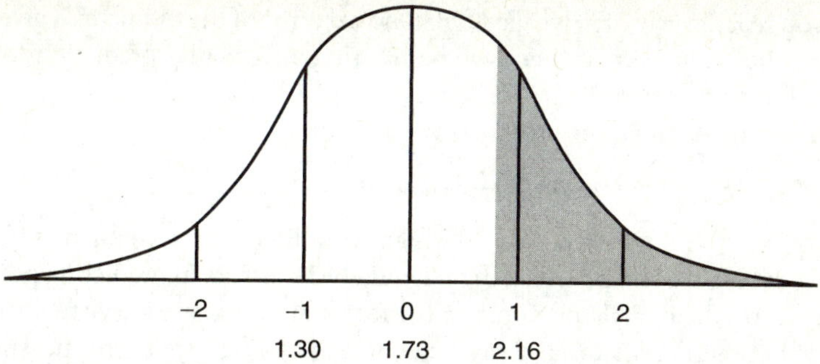

FIGURE 9-1 Proportion of GPAs of 2.0 and above.

Notice that the term $\frac{\sqrt{N-1}}{\sqrt{N-2}}$ is reduced to 1 and drops out of the equation because the sample is so large. This term doesn't matter much when your sample is large; it can matter a lot with a small sample.

You will recall from Chapter 6 that approximately 68% of the scores in a normal distribution fall between ±1 standard deviation from the mean. In this example, the standard deviation of our distribution of GPA scores from those low test-score students is 0.43. This value, 0.43, is known as the standard error of the estimate (σ_{est}). So, we conclude that 68% of the GPAs in this distribution can be expected to fall between 1.73 − 0.43 and 1.73 + 0.43, or between 1.30 and 2.16. In other words, 68% of the scores fall between ±1 standard error of the estimate from the mean.

In Figure 9-1, I've shaded the area that represents GPAs of 2.00 and above. If you define someone who graduates from college with a C average as "college material," then you can see that a fairly good percentage of those who were predicted to have a 1.73 GPA (less than a C average) actually would do all right (i.e., have a GPA higher than 2.00). In fact, using the table in Appendix B, you can figure out exactly how many students are likely to fall into this category:

1. A GPA of 2.00 is 0.27 grade points above the mean (2.00–1.73).
2. That's .27/.43 of a standard deviation, or 0.63 standard deviation above the mean.
3. Going to the table, we find that 0.26 of the distribution lies above a *Z* score of 0.63: More than a quarter of the GPAs in this distribution will be 2.00 or better.
4. About 26% of the total population of students would be mislabeled if we used a cutting point of exactly 1.73.

It's all very logical if you just take it one step at a time.

Using the standard error of the estimate, we can report predictions in a way that tells others how accurate the prediction is. If we were to say that a student who scores 34 on the admissions test will have a GPA of 1.73 ± 0.43, we would be right two-thirds of the time. (If that confuses you, better go back to Chapter 6 and read about proportions of scores under the normal curve.) And that means, of course, that we'd still be wrong about one-third of the time—about 17% of folks getting that score on the test would do better than a 1.73 GPA, and about 17% would do worse.

Do you see now why σ_{est} is called the standard error of the estimate? It gives us a way of estimating how much error there will be in using a particular prediction formula—a particular regression equation.

Look at the formula one more time:

$$\sigma_{est} = SD_y\sqrt{(1 - r_{xy}^2)}$$

Notice that if $r_{xy} = 1.00$, then $\sigma_{est} = 0$, which is another way of saying that if the correlation between *X* and *Y* were perfect, there would be no errors in predicting performance on *Y* from our predictor *X*. Unfortunately (or fortunately?), there are virtually no perfect correlations between predictor and predicted variables when we try to measure human beings. We are not able to predict individual human performance with anything near perfection at this time—and, between you and me, nor do I believe we ever will.

Problems

1. Here are some interesting (and imaginary) facts about cockroaches: The average number of roaches per home in the United States is 57; $SD = 12$. The average number of packages of roach killer purchased per family per year is 4.2; $SD = 1.1$. The correlation between roaches in the home and roach killer bought is +0.50.
   a. The Cleanly family bought 12 packages of roach killer last year. How many roaches would you predict they have in their home?
   b. The Spic-Spans have 83 roaches at their house. What would be your best prediction of how many boxes of roach killer they bought?
2. A researcher tested second-grade children for their reading skills. He used a test that had three subscales: decoding, vocabulary, and comprehension. Here's what he found:

   Decoding (*X*): $\bar{X} = 29.97$, $SD_x = 7.93$
   Vocabulary (*Y*): $\bar{Y} = 11.93$, $SD_y = 0.37$
   Comprehension (*Z*): $\bar{Z} = 42.87$, $SD_z = 23.19$
   $r_{xy} = +0.60$
   $r_{xz} = +0.77$
   $r_{yz} = +0.56$

   Find the value of *b* in the regression equation that predicts
   a. decoding score, if you know the student's vocabulary score.
   b. vocabulary score, if you know the student's comprehension score.
   c. comprehension score, if you know the student's decoding score.
   d. decoding score, if you know the student's comprehension score.

Answers to Problems

1. **a.** 99.51 roaches
   b. 5.4 packets of roach killer
2. **a.** $b = 12.86$ **b.** $b = 0.01$
   c. $b = 2.25$ **d.** $b = 0.26$

Endnote

1. It's important to remember that regression equations don't imply anything about causality—even though they may appear to do so. Regressions equations, like correlations, simply reflect the fact that two variables are related.

SECTION IV

Inferential Statistics

Three sections down, and two to go. In this section we discuss inferential statistics. Inferential statistics involve the use of statistics to infer things about larger populations by studying smaller samples of those larger populations. A word of warning: Of all the chapters in this book, Chapter 10 is probably the most important and possibly the most difficult. This chapter discusses the basic concepts underlying the use of statistics to make inferences. The difficulty of this chapter has nothing to do with the complexity of the math involved—because there is very little math in this chapter—and everything to do with the abstractness of the ideas involved in using statistics to test hypotheses. If you grasp the main concepts in this chapter, the rest of the book will be a piece of cake. So take your time reading Chapter 10. Chapter 11 discusses how to use the basic concepts covered in the preceding chapter to examine differences between the means of two groups with the *t* Test. Chapter 12 covers analysis of variance (ANOVA), a method for analyzing differences between the means of two or more groups.

CHAPTER

10 Introduction to Inferential Statistics

- **The Sampling Experiment**
- **Sample Values (Statistics) and Population Values (Parameters)**
- **The Null Hypothesis**
- **Type I and Type II Errors**
- **Statistical Significance and Type I Error**
- **Problems**
- **Answers to Problems**

The larger the sample size (n) the more confident you can be that your sample mean is a good representation of the population mean. In other words, the "n" justifies the means.

We've all had the experience of flipping on the evening news and getting the weather forecast. In Chapter 9, we talked about the kind of forecast the weatherperson would have to make if he or she had no information at all except the most common weather situation that occurs in that location. For Oregon, that would likely be "tomorrow it will rain." But the weatherperson doesn't say that; the forecast is more like, "Tomorrow there is an 80% chance of showers." What, exactly, does that "80% chance of showers" mean? Will it rain 80% of the time tomorrow? Or, maybe, 80% of us will get rained on? Or, we'll have 80% of a full rainstorm sometime during the day? Those are pretty silly interpretations; we all know that an "80% chance of rain" means that it's very likely to rain—but then again, maybe it won't. More precisely, it means that in the past, with conditions like this, there was rain the next day 80% of the time. And, one time out of five, the rain didn't happen.

"There's an 80% chance of rain tomorrow" is a probability statement. Such statements tell us how likely—how probable—it is that a particular event will occur. Probability statements are statistical statements, but, unlike the kind of statistics we've been looking at so far, they go beyond simply describing a set of data that we have in hand. They represent ways of describing and predicting what we don't know, on the basis of current data.

As we'll see in later chapters of this book, probability statements play an important role in research. The whole notion of statistical significance rests on probability statements. *Significance* here has a very specific meaning, but I think I'll wait to give you the formal definition later, when it will make more sense. For now, I just want to introduce you to some of the concepts of simple probability.

Almost every explanation of probability starts with a description of the process of flipping coins, and this will be no exception. I'm tired of "heads" and "tails," though. My coin will be a Canadian $1 coin, generally known as a "loony" because it has a picture of a loon on one side (the other side depicts the queen). So, instead of "heads" and "tails," we'll be talking about "loons" and "queens."

If I flip my coin 600 times, and if it's a fair coin (equally likely to come up either way), how many of those times should I expect it to come up loons? Right, half the time—300 loons. And 300 queens. We would say that the probability of getting a loon is 50%, or 0.50. What if I'm throwing a die instead of flipping a coin? A die has six sides, and if it's a fair die, each side is equally likely to come up. So I would expect that my 600 throws would yield 100 ones, 100 twos, 100 threes, and so on.

Will I always get the same numbers if I repeat the coin-tossing experiment over and over again? Nope, there'll be some randomness in the data I generate. I might get 305 loons and only 295 queens in one set of coin flips, or 289 loons and 311 queens in another. And there would be similar fluctuations if I repeated the die-throwing experiment over and over again. But, over many, many sets of coin flips or die throws, the deviations would even out. The more often I repeated the experiment, the more closely my total data would approximate the predicted percentages. Over an infinite number of experiments, the numbers of loons and queens—or of ones, twos, threes, fours, fives ,sixes—would be exactly as predicted. Probability statements don't tell us exactly what will happen, but they are our best guess about what will happen. Making our predictions about events based on known probabilities will, over the long run, result in less error than making them any other way.

There are a couple of things that I'd like you to notice about those two situations, flipping the coin or throwing a die. First, each throw comes out only one way—it's an all-or-nothing situation. You can't flip a coin and have it come out half loon and half queen (unless it stands on edge, and I won't let that happen); you can't throw a die and get 2.35 as a result. Second, each possible outcome is known. There are only two ways that my coin can land, and there are exactly six possible outcomes when we throw a die. So we know exactly what those possible outcomes are.

Okay, I'm going to flip that loony again. This time, though, I want you to tell me the probability of getting either a loon *or* a queen. Silly question, you say—I'll always get one or the other. Exactly right: The probability of getting either a loon or a queen is 100%, or 1.00. The probability of getting a loon is 0.50, the probability of getting a queen is 0.50, and the probability of getting a loon or a queen is 1.00. Do you see a rule coming? When two mutually exclusive[1] outcomes have known probabilities, the probability of getting either the one or the other in a given experiment is the sum of their individual probabilities. What's the probability of our die throw yielding either a five or a six? If you added $\frac{1}{6}$ and $\frac{1}{6}$ and got $\frac{2}{6}$, or $\frac{1}{3}$, or 0.33, you've got the idea!

Let's do just one more loony experiment (yes, I really said that) and then move on to something more interesting. This time we're going to flip two coins. How many possible outcomes are there, and what is the probability of each? Before you answer, let me warn you that this is a trick question. The most obvious answer is that there are three possible outcomes: two loons, or two queens, or a loon and a queen. So far, so good. But, if you go on to say that since the coins are all fair coins, and loons and queens are equally likely, the probability of each of those three outcomes is 0.33, then you've fallen for the trick. Look at the possible outcomes more closely:

Outcome	Coin A	Coin B
1	Loon	Loon
2	Loon	Queen
3	Queen	Loon
4	Queen	Queen

Even though it looks, on the surface, as if only three different things can happen, there are actually four possible outcomes, and each is equally likely. Knowing that, we can easily determine the probabilities of tossing 2 loons, 2 queens, or a queen and a loon. The probability of two loons is 1 in 4, or 0.25. The probability of 2 queens is the same, 0.25. And the probability of a loon and a queen is the sum of the probabilities of the two ways of getting that outcome: Loon on Coin A and queen on Coin B has a probability of 0.25; queen on Coin A and loon on Coin B has a probability of 0.25; the probability of getting exactly one loon and one queen when we toss two coins is 0.25 + 0.25, or 0.50. Putting it in standard symbols:

$$p_{L,Q} = 0.50$$

THE SAMPLING EXPERIMENT

Most of the time, in the kinds of research that call for statistical procedures, we aren't able to look at the total population in which we are interested. Gathering data on everyone in a population—such as all the children in special education in the United States—is almost always too time-consuming or expensive. We therefore have to use relatively small samples to represent the much larger populations. If I do an experiment that involves testing the reading skills of third-graders, I might work with a sample of 50 or 100 children in the third grade. But I'm not really interested in just those 50 or 100 children; I want to say something that will hold true for all third-graders. Agriculturists who test the usefulness of fertilizers or pesticides want to make predictions about how those fertilizers or pesticides will work for all the crops on which they might be used, not just describe the small sample they've tested. And looking at the effects of a new vaccine on a sample of twenty volunteers would be pretty useless unless we expected to generalize those results to lots and lots of other folks. Sampling, and predicting outcomes on the basis of those samples, is a fundamental idea in research. That's why we need to understand the concept of probability in sampling.

We'll start with some definitions. I've already used the words, and I hope you've understood what they mean, but it's a good idea to get the precise definitions out on the table:

• ***Population:*** A large (sometimes infinitely large) group about which some information is desired. Examples include:

All third-grade children in the United States

All the wheat crops in North America

Height of all men entering basic training in the armed forces

All the beans in a five-gallon jar

• ***Sample:*** A subset of a population; a smaller group selected from the population. Examples include:

First-grade children in Mrs. Walton's class at Wiles Elementary School

Southernmost acre of wheat in each farm in Ayres County

Height of the first 100 men entering Army training in Florida in January, 2005

The first ten beans drawn from a five-gallon jar of beans

• ***Random sample:*** A sample selected in such a way that (a) every member of the population from which it is drawn has an equal chance of being selected, and (b) selection of one member has no effect on the selection of any other member.

The randomness of a sample is very, very important, because everything we are going to say about samples and populations only holds (for sure) when the sample is truly random. That's why I put that jar of beans in as an example: If we stir up the beans very thoroughly, and then pull out a sample with our eyes shut, then every bean has an equal chance of ending up in our sample. Jars of beans are favorite tools for statistics teachers, because they do yield random samples.

Our jar of beans, by the way, has two colors of beans in it—red and white. Exactly half of the beans are red and exactly half are white. Okay, stir them up, close your eyes, and pull one out. Don't look at it yet! Before you open your eyes, what color bean do you think you drew? Of course, you can't make a very good guess—since half of the beans are red and half are white, you have an equal chance of drawing a red bean or a white one. Over in Jar 2, 80% of the beans are red. Mix them up, close your eyes, draw one, and guess its color. You'll guess red, of course, and in the long run that guess will be correct 80% of the time. The probability of getting a red bean is equal to the proportion of red beans in the total population. For Jar 1, $\rho_{\text{Red}} = 0.50$; for Jar 2, $\rho_{\text{Red}} = 0.80$.

If you drew a random sample of not one bean but ten beans from each jar, what would those samples look like? Intuitively, we know the answer: The sample from Jar 1 would have about half red and half white beans; the sample from Jar 2 would have about 80% red beans. Samples tend to resemble the populations from which they are drawn. More specifically, over time, the proportions of the sample (for the characteristic of interest) approximate more and more closely the proportions of that characteristic in the parent population. And the bigger the sample, the more likely it is to resemble the parent population. The more experiments we do with Jar 1, the more the number of red and white beans will tend to equal out. The larger the samples we draw from Jar 2, the closer our samples will come to having exactly 80% red and 20% white beans. If we had a magic jar, with an infinite supply of beans, these statements would be true whether or not we put each sample back into the jar before we took another. This basic characteristic of random samples—that over time and with increasing size they come to resemble the parent population more and more closely—is true for samples taken with or without replacement.

SAMPLE VALUES (STATISTICS) AND POPULATION VALUES (PARAMETERS)

You can see where all this is going, can't you? Since it's often difficult or even impossible to measure an entire population, it makes sense to get a sample from that population and measure it instead. What's the average weight of ten-year-olds? Get a sample of ten-year-olds and weigh them. How much do North Americans spend on groceries every week? Get fifty or so folks to let you keep track of what they do in the supermarket. What's the effect of secondhand smoke on the water intake of white rats? Put a dozen rats in a cage and blow smoke at them, and measure what they drink. We can find the means and standard deviations of samples like this and use them to estimate the same values in the populations from which they came. Or can we?

There are a couple of problems that must be overcome in order to use sample values (technically, these are called "statistics") to estimate population values (called "parameters"). One has to do with the representativeness of the sample: If we are going to use sample measurements to estimate population values, the sample has to be truly representative of the population. The experiment with the ten-year-olds wouldn't yield very useful data, for instance, if we got the children in our sample from a group of young gymnasts. Kids involved in gymnastics tend to be thinner than the general population of kids. The easiest way to ensure that our sample is representative is to select it randomly.[2] That way, even though it may not be exactly like the parent population, the differences will at least tend to even out over a large number of samples, or as a single sample gets larger. Samples that are truly representative of their parent population are said to be unbiased. Perhaps the most notorious biased sample was taken inadvertently in 1936, when the *Literary Digest* predicted on the basis of its sample of automobile and telephone users that Alf Landon, the Republican candidate, would win the presidential election by a landslide. In 1936, many voters didn't have telephones or cars, and the ones who didn't have them were more likely to be Democrats than Republicans. Of course, Alf Landon didn't win by a landslide; he lost to Franklin D. Roosevelt.

Even with an unbiased sample, however, bias can creep into some estimates of population values. Some statistics—mathematical descriptions—are inherently biased, and some aren't. The two statistics that are most important to us at this point are the mean and the standard deviation. The mean of a sample is an *unbiased* estimate of the mean of the population from which it came. Hmm . . . that's a complicated-sounding sentence. Let's introduce a couple of new symbols to simplify things. The mean of a population is designated by μ, the Greek letter mu. (If we're talking about samples, we use our standard English $\overline{X}$ for the mean; and if we're talking about populations, we use the Greek μ. Similarly with the variance and standard deviation: For samples, we use the English SD^2 for the variance and SD for the standard deviation; and for populations we use the Greek lowercase σ^2 and σ.) Now, getting back to business: If we take lots and lots of samples from a given population, the means of those samples ($\overline{X}$) will form a distribution that clusters around the mean of the population (μ). What's more, that distribution will be normal—but that's another story, one we'll save for later.

Do you remember, back when we first talked about the variance, I mentioned in Chapter 5 that you will often see the squared deviations from the mean divided by $N - 1$ instead of by N, in order to get SD^2? Well, now we're ready to talk about why that is. When we compute the variance of a sample, we are actually estimating the variance of the population from which the sample was drawn. If we wanted to find the true "average squared deviation," we would use this formula:

$$SD_x^2 = \frac{\sum (X - \overline{X})^2}{N}$$

Using this formula, which involves dividing by N, we would get the variance of the sample itself, but this value would not be an unbiased estimate of the population variance. This value would tend to be smaller than the population variance. The smaller the sample, the greater this error is likely to be. Dividing by $N - 1$ instead of by N is a way of correcting the problem—that is, of correcting for bias in estimating the population value. When the sample is very large, the difference between N and $N - 1$ is negligible; little correction is made, and little is needed. With small samples, the correction is larger. Just as it should be.

Perhaps looking at two extreme situations will help you see how this works. What's the smallest sample you could draw? That's right, just one case: $N = 1$. If we were to find one without correcting for bias, we'd get

$$SD_x^2 = \frac{\sum (X - \overline{X})^2}{N} = \frac{\sum (0)^2}{1} = 0$$

No matter how large the population variance might be, this "sample" wouldn't reflect any of it at all.

What's the biggest sample you could draw? Right again, one the size of the whole population. And its variance (again, uncorrected) would be exactly the same as SD_x^2. So, we have this situation shown in Figure 10-1.

It turns out, by the way, that the points in between those two check marks don't fall in a straight line—SD^2 and σ^2—and therefore aren't linearly related. Instead, SD^2 and σ^2 can be quite different when the sample is small, but the difference levels out relatively quickly, something like that shown in Figure 10-2.

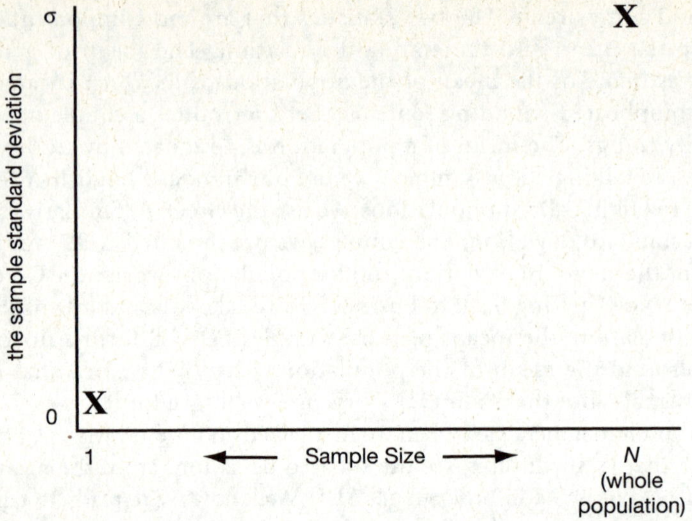

FIGURE 10-1 Uncorrected values of SD^2 for small and large samples.

This situation leads to a very handy fact. Since the amount of bias in using SD^2 to estimate σ^2 is proportional to the size of the sample (N), we can correct for that bias by substituting $N - 1$ for N in the formula for the variance:

$$SD_x^2 = \frac{\sum (X - \bar{X})^2}{N - 1}$$

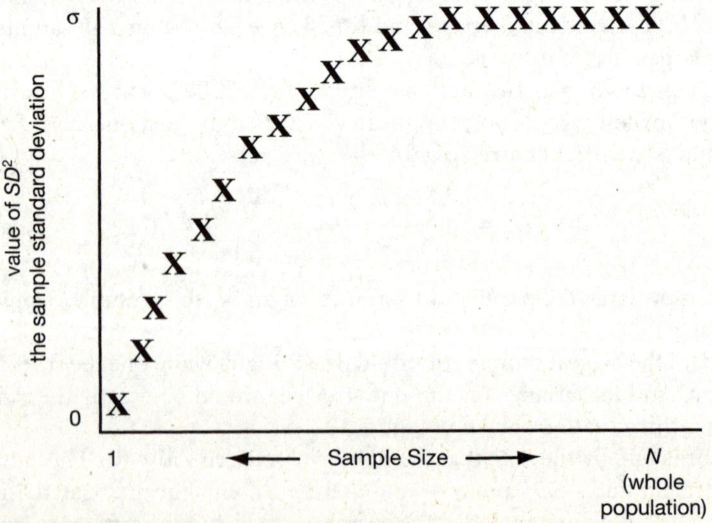

FIGURE 10-2 Uncorrected values of SD^2 for a range of sample sizes.

The computational formula becomes

$$SD_x^2 = \frac{\sum X^2 - \frac{\left(\sum X\right)^2}{N}}{N - 1}$$

THE NULL HYPOTHESIS

Ordinarily, researchers are interested in demonstrating the truth of some hypothesis of interest: that some relationship exists between two variables; that two groups differ in some important way; that Population A is bigger, stronger, smarter, more anxious, and so on, than Population B. We need statistical procedures to test such hypotheses. The problem is, though, that it's almost impossible (with most statistical techniques) to demonstrate that something is true. Statistical techniques are much better at demonstrating that a particular hypothesis is false, that it's very unlikely that the hypothesis could really hold up.

So we have an interesting dilemma. We want to show that something is true, but our best tools only know how to show that something is false. The solution is both logical and elegant: State the exact opposite of what we want to demonstrate to be true, disprove that, and what's left—what hasn't been disproved—must be true.

In case you are now thoroughly confused, here's an example: A researcher wants to show that boys, in general, have larger ears than girls. (I know, it's a dumb idea, but research grants have been awarded for stranger things.) She knows that her statistical tools can't be used to demonstrate the truth of her hypothesis. So she constructs what's known as a null hypothesis, which takes in every possibility except the one thing she wants to prove: Boys' ears are either smaller than or just the same size as girls' ears. If she can use her statistical techniques to disprove or reject this null hypothesis, then there's only one thing left to believe about boys' and girls' ears—the very thing she wanted to prove in the first place.

So, if you can rule out all the gray parts, the only thing left (the thing that must be true) is the white part—exactly what you wanted to prove all along. See Figure 10-3.

The hypothesis that the scientist wants to support or prove is known as the research hypothesis, symbolized H_1; the "everything else" hypothesis is called the null hypothesis and is symbolized as H_0. A primary use of inferential statistics is that of attempting to reject H_0.

Okay, time for another example. Suppose we wanted to compare the math anxiety of male and female graduate students in the United States. In theory, we could administer a math anxiety test to all female and male graduate students in the country, score the tests, and compare the μ's for the two populations. Chances are good, however, that our resources would not allow us to conduct such a study. So we decide to use statistics. If we suspect that there is a difference in the two populations, and that's what we want to demonstrate, then our H_0 is that there is no difference. In statistical notation:

$$H_0\colon \mu_{Females} = \mu_{Males}$$

The purpose of our study is to decide whether H_0 is probably true or probably false.

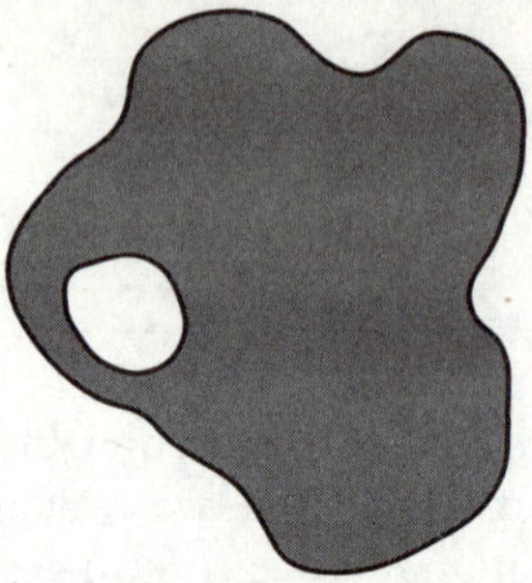

FIGURE 10-3 A blob diagram of the world.

Suppose we drew 50 subjects (using a random sampling method, of course) from each of the two populations, male graduate students and female graduate students, and tested them for math anxiety. Suppose also that the mean of our female sample was 60 and the mean for our male sample was 50:

$$\overline{X}_{Females} = 60 \qquad \overline{X}_{Males} = 50$$

Obviously, the mean of our female sample was higher than that for males. But how do we use this fact to justify throwing out—that is, rejecting—the null hypothesis, so as to be left with the hypothesis we are trying to prove?

There are two possible explanations for our observed difference between male and female sample means: (a) There is, in fact, a difference in math anxiety between the male and female population means—that is, $\overline{X}_{Female} \neq \overline{X}_{Males}$—and the difference we see between the samples reflects this fact; or (b) there is no appreciable difference in anxiety between the means of the male and female graduate student populations—that is, $\overline{X}_{Female} = \overline{X}_{Males}$—and the difference we observe between the sample means is due to chance or sampling error (this would be analogous to drawing more white beans than red even though there is no difference in the proportion of the two in the jar from which the sample was drawn).

If the null hypothesis really is true, then the differences we observe between sample means is due to chance. The statistical tests you will study in later chapters, such as the *t* Test in Chapter 11 or analysis of variance (ANOVA) in Chapter 12, will help you to decide if your obtained result is likely to have been due to chance or if there probably is a difference in the two populations. If the result of your study is that the difference you observe is "statistically significant," then you will reject the null hypothesis and conclude that you believe there is a real difference in the two populations. Of course, even after concluding that the difference was real, you would still have to decide whether it was large enough, in the context of your research situation, to have practical usefulness. Researchers call this the "magnitude of effect" question.

TYPE I AND TYPE II ERRORS

Your decision either to reject or not to reject the null hypothesis is subject to error. Because you have not studied all members of both populations and because statistics (such as $\bar{X}$ and S_x) are subject to sampling error, you can never be completely sure whether H_0 is true or not. In drawing your conclusion about H_0, you can make two kinds of errors, known (cleverly) as Type I and Type II errors. Rejection of a true null hypothesis is a Type I error, and failure to reject a false null hypothesis is a Type II error. Perhaps the following table will help you to understand the difference.

	The Real Situation (unknown to the investigator)	
Investigator's Decision	**H_0 Is True**	**H_0 Is False**
Reject H_0	Investigator makes a Type I error	Investigator makes a Correct decision
Do not reject H_0	Investigator makes a Correct decision	Investigator makes a Type II error

If the real situation is that there is no difference in math anxiety between males and females, but you reject H_0, then you have made a Type I error; if you do not reject H_0, then you have made a correct decision. On the other hand, if there is a real difference between the population means of males and females and you reject H_0, you have made a correct decision, but if you fail to reject H_0, you have made a Type II error.

The primary purpose of inferential statistics is to help you to decide whether to reject the null hypothesis and to estimate the probability of a Type I or Type II error when making your decision. Inferential statistics can't tell you for sure whether you've made either a Type I or a Type II error, but they can tell you how likely it is that you have made one.

One last point: Notice that you do not have the option of accepting the null hypothesis. That would amount to using your statistical test to "prove" that the null hypothesis is true, and you can't do that. Your two possible decisions really amount to either (a) I reject the null hypothesis, and so I believe that there really are important differences between the two populations, or (b) I failed to reject the null hypothesis, and I still don't know whether there are important differences or not. For this reason, Type I errors are generally considered to be more serious than Type II errors. Claiming significant results when there really are no differences between the populations is held to be a more serious mistake than saying that you don't know for sure, even when those differences might exist. As you will see, statistical decisions are usually made so as to minimize the likelihood of a Type I error, even at the risk of making lots of Type II errors.

STATISTICAL SIGNIFICANCE AND TYPE I ERROR

Suppose that a colleague of yours actually did the study of math anxiety that we've been talking about and concluded that the difference between male and female sample means was "statistically significant at the 0.05 (or the 5%) level." This statement would mean that a difference as big as or bigger than what he observed between the sample means could have occurred only 5 times out of 100 by chance alone. Since it could have happened only 5 times out of 100 just by chance, your colleague may be willing to bet that there is a real difference in the populations of male and female graduate students and will reject the null hypothesis.

You must realize, however, that whenever you reject the null hypothesis, you may be making an error. Perhaps the null hypothesis really is true, and this is one of those 5 times out of 100 when, by chance alone, you got this large a difference in sample means. Another way of saying the same thing is that, if the null hypothesis were true, 5 times out of 100 you would make a Type I error when you use this decision rule. You would reject the null hypothesis when it was, in fact, true 5% of the time.

You might say, "But, I don't want to make errors! Why can't I use the 0.01 (or 1%) level of significance instead of the 0.05 level? That way, I reduce the likelihood of a Type I error to 1 out of 100 times." You can do that, of course, but when you do so, you increase the probability of a Type II error. That's because you reduce the probability of a Type I error by insisting on more stringent conditions for accepting your research hypothesis—that is, you fail to reject H_0 even when H_0 is fairly unlikely. Reducing the probability of a Type I error from 0.05 to 0.01 means that you'll fail to reject H_0 even if the odds are 98 out of 100 that it is untrue. In educational and psychological research, it is conventional to set the 0.05 level of significance as a minimum standard for the rejection of the null hypothesis. Typically, if an obtained result is significant at, say, the 0.08 level, a researcher will conclude that he or she was unable to reject the null hypothesis or that the results were not statistically significant.

Making a Type II error—failing to reject the null hypothesis when it's really not true—is rather like missing your plane at the airport. You didn't do the right thing this time, but you can still catch another plane. Making a Type I error is like getting on the wrong plane—not only did you miss the right one, but now you're headed in the wrong direction! With a result significant at the 0.08 level, the odds still suggest that the null hypothesis is false (you'd only get this large a difference by chance 8 times in 100). But researchers don't want to get on the wrong airplane; they'd rather make a Type II error and wait for another chance to reject H_0 in some future study.

Remember our discussion about magnitude of effect, when we were looking at correlation coefficients? Just because an observed difference may be significant (i.e., may represent real differences between populations), it is not necessarily useful. We might reject the null hypothesis with regard to differences between male and female math anxiety scores, but if the real difference were only 1 or 2 points, with means of 50 and 60, would those differences be worth paying attention to?

Magnitude of effect is often ignored in media reports of medical discoveries. "Using toothpicks linked to the rare disease archeomelanitis!" trumpet the headlines, and the news story goes on to say that researchers have shown that people who use toothpicks are 1.5 times more likely to get archeomelanitis than people who don't. But if you look at the actual numbers, the likelihood of getting archeomelanitis (with no toothpicks) is one in a million, and so using a toothpick increases those odds to 1.5 in a million. Are you going to worry about raising your risk from 0.00001 to 0.000015? I'm not.

Mrs. Zackford liked her students to feel the full shock effect of a pop quiz.

Problems

1. Answer the following questions:
   a. What is the difference between $\overline{X}$ and μ? Between SD_x and σ?
   b. Which of the four preceding symbols represents a value that has been corrected for bias? Why not the others?
2. Which of the following would not be a truly random sample, and why?
   a. To get a sample of children attending a particular grade school, the researcher numbered all the children on the playground at recess time and used a random-number table to select fifty of them.
   b. Another researcher, at a different school, got a list of all the families who had kids in that school. She wrote each name on a slip of paper, mixed up the slips, and drew out a name. All kids with that last name went into the sample; she kept this up until she had fifty kids.
   c. A third researcher took a ruler to the school office, where student files were kept. She used a random-number table to get a number, measured that distance into the files, and the child whose file she was over at that point was selected for the sample. She did this fifty times and selected fifty kids.
   d. A fourth researcher listed all the kids in the school and numbered the names. He then used a random-number table to pick out fifty names.
3. What is the appropriate H_0 for the following research situation? A study designed to investigate possible differences in academic achievement between right- and left-handed children.
4. Assume that each of the following statements is in error: Each describes a researcher's conclusions, but the researcher is mistaken. Indicate whether the error is Type I or Type II.
   a. "The data indicate that there are significant differences between males and females in their ability to perform Task 1."
   b. "There are no significant differences between males and females in their ability to perform Task 2."
   c. "On the basis of our data, we reject the null hypothesis."
5. Answer the following questions.
   a. Explain the meaning of the following: "The difference between Group 1 and Group 2 is significant at the 0.05 level."
   b. When would a researcher be likely to use the 0.01 level of significance rather than the 0.05 level? What is the drawback of using the 0.01 level?

Answers to Problems

1. **a.** $\overline{X}$ and SD_x are sample values, and μ and σ are population values.
   b. The value of SD_x, like the value of S_x^2, is obtained from a formula that includes a correction for bias. If this correction wasn't in the formula, the obtained value would tend to be too small. $\overline{X}$ doesn't need such a correction because it is already an unbiased estimate. μ and σ don't need correction, because they are themselves population values.
2. **a.** Not random because all members of the population didn't have an equal chance of being included (kids who were ill or stayed inside during recess couldn't be chosen).
   b. Not random because selection wasn't independent (once a given child was selected, anyone else with that last name was included, too).
   c. Not random, because kids who had very thick files (which usually means they

caused some sort of problem) would have a better chance of being selected).

d. (Okay, okay, so it was too easy . . .) Random.

3. a. $\mu_{Left} = \mu_{Right}$

4. a. Type I **b.** Type II **c.** Type I

5. a. If we performed this experiment over and over, and if the null hypothesis were true, we could expect to get these results just by chance only 5 times out of 100.

b. We use the 0.01 level when we need to be very sure that we are not making a Type I error. The drawback is that as we reduce the probability of a Type I error, the likelihood of a Type II error goes up.

Endnotes

1. "Mutually exclusive" is a fancy way of saying that you can have one or the other but not both at the same time.
2. One of the easiest ways to get an (approximately) random sample is by using a random-number table. Such a table, together with instructions for how to use it, is found in Appendix B.

CHAPTER

11 The *t* Test

- **The *t* Test for Independent Samples**
- **Formulas for the *t* Test for Independent Samples**
- **The Critical Value of *t*: t_{crit}**
- **Requirements for Using the *t* Test for Independent Samples**
- **The *t* Test for Dependent (Matched) Samples**
- **Directional Versus Nondirectional Tests**
- **Problems**
- **Answers to Problems**

Top Ten Reasons to Be a Statistician

1. Estimating parameters is easier than dealing with real life.
2. Statisticians are significant.
3. I always wanted to learn the entire Greek alphabet.
4. The probability that a statistician major will get a job is > 0.9999.
5. If I flunk out, I can always transfer to Engineering.
6. We do it with confidence, frequency, and variability.
7. You never have to be right—only close.
8. We're normal and everyone else is skewed.
9. The regression line looks better than the unemployment line.
10. No one knows what we do, so we are always right.

The *t* Test is one of the most commonly used statistical tests. Its primary purpose is to determine whether the means of two groups of scores differ to a statistically significant degree. Here's an example: Suppose you randomly assigned 12 subjects each to Group 1, a counseling group, and to Group 2, a waiting-list control group. Suppose also that after those in Group 1 had been counseled, you administered a measure of psychological adjustment to the two groups, with results as follows:

Counseled Group Scores	Control Group Scores
25	14
14	11
23	13
21	9
24	15
17	12
19	9
20	11
15	8
22	13
16	12
21	14
$\overline{X}_1 = 19.75$	$\overline{X}_2 = 11.75$
$n_1 = 12$	$n_2 = 12$
$SD_1^2 = 12.93$	$SD_2^2 = 4.93$

Since you hope to show that the two groups are really different, your null hypothesis is

$$H_0: \mu_1 = \mu_2$$

The null hypothesis states that there is no difference in mean adjustment level between those in the population who receive counseling and those who don't. As you can see, there is a difference in the two sample means, but it may be that this observed difference occurred by chance and there really is no difference in the population means. We need to find out if the difference is statistically significant. If the difference between $\overline{X}_1$ and $\overline{X}_2$ is statistically significant, you will reject the null hypothesis and conclude that there is a difference in the adjustment level between the people who have had counseling and those who have not.

There are two kinds of *t* Tests: those for groups whose members are independent of each and those for two groups whose members are paired in some way (like pretreatment and posttreatment measures, for instance, or pairs of siblings). Since the counseled and control groups in our hypothetical study were not paired in any way, we would use the *t* Test for independent samples. Here we go!

THE *t* TEST FOR INDEPENDENT SAMPLES

The *t* Test, like most other statistical tests, consists of a set of mathematical procedures that yields a numerical value. In the case of the *t* Test, the value that is obtained is called t_{obt}. The larger the absolute value of t_{obt}, the more likely it is to reflect a statistically significant

"In an increasingly complex world, sometimes old questions require new answers."

difference between the two groups under comparison. We'll learn how to compute the value of t_{obt} in the next few pages; first, though, let's think about what a *t* Test really examines.

A major application of the *t* Test for independent samples is found in experimental research like the study in our example. Researchers often draw a sample from one population and randomly assign half of the subjects to an experimental group and the other half to a control group, or to some other comparison group (see Appendix B for a method of assigning subjects at random to two or more groups). They then administer some sort of treatment to the experimental group. Since the subjects were assigned to their two groups by chance (i.e., at random), the means of the two groups should not differ from each other at the beginning of the experiment any more than would be expected on the basis of chance alone. If a *t* Test were done at the beginning of the experiment, the difference between the means would probably not be statistically significant.[1] After the treatment, the means of the two groups are compared using the *t* Test. If the absolute value of t_{obt} is large enough to be statistically significant, the experimenter rejects H_0. Since the two groups have now been shown to differ more than would be expected on the basis of chance alone, and since the only difference between them (that we know of) is the experimental treatment, it is reasonable to conclude that this treatment is responsible for the differences that were observed.

FORMULAS FOR THE *t* TEST FOR INDEPENDENT SAMPLES

The formulas for the *t* Test look pretty horrendous at first, especially this first one. Just remember to relax and work on one step at a time, from the inside out. When you look closely, you will see that you already learned how to do most of the computations in earlier chapters. This formula for the *t* Test for independent samples can be used with samples of equal and unequal sizes:

$$t_{obt} = \frac{\bar{X}_1 - \bar{X}_2}{\sqrt{\left[\frac{(n_1 - 1)SD_1^2 + (n_2 - 1)SD_2^2}{n_1 + n_2 - 2}\right]\left(\frac{1}{n_1} + \frac{1}{n_2}\right)}}$$

Where: t_{obt} = the value of *t* obtained through your data

n_1, n_2 = the number of participants in Group 1 (n_1) and Group 2 (n_2)

SD_1^2, SD_2^2 = the estimates of the variances of the two populations

$\bar{X}_1, \bar{X}_2$ = the means of the two groups

When you look at it, all you have to do is find the means and standard deviations of the two groups, plug the numbers into the formula, and then work out the problem. Piece of cake! If the two sample sizes are equal—that is, if $n_1 = n_2 = n$—then you can use this simpler formula:

$$t_{obt} = \frac{\bar{X}_1 - \bar{X}_2}{\sqrt{\dfrac{SD_1^2 + SD_2^2}{n}}}$$

Next, we'll work out an example together using the data of the counseling and no-counseling groups. You might want to see if you can do it on your own before you look at the example. Remember to work from the inside out when working out the problem and to show your work so you don't make a silly error. And don't get discouraged if you can't do it on the first try, because I'll go through the computations with you a step at a time. Here's the computation of t_{obt} for counseled and control groups in the example data:

$$t_{obt} = \frac{\bar{X}_1 - \bar{X}_2}{\sqrt{\left[\dfrac{(n_1 - 1)SD_1^2 + (n_2 - 1)SD_2^2}{n_1 + n_2 - 2}\right]\left(\dfrac{1}{n_1} + \dfrac{1}{n_2}\right)}}$$

$$= \frac{19.75 - 11.75}{\sqrt{\left[\dfrac{(12 - 1)12.93 + (12 - 1)4.93}{12 + 12 - 2}\right]\left(\dfrac{1}{12} + \dfrac{1}{12}\right)}}$$

$$= \frac{8.00}{\sqrt{\left[\dfrac{(11)12.93 + (11)4.93}{22}\right]\left(\dfrac{2}{12}\right)}} = \frac{8.00}{\sqrt{\left[\dfrac{142.23 + 54.23}{22}\right](0.17)}}$$

$$= \frac{8.00}{\sqrt{(8.93)(0.17)}} = \frac{8.00}{\sqrt{1.52}} = \frac{8.00}{1.23} = 6.50$$

That wasn't so bad, was it? Actually, because we had equal sample sizes, we could've used the simpler formula. Here it is with these data:

$$t_{obt} = \frac{\bar{X}_1 - \bar{X}_2}{\sqrt{\dfrac{SD_1^2 + SD_2^2}{n}}} = \frac{19.75 - 11.75}{\sqrt{\dfrac{12.93 + 4.93}{12}}} = \frac{8.00}{\sqrt{\dfrac{17.86}{12}}} = \frac{8.00}{\sqrt{1.49}} = \frac{8.00}{1.22} = 6.56$$

As you can see, both formulas arrive at the same value of about 6.5 (plus or minus a little rounding error). Notice that this computation requires that you know the number of subjects (n), the mean ($\bar{X}$), and the variance (SD^2) for each of your groups. If you go back to the beginning of this chapter, you will see that $n_1 = n_2 = n = 12$, $\overline{X}_1 = 19.75$, $\overline{X}_2 = 11.75$, and $SD_1^2 = 12.93$, $SD_2^2 = 4.93$. If you were doing your own study, you would, of course, have to compute both of those means and variances. But you know how to do that, right? Also, remember that the *n* used here is the number in both groups, not the sum of the number in both groups.

By the way, notice that the decision of which sample mean is subtracted from the other is purely arbitrary; we could just as well have used $\overline{X}_2 - \overline{X}_1$ for the numerator of that last equation. Had we done so, the value of t_{obt} would have been negative rather than positive. When the direction of the difference we are interested in is unimportant, the *t* Test is nondirectional and we use the absolute value of t_{obt}. With a negative value, we would just drop the negative sign and proceed as if we had subtracted in the other direction.

THE CRITICAL VALUE OF *t*: t_{crit}

"Okay," you might say, "I've done all the computations. Now what does my t_{obt} mean?" Good question. To find out whether your t_{obt} is statistically significant—that is, if it is large enough so that it probably reflects more than chance or random differences between the two samples—you will have to compare it with what is known as the critical value of t (t_{crit}). To find t_{crit}, go to Appendix C. Look at the left-hand set of values (labeled "Two-Tailed or Nondirectional Test"[2]) and notice that the farthest column to the left is headed with the letters *df*. The abbreviation *df* means "degrees of freedom." To find the degrees of freedom for a *t* Test for independent samples, just subtract 2 from the total number of subjects in your study. In our example, $df = n_1 + n_2 - 2 = 12 + 12 - 2 = 22$.

The value of t_{crit} is determined by *df* and by your selected level of significance. Suppose you selected the 0.05 level of significance (the most commonly chosen value). Go down the *df* column to 22, the number of *df* in our example, and across to the value in the column to the right (headed with 0.05). There you will see the number 2.074. That is the critical value of *t*, or t_{crit}, for the 0.05 level of significance when $df = 22$. If your t_{obt} is equal to or greater than t_{crit}, your results are statistically significant at the 0.05 level. Another way of saying this is that there are fewer than 5 chances out of 100 that a value of t (t_{obt}) this large could have occurred by chance alone. The statistician's way of saying it is $p < 0.05$.

The level of significance chosen is known as α (alpha). Why α, rather than *p*? It's a pretty niggling difference, but α is the probability of a Type I error, and *p* refers to the probability of getting the actual results you got just by chance. The most typical alpha level for social science research is $\alpha = 0.05$. As indicated in Chapter 10, you might choose $\alpha = 0.01$ if you want to be super-careful to avoid committing a Type I error. If a significant result would commit you to investing a great deal of money in program changes, or would lead to other important policy decisions, for example, then a Type I error would be quite dangerous and you would want to be very cautious indeed in setting your α level. Got it?

The t_{obt} in our example was 6.56. This is obviously larger than $t_{crit} = 2.074$; therefore, your results are significant at the .05 level. In fact, if you go across the $df = 22$ row, you will see that your $t_{obt} = 6.56$ is greater than the t_{crit} for the 0.01 level (2.819) and for the 0.001 level (3.792). You cannot claim that your results are significant at the 0.001 level, though; to do that, you'd have to say ahead of time that you would only reject H_0 if you got such an extreme value. You must decide what level of significance will justify rejecting H_0 before you look at your data; that's the rule. But you're still okay; you got what you were looking for—a t_{obt} that will allow you to reject H_0 at the 0.05 level. You conclude that the differences between your samples of counseled and control subjects reflect a real difference in the populations of counseled and non-counseled people.

Let's do one more example, going through each step in a typical study comparing two groups. Suppose you wanted to test the hypothesis that men and women differ in the degree of empathy that they show to a stranger. You could select representative samples of men and women, tape-record their conversations with your research associate, and use some sort of test to measure their degree of empathy. Imagine that your results were as follows (the higher the score, the greater the degree of empathy shown):

Group 1 Men's Empathy Scores	Group 2 Women's Empathy Scores
7	7
5	8
3	10
4	7
1	

STEP 1: STATE YOUR HYPOTHESIS. The statistical hypothesis you will be testing is the null hypothesis. In this example, the null hypothesis is that there is no difference between populations of men and women in the level of empathy that they offer to a stranger. In statistical terms,

$$H_0: \mu_1 = \mu_2$$

Sometimes hypotheses are stated as alternative or research hypotheses, which represent the thing you want to show to be true. Alternative or research hypotheses are the opposite of the null hypothesis. In this case, the alternative hypothesis would be that there is a difference between populations of men and women in the degree of empathy that they offer to a stranger:

$$H_A: \mu_1 \neq \mu_2$$

STEP 2: SELECT α, YOUR SIGNIFICANCE LEVEL. Let's choose $\alpha = .05$.

STEP 3: COMPUTE t_{obt}

a. Find $n, \overline{X}, SD^2$ for each group:

Group 1 (males): $n_1 = 5, \overline{X}_1 = 4, SD_1^2 = 5$

Group 2 (females): $n_2 = 4, \overline{X}_2 = 8, SD_2^2 = 2$

b. Plug these values into the formula:

$$t_{obt} = \frac{\overline{X}_1 - \overline{X}_2}{\sqrt{\left[\frac{(n_1 - 1)SD_1^2 + (n_2 - 1)SD_2^2}{n_1 + n_2 - 2}\right]\left(\frac{1}{n_1} + \frac{1}{n_2}\right)}}$$

$$= \frac{4 - 8}{\sqrt{\left[\frac{(5 - 1)5 + (4 - 1)2}{5 + 4 - 2}\right]\left(\frac{1}{5} + \frac{1}{4}\right)}}$$

$$= \frac{-4}{\sqrt{\left[\frac{(4)5 + (3)2}{7}\right]\left(\frac{9}{20}\right)}} = \frac{-4}{\sqrt{\left(\frac{26}{7}\right)\left(\frac{9}{20}\right)}}$$

$$= \frac{-4}{\sqrt{(3.71)(0.45)}} = \frac{-4}{\sqrt{1.67}} = \frac{-4}{1.29} = -3.10$$

$$t_{obt} = -3.10$$

STEP 4: FIND t_{crit}. Entering Appendix C with $df = n_1 + n_2 - 2 = 5 + 4 - 2 = 7$, and with $\alpha = 0.05$, you can see that $t_{crit} = 2.365$.

STEP 5: DECIDE WHETHER OR NOT TO REJECT THE NULL HYPOTHESIS. As I pointed out earlier, the sign of t_{obt} will depend on which sample mean you happened to label $\overline{X}_1$ and which one you labeled $\overline{X}_2$. For the hypothesis you are testing now, it doesn't really matter which sample mean is larger; you're only interested in whether they're different. For this reason, use the absolute value of t_{obt}: If you get a negative value for t_{obt}, just change the sign to positive before comparing it to the tabled value. If t_{obt} has an absolute value equal to or greater than t_{crit}, you will reject H_0. Comparing $t_{obt} = 3.10$ with $t_{crit} = 2.365$, we decide to reject the null hypothesis, because $t_{obt} = 3.10 \rangle t_{crit} = 2.365$. Our results are significant at the 0.05 level. Not only is t_{obt} significant, but the actual values of the means look quite different—the magnitude of effect is large. It is reasonable to conclude on the basis of our study that female counselors offer a higher level of empathy to strangers than do male counselors and that this difference may be of practical interest.

REQUIREMENTS FOR USING THE *t* TEST FOR INDEPENDENT SAMPLES

The *t* Test you have just learned requires that you have two independent samples, which means that the subjects for one group were selected independently from those in the second group. That is, the measurements from the two groups aren't paired in any way; a given measurement from Group 1 doesn't "go with" a particular measurement from Group 2. Sometimes you want to do a study in which this is not the case; for paired data you will use the *t* Test for non-independent (matched) groups.

Also, *t* Tests assume that both of the populations being considered are essentially normally distributed. I say "essentially," because a really close fit to the normal distribution isn't necessary. The *t* Test is considered "robust" with respect to this assumption—

that is, we can violate the assumption without putting too much strain on our findings, especially if we have large samples. If you have only small samples (as in the last example we worked), and if the populations they came from are likely to be quite skewed, then you should not use a *t* Test—you should use a nonparametric test. An example of a widely used nonparametric test is chi-square, which we'll discuss in Chapter 13.

THE *t* TEST FOR DEPENDENT (MATCHED) SAMPLES

Suppose you gave a group of ten subjects a test both before and after a movie intended to influence attitudes toward public schools. You had two sets of scores, one from the pretest and the other from the posttest, and you wanted to find out if attitudes as measured by the tests were more or less favorable after seeing the movie than they were before. You now have pairs of scores—a score for each subject on the pretest and another score from each subject for the posttest. You have two groups of scores, but they are not independent of each other; they are matched.

Participants	Pretest	Posttest	Posttest-Pretest *D*	D^2
1	84	89	+5	25
2	87	92	+5	25
3	87	98	+11	121
4	90	95	+5	25
5	90	95	+5	25
6	90	95	+5	25
7	90	95	+5	25
8	93	92	−1	2
9	93	98	+5	25
10	96	101	+5	25
$\overline{X}$	90.00	95.00		
SD	3.46	3.46		
r_{12}	+0.67			

The results are shown in the preceding table, in which pretest and posttest scores are in Columns 2 and 3, Column 4 is the difference between each pair of scores (D), and Column 5 is the square of that difference (D^2).

The most important thing to notice about these data, when deciding what statistical test to use, is that the scores are paired. The pretest score of 84 goes with the posttest score of 89, and it is the fact that Participant 1 raised his or her score by 5 points that is important, rather than the values of the two scores by themselves. It wouldn't make sense to scramble the posttest scores and then look at the difference between pretest and posttest scores. Each pretest score is logically linked to one, and only one, posttest score. That's the definition of non-independent samples; whenever that condition holds, then a non-independent samples test is appropriate.

Here is the conceptual formula for the dependent-sample *t* Test:

$$t^{*}_{obt} = \frac{\overline{X}_1 - \overline{X}_2}{\sqrt{S^2_{\overline{X}_1} + S^2_{\overline{X}_2} - 2r_{12}S_{\overline{X}_1}S_{\overline{X}_2}}}$$

Where: $\overline{X}_1, \overline{X}_2$ are the means of the two measurement

$S_{\overline{X}_1}S_{\overline{X}_2}$ are the standard error of the means $\left(\frac{SD}{\sqrt{N}}\right)$

r_{12} is the correlation between the two measurements

Here we go, step by step, to conduct the dependent samples *t* Test:

STEP 1: STATE YOUR HYPOTHESIS. Your null hypothesis is that there is no difference between attitudes before the movie and attitudes after the movie—that is,

$$H_o: \mu_1 = \mu_2$$

Your alternative, or research, hypothesis is that there is a difference between attitudes before and after the movie:

$$H_A: \mu_1 \neq \mu_2$$

STEP 2: SELECT YOUR LEVEL OF SIGNIFICANCE. For this example, we arbitrarily select the 0.05 level of significance, $\alpha = 0.05$.

STEP 3: COMPUTE T_{obt}. The formula, with appropriate numbers plugged in from the preceding table, is:

$$t^{*}_{obt} = \frac{\overline{X}_1 - \overline{X}_2}{\sqrt{S^2_{\overline{X}_1} + S^2_{\overline{X}_2} - 2r_{12}S_{\overline{X}_1}S_{\overline{X}_2}}}$$

$$= \frac{90.0 - 95.0}{\sqrt{\left(\frac{3.46}{\sqrt{10}}\right)^2 + \left(\frac{3.46}{\sqrt{10}}\right)^2 - 2(0.67)\left(\frac{3.46}{\sqrt{10}}\right)\left(\frac{3.46}{\sqrt{10}}\right)}}$$

$$= \frac{90.0 - 95.0}{\sqrt{\left(\frac{3.46}{\sqrt{10}}\right)^2 + \left(\frac{3.46}{\sqrt{10}}\right)^2 - 2(.67)\left(\frac{3.46}{\sqrt{10}}\right)\left(\frac{3.46}{\sqrt{10}}\right)}}$$

$$= \frac{90.0 - 95.0}{\sqrt{(1.09)^2 + (1.09)^2 - 2(0.67)(1.09)(1.09)}}$$

$$= \frac{90.0 - 95.0}{\sqrt{(1.19) + (1.19) - 2(.67)(1.09)(1.09)}}$$

$$= \frac{-5.0}{\sqrt{2.38 - 1.59}} = -5.62$$

STEP 4: FIND t_{crit}. As was true for the *t* test for independent samples, we enter the table in Appendix C to find t_{crit}. In the case of the *t* for non-independent samples, however, $df = N - 1$, where *N* is the number of subjects (again, the number of pairs of scores, not the total number of scores). Thus, in our example, $df = 10 - 1 = 9$ and $t_{crit} = 2.262$ at the 0.05 level of significance.

STEP 5: DECIDE WHETHER TO REJECT H_O. As was the case with independent *t* Tests, we compare our t_{obt} with t_{crit}. If t_{obt} (either positive or negative) is equal to or greater than t_{crit}, then we reject H_o and conclude that our results are significant at the chosen level of α. Since in our example t_{obt} is greater than t_{crit}, we reject the null hypothesis and conclude that the movie appeared to have a positive effect on attitudes toward public schools. We don't conclude that attitudes were unchanged—that would be accepting H_o, and we can't do that.

As you probably expected, there is also a computational formula for the *t* Test of dependent samples. Here it is:

$$t_{obt} = \frac{\overline{\Delta}}{\left(\frac{S_\Delta}{\sqrt{n}}\right)}$$

Where: $\overline{\Delta}$ is the mean of the difference between the participants scores on the pretest and posttest

S_Δ is the standard deviation of the difference scores

n is the number of pairs of scores

Here we go, step by step.

STEP 1: STATE YOUR HYPOTHESIS. The null hypothesis is the same as for the conceptual formula.

$$H_o: \mu_1 = \mu_2$$

Your alternative, or research, hypothesis is also the same:

$$H_o: \mu_1 \neq \mu_2$$

STEP 2: SELECT YOUR LEVEL OF SIGNIFICANCE. Same here: $\alpha = .05$.

STEP 3: COMPUTE t_{obt}. This step is, of course, a little different. The formula, with appropriate numbers plugged in, is:

$$t_{obt} = \frac{\overline{\Delta}}{\left(\frac{S_\Delta}{\sqrt{n}}\right)} = \frac{5.00}{\left(\frac{2.83}{\sqrt{10}}\right)} = \frac{5.00}{\left(\frac{2.83}{3.16}\right)} = \frac{5.00}{0.90} = 5.56$$

Where: $n = 10, \overline{\Delta} = 5.00, S_\Delta = 2.83$

Notice that I subtracted each subject's pretest score from his or her posttest score. I could have subtracted posttest from pretest scores, in which case most of my *D* values would have been negative and my t_{obt} would also have been negative. It wouldn't have made any difference, however, as long as I did it the same way for every pair. If the absolute value of t_{obt} is greater than t_{crit}, then the difference between the two groups is statistically significant. Also, $n =$ the number of pairs of scores. In our example, $n = 10$.

STEP 4: FIND t_{crit}. We of course use the same critical value for this test as mentioned earlier $t_{crit} = 2.262$ at the 0.05 level of significance.

STEP 5: DECIDE WHETHER TO REJECT H_O. And, finally, we compare our t_{obt} with t_{crit}. We conclude that the difference in dependent means is statistically significantly different. On the basis of this result, we would decide that attitudes toward public schools are indeed more favorable after seeing the movie than before.

DIRECTIONAL VERSUS NONDIRECTIONAL TESTS

When you as a researcher are quite confident, on the basis of previous research or theory, that the mean of one group should be higher than that of some other group (or that you are only interested in demonstrating that it is higher), and you predict the direction of the difference before you collect your data, you can then use what is called a one-tailed, or directional, *t* Test. When conducting a one-tailed test, the t_{obt} formulas will be the same, but the value of t_{crit} will be different.

Suppose you predicted in advance that the mean weight of a group who had participated in a Weight Watchers program ($n = 12$) would be lower than the mean of a control group who hadn't been in Weight Watchers ($n = 12$). Suppose also that $t_{obt} = 2.00$. If you were conducting a two-tailed test, you would look up t_{crit} with 22 degrees of freedom. (Do you know why $df = 22$ and not 11? Because these data are not paired; a given subject in the treatment group isn't logically linked to some particular subject in the control group.) This time, though, you'd look in the column labeled "One-Tailed or Directional Test," and the value of t_{crit} would be 1.717 at the 0.05 level of significance. Since t_{obt} is larger than t_{crit}, the result is statistically significant.

If you had not predicted the direction of the difference in advance of your study, you would have to use a two-tailed test and use the t_{crit} values from the left-hand side of Appendix C. As you can see from that table, with $df = 22$, $t_{crit} = 2.074$ for a two-tailed test. The t_{obt} is still 2.00, but your results would not be statistically significant at the 0.05 level.

The diagrams at the top of Appendix C show how a value of t_{obt} can be significant for a one-tailed test but not for a two-tailed test. In a one-tailed test, we are interested in differences in one direction—that is, in only one tail of the distribution. If a t_{obt} is large enough to fall beyond the value of t_{crit} in that tail, t_{obt} is significant. With a two-tailed test, differences in either direction are important, and so we have to split the value of α and put half into each tail of the distribution. With $\alpha = 0.05$, t_{crit} will mark off 0.025 at either end. Because the area marked off is smaller, t_{crit} must "slide" farther out away from 0, the mean, and the farther it slides away from the mean, the bigger it gets.[3] With everything else equal, the value of t_{crit} will always be larger for a two-tailed test than for a one-tailed test. It's easier to get significant results with a one-tailed test, because t_{obt} doesn't have to be so large.

So why not always use a one-tailed test? To use the one-tailed test legitimately, you must make your predictions prior to data collection. To do otherwise would be analogous to placing your bets after you see the outcome of an event. When in doubt, it is better to do two-tailed tests, if only to avoid temptation. However, doing a two-tailed test does increase the likelihood of a Type II error—that is, of not rejecting the null hypothesis when it should be rejected. If a significant outcome of your research would make sense only if the observed differences are in a particular direction (if you'd dismiss anything else as chance or random differences, no matter how unlikely), then do a one-tailed test. Remember, though, that if you choose to do a one-tailed test and your data show "significant" differences in the opposite direction, you may not reject H_0. By choosing a one-tailed approach, you have committed yourself to assuming that any differences in the non-predicted direction are due to chance or error.

Problems

For each problem, be sure to specify the null hypothesis being tested and whether you will use a *t* test for independent samples or a *t* test for non-independent samples; also, specify whether you will use a one-tailed or two-tailed test.

1. In a study designed to discover whether men or women drink more coffee, a researcher (working on a very limited budget) observes five men and five women randomly selected from her university department. Here's what she found:

Men	Women
5	8
1	3
4	7
2	3
3	5

a. Run the appropriate test, assuming that both men and women were originally part of one random sample, with $n = 10$, and were then divided into men's and women's groups.

2. Using hospital and agency records, you locate six pairs of identical twins, one of whom was adopted at birth and the other of whom was in foster care for at least three years. All the twins are now five years old. You want to show that early adoption leads to better intellectual ability, so you test all the twins with the Wechsler Intelligence Scale for Children (WISC). Your results are as follows:

Twin Pair No.	Adopted Twin	Foster-Care Twin
1	105	103
2	99	97
3	112	105
4	101	99
5	124	104
6	100	110

3. The following table contains scores on an index of depression for three groups of clients at a college counseling center. Group 1 clients have received six sessions of counseling; Group 2 clients were put on a waiting list for six weeks and asked to keep a personal journal during that time; Group 3 clients were put on the waiting list with no other instructions. Use a *t* Test to decide whether:

a. Group 2 (journal) clients scored differently from Group 3 (control) clients
b. Group 1 (counseled) clients scored differently from Group 2 (journal) clients
c. Group 1 (counseled) clients scored higher than Group 3 (control) clients

Group 1 (Counseled)	Group 2 (Journal)	Group 3 (Control)
22	6	8
16	10	6
17	13	4
18	13	5
	8	2
	4	

4. A researcher tests the high-frequency hearing acuity of a group of teens two days before they attend a rock concert; two days after the concert, she tests them again. Here are her results; she expects to find that the teens hear better before the concert than afterward (the higher the score on this test, the poorer the hearing).

Subject	Pre-Concert	Post-Concert
Tom	12	18
Dan	2	3
Sue	6	5
Terri	13	10
Karen	10	15
Lance	10	15
Christy	5	6
Jan	2	9
Lenora	7	7
Roberta	9	9
Dave	10	11
Victoria	14	13

Answers to Problems

1. t Test for independent samples; two-tailed test; $t_{obt} = 1.77$; $df = 8$; $t_{crit} = 2.306$; do not reject H_o.
2. t. Test for non-independent samples; one-tailed test; $t_{obt} = 0.96$; $df = 5$; $t_{crit} = 2.571$; do not reject H_o.
3. **a.** t Test for independent samples; two-tailed test; $t_{obt} = 2.10$; $df = 9$; $t_{crit} = 2.262$; do not reject H_o.
   b. t Test for independent samples; two-tailed test; $t_{obt} = 4.28$; $df = 8$; $t_{crit} = 2.306$; reject H_o.
   c. t Test for independent samples; one-tailed test; $t_{obt} = 8.20$; $df = 7$; $t_{crit} = 1.895$; reject H_o.
4. t Test for dependent samples; one-tailed test; $t_{obt} = -1.89$; $df = 11$; $t_{crit} = 1.796$; do not reject H_o.

Endnotes

1. If we are to be very precise here, we would say that the difference between the means would be significant at the 0.05 level only 5 times out of 100 or would be significant at the 0.01 level only once in 100 such experiments.
2. Don't worry too much about what "two-tailed" means; we'll get back to it after you've learned how to do this first kind of *t* Test.
3. Why is the mean taken to be 0? Because the table is giving values for the null hypothesis, that there is no difference between the two groups. If there is no difference, the differences between sample means will form a distribution that has some negative values (Group A will, by chance, be slightly smaller than Group B) and some positive values (Group B will, by chance, be slightly smaller than Group A), with a mean of 0.

CHAPTER

12 Analysis of Variance (ANOVA)

- **Computation Steps**
- **Strength of Association**
- **Post hoc Analyses**
- **The Scheffé Method of Post hoc Analysis**
- **Problems**
- **Answers to Problems**

The Top Ten Reasons Why Statisticians Are Misunderstood

1. They speak only the Greek language.
2. They usually have long, threatening names, such as Bonferonni, Scheffe, Tchebycheff, Schatzoff, Hotelling, and Godambe. Where are the statisticians with names such as Smith, Brown, or Johnson?
3. They are fond of all snakes and typically own as a pet a large South American snake called an ANOCOVA.
4. For perverse reasons, rather than view a matrix right side up, they prefer to invert it.
5. Rather than moonlighting by holding Amway parties, they earn a few extra bucks by holding pocket-protector parties.
6. They are frequently seen in their backyards on clear nights gazing through powerful amateur telescopes looking for distant star constellations called ANOVAs.
7. They are 99% confident that sleep cannot be induced in an introductory statistics class by lecturing on *Z* scores.
8. Their idea of a scenic and exotic trip is traveling three standard deviations above the mean in a normal distribution.
9. They manifest many psychological disorders, because as young statisticians many of their statistical hypotheses were rejected.

10. They express a deep-seated fear that society will someday construct tests that will enable everyone to make the same score. Without variation or individual differences, the field of statistics has no real function, and a statistician becomes a penniless ward of the state.

In Chapter 11, you learned how to determine if the means of two groups differ to a statistically significant degree. In this chapter, you will learn how to test for differences among the means of two *or more* groups. Hey, I bet you thought you were having fun before!

Suppose you assigned subjects to one of three groups: a peer support group (Group 1), an exercise/diet group (Group 2), and a no-treatment control group (Group 3), with posttreatment adjustment test scores as follows:

Group 1 Peer Support	Group 2 Exercise/Diet	Group 3 Control
22	6	8
16	10	6
17	13	4
18	13	5
	8	2
	4	

You could test for the differences between pairs of means with the *t* Test: You could test for the significance of difference for $\overline{X}_1$ versus $\overline{X}_2$, $\overline{X}_1$ versus $\overline{X}_3$, and $\overline{X}_2$ versus $\overline{X}_3$. There are at least two reasons why it would not be a good idea to do this kind of analysis, however.

1. It's tedious. If you do *t* Tests, you will have to compute $\frac{K(K-1)}{2}$ of them, where K is the number of groups. In our example, $\frac{K(K-1)}{2} = \frac{3(3-1)}{2} = \frac{6}{2} = 3$. This isn't too bad, but if you were comparing means among, say, ten groups, you would have to compute forty-five *t* Tests!

2. More important, when you select, for example, the 0.05 level of significance, you expect to make a Type I error 5 times out of 100 by sampling error alone for each test. If you performed 20*t* Tests and 1 of them reached the 0.05 level of significance, would that be a chance occurrence or not? What if 3 of the 20 were significant? Which would be chance and which would be a "real" difference? With multiple *t* Tests, the probability (p) of a Type I error is

$$p = 1 - (1 - \alpha)^c$$

Where: α = alpha level
c = number of comparisons

For our example, if $c = 3$ and $\alpha = 0.05$, then

$$p = 1 - (1 - \alpha)^c = 1 - (1 - 0.05)^3 = 1 - 0.93^3 = 0.14$$

So, instead of a 5% chance of making a Type I error, when you conduct three *t* Tests you have a 14% chance of committing a Type I error.

You can take care of both of these problems by using *analysis of variance* (ANOVA) to test for statistical significance of the differences among the means of two or more groups. It may be important to note here that, even though the name of this statistic has the word *variance* in it, it is used to test for significant differences among means. The test looks at the amount of variability (the differences) between the means of the groups, compared with the amount of variability among the individual scores in each group—that is, the variance between groups versus the variance within groups—and that's where the name comes from. The ANOVA starts with the total amount of variability (i.e., variance) in the data and divides it up (statisticians call it "partitioning") into various categories. Eventually, the technique allows us to compare the variability among the group means with the variability that occurred just by chance or error—and that's exactly what we need to be able to do.

Perhaps you recall the formula for the variance, given to you in Chapter 5.

Remember that when we are estimating the variance of the population from which the sample was drawn, we divide the sum of the deviation scores by $N - 1$, rather than just N: Just getting the average of the sample members' deviations around the mean would yield a biased estimate of the population value. $N - 1$, one less than the number of things in the sample (scores, people, hot fudge sundaes) is known as the sample's *degrees of freedom.* So when we estimate the variance of the population, we must use the following formula:

$$SD_x^2 = \frac{(X - \overline{X})^2}{N - 1}$$

Degrees of freedom is a concept you may not understand yet, although we've used the term several times already. The basic idea has to do with the number of scores in a group of scores that are free to vary. In a group of 10 scores that sum up to 100, you could let 9 of the scores be anything you wanted. Once you had decided what those 9 scores were, the value of the 10th score would be determined. Let's say we made the first 9 scores each equal to 2. They'd add up to a total of 18; if the sum has to be 100, then the 10th score has to be 82. The group of 10 scores has only 9 degrees of freedom, 9 scores that are free to vary, $df = 9$. Why is this important? Because the calculations for an ANOVA involve degrees of freedom, and you need to be able to figure out what those *df* are. But we need to do a few other things first.

The first step in carrying out an ANOVA is to compute the variance of the total number of subjects in the study—we put them all together, regardless of the group to which they've been assigned, and find the variance of the whole thing. We do this using $N_T - 1$ (the total degrees of freedom) for the denominator of the formula:

$$s_T^2 = \frac{\Sigma(X - \overline{X}_T)^2}{N_T - 1}$$

Nothing new so far; this is just our old friend, the formula for estimating a population variance based on a sample drawn from that population. We do have a couple of new names for things, though. The numerator of this formula is called the "total sum of squares," abbreviated SS_T—"total," because it's calculated across the total number of scores, combining all the groups. SS_T is the basis for all the partitioning that will follow. Notice, too, that the formula uses $\overline{X}_T$ as the symbol for the overall mean of all scores (some authors use "GM," for "grand mean") and N_T, the total number of subjects. The denominator of the formula is known as the total degrees of freedom, or df_T. Translating the old variance formula to these new terms, we get

$$s_T^2 = \frac{\Sigma(X - \overline{X}_T)^2}{N_T - 1} = \frac{SS_T}{df_T}$$

In ANOVA calculations, this pattern—dividing a sum of squares by an associated *df*—is repeated again and again. The number that you get when you divide a sum of squares by the appropriate *df* is called a mean square (MS). So,

$$s_T^2 = MS_T = \frac{SS_T}{df_T}$$

I want to pause here to remind you of something I said way back at the very beginning of this book: Mathematical formulas take much longer to read and understand than do most other kinds of reading. You struggled through a lot of formulas in Chapter 11, and we're going to be dealing with lots more of them here. So, please, remember to take your time! Pause, translate the formula into words, and make sure you understand how it relates to what went before. This last formula, for instance, says that the total mean square of a group of scores is the sum of squares for that group, divided by the degrees of freedom. And what are the sum of squares and the degrees of freedom? Go back, read again, and put it together in your head. Understand each piece before you go on to the next. Reading this way will actually prove to be a faster way to learn in the long run.

In a simple ANOVA, the total sum of squares (SS_T) is broken down into two parts: (a) a *sum of squares within groups*, SS_W, which reflects the degree of variability within groups but is not sensitive to overall differences between the groups; and (b) a *sum of squares between groups*, SS_B, which reflects differences between groups but is not sensitive to variability within groups. The total sum of squares is the sum of the sum of squares within and the sum of squares between:

$$SS_T = SS_W + SS_B$$

The total degrees of freedom can be broken down as well:

$$df_T = df_W + df_B$$

To find df_w, add up the dfs within all the groups:

$$df_W = (n_1 - 1) + (n_2 - 1) + \cdots + (n_{Last} - 1)$$

And df_B is the number of groups minus 1: $K - 1$.

For the groups in our example,

$$df_W = (4 - 1) + (6 - 1) + (5 - 1) = 3 + 5 + 4 = 12$$
$$df_B = 3 - 1 = 2$$

If we did our math right, $df_W + df_B$ should equal df_T:

$$[(4 - 1) + (6 - 1) + (5 - 1)] + (3 - 1) = (3 + 5 + 4) + 2$$
$$12 + 2 = 14$$

Dividing SS_W by df_W gives us what is known as the mean square within, a measure of the variability within groups:

$$MS_W = \frac{SS_W}{df_W}$$

And dividing SS_B by df_B gives us the mean square between, a measure of variability between groups:

$$MS_B = \frac{SS_B}{df_B}$$

I know you haven't been told how to find SS_W and SS_B yet—that comes next. For now, just look at the logic of the process.

With MS_B, we have a measure of variability *between* the groups—that is, a measure that reflects how different they are from each other. And with MS_W we have a measure of the variability *inside* the groups—that is, variability that can be attributed to chance or error. Ultimately, of course, we want to know if the between-group differences are significantly greater than chance. So we will compare the two by computing their ratio:

$$F_{obt} = \frac{MS_B}{MS_W}$$

F is the ratio of a mean square between groups to a mean square within groups. (It's named after Sir Roland Fisher, who invented it.) The *obt* subscript means that, as usual, we will compare this obtained value of *F* with some critical value (F_{crit}), which will tell us how likely it is that our F_{obt} could have happened just by chance. The values of F_{crit} are found in Appendix D. (I'll show you how to look up the values of F_{crit} later.) If F_{obt} is equal to or greater than F_{crit}, then we reject the null hypothesis.

You may have guessed that when comparing three group means the null hypothesis is

$$H_0 : \mu_1 = \mu_2 = \mu_3$$

The only hard part about ANOVA is learning how to compute SS_W and SS_B. You can do it, though. It's no harder than some of the other computations we've done.

TABLE 12-1 Computation of values for one-way ANOVA.

Step		Group 1	Group 2	Group 3	
		22	6	8	
		16	10	6	
		17	13	4	
		18	13	5	
			8	2	
			4		
1	N	4	6	5	$N_T = \Sigma N = 15$
2	ΣX	73	54	25	$\Sigma X_T = 152$
3					$I = \frac{(\Sigma X_T)^2}{N_T}$ **I = 1,540.27**
4	ΣX^2	1,353	554	145	**II** $= \Sigma\Sigma X^2 =$ **2,052**
5	$\frac{(\Sigma X)^2}{N}$	$\frac{(73)^2}{4}$	$\frac{(54)^2}{6}$	$\frac{(25)^2}{5}$	$III = \Sigma\frac{(\Sigma X)^2}{N} = \frac{\Sigma(\Sigma X)^2}{N}$ **III = 1,943.25**
6	M	18.25	9	5	

The scores from our hypothetical study are shown again in Table 12-1. Under the scores, you'll see some rows of computations, which I'll explain as we go along. In this computational table, we'll end up with intermediate values—which I've labeled I, II, and III—which we'll use to compute our SS_W and SS_B.

COMPUTATION STEPS

STEP 1. FIND N_T. N_T stands for the total number of subjects in the entire study. Under each column of scores, you will see the number of subjects (N) for each group. In the last column in Row 1, you will see N_T, which is the total number of subjects in the study. You get that, of course, by adding the Ns of the columns:

$$N_T = N_1 + N_2 + N_3 = 4 + 6 + 5 = 15$$

STEP 2. FIND ΣX_T. ΣX_T stands for the grand total of all the scores. Start by finding ΣX_T for each column. For example, for Group 1, $\Sigma X = 73$. Then find ΣX_T by adding the sum of each column:

$$\Sigma X_T = 73 + 54 + 25 = 152$$

STEP 3. FIND *I*. **I** is the first intermediate value we will compute. As the formula indicates, **I** is found by squaring ΣX_T (found in Row 2) and dividing that by N_T (found in Step 1).

$$\mathbf{I} = \frac{(\Sigma X_T)^2}{N_T} = \frac{152^2}{15} = \frac{23{,}104}{15} = 1{,}540.27$$

STEP 4. FIND *II*. II is the total sum of X^2 for the entire set of scores across all groups, or $\sum(\sum X^2)$. First, find $\sum X^2$ for each column (square each score first, then find the sum of the squares—remember?), and then compute **II** by adding those sums of squares:

$$\mathbf{II} = \sum(\sum X^2) = 1{,}353 + 554 + 145 = 2{,}052$$

STEP 5. FIND *III*. To find **III**, $\sum\frac{\sum(X)^2}{N}$, first find the sum of all scores in each column, or $\sum X$. Now square that value—$(\sum X)^2$. After that, divide $(\sum X)^2$ by the N for each column. Finally, sum those values for all groups:

$$\sum\frac{\sum(X)^2}{N} = \frac{(73)^2}{4} + \frac{(54)^2}{6} + \frac{(25)^2}{5} = 1{,}332.25 + 486 + 125 = 1{,}943.25$$

STEP 6. FIND THE MEAN ($\overline{X}$) OF EACH GROUP. This is an "extra" step that I added because you're going to need the group means shortly. As you no doubt recall with fondness, we learned how to find $\overline{X}$ way back in Chapter 5.

Now use the intermediate values to compute the sums of squares with the following formulas:

$$SS_B = \mathbf{III} - \mathbf{I} = 1{,}943.25 - 1{,}540.27 = 402.98$$
$$SS_W = \mathbf{II} - \mathbf{III} = 2052 - 1943.25 = 108.75$$

We will also need to know the degrees of freedom for both between and within groups. In the following formulas, K stands for the number of groups. In our example, $K = 3$. Also, remember that N_T is the total number of subjects in the study:

$$df_B = K - 1 = 3 - 1 = 2$$
$$df_W = N - K = 15 - 3 = 12$$

Here's a chance for another quick arithmetic check. Since the total df is equal to $N_T - 1$ (in our study, $15 - 1$, or 14), the df_B and the df_W should add up to that number. And they do: $12 + 2 = 14$.

Now we can fill in what is known as an ANOVA summary table (see Table 12-2). Look carefully in each column of the table and you will find all the numbers we calculated in Steps 1–5, plus the df. As you can see in the table,

$$F_{obt} = \frac{MS_B}{MS_W} = \frac{201.49}{9.06} = 22.24$$

As was true for the t Test, to find out whether your F_{obt} is statistically significant, you will need to compare it with F_{crit}. You will find the value for F_{crit} in Appendix D. Go across the table until you come to the column headed by the df_B for the F_{obt} you are interested in (in our example, there is only one F_{obt} to worry about, and $df_B = 2$). Look down that column until you are directly across from your df_W (in our example, $df_W = 12$). Appendix D includes critical values of F for both the 0.05 and the 0.01 levels of significance; the 0.01 level is in boldface type. As you can see, for $df_B = 2$ and $df_W = 12$, F_{crit} at the 0.05 level of significance is 3.88, and at the 0.01 level, F_{crit} is 6.93. Since your $F_{obt} = 22.24$ is larger than F_{crit} for either the 0.05 or the 0.01 levels

TABLE 12-2 ANOVA summary table.

Source of Variation	Degrees of Freedom (df)	Sum of Squares	Mean Squares	F
Between (*B*)	$k - 1 = 3 - 1 = 2$	$SS_B = \text{III} - \text{I}$	$MS_B = \frac{SS_B}{df_B}$	$F_{obt} = \frac{MS_B}{MS_W}$
		$= 402.98$		
			$= \frac{402.98}{2}$	$= 22.24^{**}$
			$= 201.49$	
Within (*W*)	$N_T - k = 15 - 3$	$SS_W = \text{II} - \text{III}$	$MS_W = \frac{SS_W}{df}$	
	$= 12$	$= 108.75$	$= \frac{108.75}{12}$	
Total	$N - 1 = 14$	$SS_T = 511.73$		

of significance, you reject the null hypothesis (that there is no difference among means) and conclude that at least one of the means is significantly different from at least one of the others. Conventionally, a value of F_{obt} that exceeds F_{crit} for the 0.05 level is followed by a single asterisk; if it exceeds F_{crit} for the 0.01 level, it gets two asterisks. In the table, because the F_{obt} exceeds the F_{crit} at the 0.01 level, there are two asterisks.

A statistically significant *F* test in ANOVA tells us that at least one of the means is significantly different from at least one of the others, but it doesn't tell us which means are significantly different. Eyeballing the means of the three groups in our example, we can see that the mean of Group 1, the peer support group ($\overline{X}_1 = 18.25$), is much larger than the mean of Group 3, the control group ($\overline{X}_2 = 5.0$). It seems likely that these two means are statistically significantly different. We also might wonder, however, if the mean of Group 1 is different from the mean of Group 2, the exercise/diet group ($\overline{X}_3 = 9.0$), and if the exercise/diet group is significantly different from the control group. To answer these questions, you will need to learn how to do what is known as post hoc analysis. But first, let's talk about strength of association.

STRENGTH OF ASSOCIATION

With ANOVA, the overall *F* test tells us whether the means of the treatment groups were statistically significantly different. The overall *F* test does not, however, tell us anything about the strength of the treatment effect. With very large samples, you often find differences between means that are statistically significant but not very important in terms of practical significance. For this reason, whenever you find a statistically significant overall *F* test, you also need to determine the strength of association for the treatment effects.

One way to do that is to find proportion of total variability that can be accounted for by the treatment effects with the Omega-square $\hat{\omega}^2$):

$$\hat{\omega}^2 = \frac{SS_B - (K - 1)MS_W}{SS_T + MS_W}$$

To find the strength of association between treatments and adjustment test scores for our example, we simply plug in the numbers from our ANOVA summary table and find the answer:

$$\hat{\omega}^2 = \frac{SS_B - (K - 1)MS_W}{SS_T + MS_W} = \frac{402.98 - (3 - 1)9.06}{511.73 + 9.06}$$

$$= \frac{402.98 - 18.12}{520.79} = \frac{384.86}{520.79} = 0.74$$

The $\hat{\omega}^2$ is interpreted in the same way as the coefficient of determination, r^2_{xy}. If that concept is a bit fuzzy, go back to Chapter 8 for a quick review. For our example, $\hat{\omega}^2 = 0.74$. This indicates that the treatment effects in our example account for a large amount of variance—74%, in fact—in post-treatment adjustment test scores. Pretty easy stuff, right?

POST HOC ANALYSIS

Post hoc analyses are used after an ANOVA has been done and the null hypothesis of no difference among means has been rejected. Let's look at another example. Consider a study of five different teaching methods. Five groups of students were taught a unit, each group being exposed to a different teaching method, and then the groups of students were tested for how much they had learned. Even if an ANOVA were to show the differences among the five means to be statistically significant, we still would not know which of the pairs of means were significantly different: Is $\overline{X}_1$ significantly different from $\overline{X}_2$? How about the difference between $\overline{X}_2$ and $\overline{X}_3$? If we looked at each possible combination, we would have $5(5 - 1)/2 = 10$ pairs of means to analyze. You will recall from the discussion at the beginning of this chapter that it is not good practice to analyze differences among pairs of means with the *t* Test because of the increased probability of a Type I error; the same criticism can be leveled at any large set of independent comparisons.

Many procedures have been developed to do what is called post hoc analysis (tests used after an F_{obt} has been found to be statistically significant in an ANOVA). This book will present only one of these methods, the Scheffé method, which can be used for groups of equal or unequal *N*s.

THE SCHEFFÉ METHOD OF POST HOC ANALYSIS

The statistic you will compute in the Scheffé method is designated as *C*. A value of *C* is computed for any pair of means that you want to compare; unlike the *t* Test, *C* is designed to allow multiple comparisons without affecting the likelihood of a Type I error. Moreover, if all the groups are the same size, you don't have to compute *C* for every single pair of means; once a significant *C* has been found for a given pair, you can assume that any other pair that is at least this far apart will also be significantly different. (With a *t* Test, this is not necessarily true; nor is it always true for *C* when the group *N*s are unequal.)

As is the usual procedure, you will compare your C_{obt} with a C_{crit}; if C_{obt} is equal to or greater than C_{crit}, you will reject the null hypothesis for that pair of means. In the Scheffé test, you don't look up C_{crit} in a table; I'll show you how to compute it for yourself. First, though, we'll deal with C_{obt}:

$$C_{obt} = \frac{\overline{X}_1 - \overline{X}_2}{\sqrt{MS_W\left(\frac{1}{N_1} + \frac{1}{N_2}\right)}}$$

Where: $\overline{X}_1, \overline{X}_2$ are the means of two groups being compared
N_1, N_2 are the *N*s of those two groups
MS_W is the within-group mean square from your ANOVA

Now let's go back to our original three groups: peer support (Group 1), exercise/ diet (Group 2), and control (Group 3). Since we were able to reject H_0, we know that at least one group is significantly different from one other group; but we don't know which groups they are. And there may be more than one significant difference; we need to check that out. We'll start with the first pair, Group 1 vs. Group 2:

$$C_{obt} = \frac{\overline{X}_1 - \overline{X}_2}{\sqrt{MS_W\left(\frac{1}{N_1} + \frac{1}{N_2}\right)}} = \frac{18.25 - 9.0}{\sqrt{9.06\left(\frac{1}{4} + \frac{1}{6}\right)}} = \frac{9.25}{1.95} = 4.74$$

For Group 1 vs. Group 3,

$$C_{obt} = \frac{\overline{X}_1 - \overline{X}_3}{\sqrt{MS_W\left(\frac{1}{N_1} + \frac{1}{N_3}\right)}} = \frac{18.25 - 5.0}{\sqrt{9.06\left(\frac{1}{4} + \frac{1}{5}\right)}} = \frac{13.25}{2.02} = 6.56$$

And for Group 2 vs. Group 3,

$$C_{obt} = \frac{\overline{X}_2 - \overline{X}_3}{\sqrt{MS_W\left(\frac{1}{N_2} + \frac{1}{N_3}\right)}} = \frac{9.0 - 5.0}{\sqrt{9.06\left(\frac{1}{6} + \frac{1}{5}\right)}} = \frac{4.0}{1.83} = 2.19$$

(Notice that, although it's still tedious to look at each possible pair, it's a lot less work than doing multiple *t* Tests!)

Now we are ready to compute C_{crit}. The general formula for C_{crit} is

$$C_{crit} = \sqrt{(K - 1)(F_{crit})}$$

Where: *K* is the number of treatment groups
F_{crit} is the critical value of *F* test from your ANOVA

United Media/United Feature Syndicate, Inc. © 1979 PEANUTS reprinted by permission of United Feature Syndicate, Inc.

At the 0.05 level of significance ($\alpha = 0.05$),

$$C_{crit} = \sqrt{(K - 1)(F_{crit})} = \sqrt{(3 - 1)(3.88)} = 2.79$$

and at the 0.01 level ($\alpha = 0.01$),

$$C_{crit} = \sqrt{(K - 1)(F_{crit})} = \sqrt{(3 - 1)(6.93)} = 3.72$$

Since it doesn't matter which group mean is subtracted from which in each computation of C_{obt}, the sign of the value you get doesn't matter either. Just treat C_{obt} as if it were positive. As you can see by comparing C_{crit} with C_{obt}, for both the 0.05 and the 0.01 levels of significance, the mean of the counseled group (Group 1) is significantly larger than either the exercise/diet or the control groups. However, the mean of the exercise/diet group is not significantly greater than that of the control group.

Once you have determined that two groups are significantly different from each other, you will still have to decide if the differences are large enough to be useful in the real world. This is the "magnitude of effect" decision, which we discussed in relation to the *t* Test. Unfortunately, there's no handy-dandy rule or formula to tell us whether we have a "large enough" magnitude of effect. It depends on what's at stake: what's to be gained by a correct decision and what's to be lost by an incorrect one and how much difference between groups is enough to be worth paying attention to. In our example, the mean of the peer support group is twice as high as the mean of the exercise/diet group and more than three times the mean of the control group. For me, differences of that magnitude would play a very important part in treatment recommendations to students or clients. How about for you?

Problems

1. A researcher is interested in differences among blondes, brunettes, and redheads in terms of introversion/extroversion. She selects random samples from a college campus, gives each subject a test of social introversion, and comes up with the following:

Blondes	Brunettes	Redheads
5	3	2
10	5	1
6	2	7
2	4	2
5	3	2
3	5	3

Use a simple ANOVA to test for differences among the groups.

2. A (hypothetical!) study of eating patterns among people in different occupations yielded the following:

	Bus Drivers ($n = 10$)	College Professors ($n = 4$)	U.S. Presidents ($n = 4$)
Mean Junk Food Score	12	17	58.3

ANOVA Source Table

Source	*df*	*SS*	*MS*	*F*
Between	2	6505	3252.5	6.1**
Within	15	11,197	533.2	

a. What do you conclude?

b. Perform the appropriate post hoc analysis.

Answers to Problems

1. (I've given you some intermediate steps here, in case you got confused.) Since F_{crit} for $\alpha = 0.05$—with 2 and 15 *df*—is 3.68, the obtained value of *F* does not reach the critical value, and we cannot reject H_0.

2. The null hypothesis can be rejected at the 0.01 level; the differences among the groups are significant ($p < 0.01$). Scheffé's test, using C_{Crit} of 2.63 (for $\alpha = 0.05$), indicates no significant differences between bus drivers and professors ($C < 1$) but significant differences between bus drivers and U.S. presidents ($C = 3.39$) and between college professors and U.S. presidents ($C = 2.53$).

	Blondes	Brunettes	Redheads	
N	6	6	6	$N_T = 18$
ΣX	31	22	17	$\Sigma X_T = 70$
ΣX^2	199	88	71	$\text{I} = \frac{(\Sigma X_T)^2}{N_T} = \frac{70^2}{18} = 272.22$
$\frac{(\Sigma X)^2}{N}$	160.17	80.67	48.17	$\text{II} = 358$ $\text{III} = 289.01$
$\bar{X}$	5.17	3.67	2.83	

ANOVA Source Table

Source	*df*	*SS*	*MS*	*F*
Between	2	16.79	8.4	1.83
Within	15	68.99	4.6	

SECTION V

Additional Topics

Nonparametric Statistics and Using Statistical Software Programs

In this final section, we cover two additional important topics. In Chapter 13, the concept of nonparametric statistics is introduced. We discuss one of the most commonly used nonparametric tests, the chi-square. Nonparametric statistics are not used to test hypotheses about specific population parameters; rather, they are used to test, for example, hypotheses about the shapes of distributions of data and their central tendency, among other things. In Chapter 14, we introduce the use of statistical software programs. The widespread use of statistical software has changed the way most people conduct statistical analyses. This chapter introduces SPSS, one of the easiest to use and most widely used statistical programs. Step-by-step instructions with multiple screen shots are provided to show you how to enter data, compute statistics, and interpret example output, using SPSS. Chapter 15 consists of the postscript in which we review how far you have come and congratulate you on a job truly well done.

CHAPTER

13 Nonparametric Statistics

Chi-Square

- **One-Way Test of Chi-Square**
- **Yates' Correction for Continuity**
- **A Bit More**
- **Problems**
- **Answers to Problems**

> *"An approximate answer to the right question is worth a good deal more than the exact answer to an approximate problem."*
>
> —JOHN TUKEY

"Nonparametric"—Oh, no! Is this something I should recognize from what has gone before? If we're going to look at nonparametric things, what in the world are parametric ones? Relax—all these questions will be answered. You should know, though, first of all, that the things we will be doing in this chapter will be easier, not harder, than what you have already done.

All the statistical procedures that you have learned so far are parametric procedures. The idea of parametric statistics involves a number of things, including the assumption that the data we work with are drawn from normally distributed populations. The most important thing, however, is that the data used in parametric tests or techniques must be scores or measurements of some sort. When comparing groups of people by means of a parametric test, we measure all the people and then use the test to determine whether the groups' measurements are significantly different from what could be expected just by chance.

But what if we are dealing with a situation in which we don't measure or test our subjects? That's not as unusual as you may imagine. Here's an example: A researcher wants to know if college students differ in terms of their use of the college counseling center by year in college. She randomly selects 100 students and asks them if they have ever used the center. Here are her findings:

Center Use	Freshman	Sophomore	Junior	Senior	Total
Used Center	20	31	28	21	100

How should this researcher analyze her data? There are no scores, no means or variances to calculate. What she has is four categories: students who used the center. Each person in the sample can be assigned to one, and only one, of these categories. What the researcher wants to know is whether the distribution she observed is significantly different from what she might expect, by chance, if the total population of students didn't differ by year.

ONE-WAY TEST OF CHI-SQUARE (χ^2)

Her question is quite easy to answer using a procedure called the chi-square test. Chi-square (symbolized by the Greek letter chi, squared: χ^2) is a nonparametric test. It doesn't require that its data meet the assumptions of parametric statistics, and it most particularly doesn't require that the data be in the form of scores or measurements. Instead, it was specifically designed to test hypotheses about categorical data. The one-way test of χ^2 can be used when the categories involve a single independent variable.

The null hypothesis for our example is that use of the counseling center doesn't differ significantly by year:

H_0: The observed frequencies (f_0) equal the expected frequencies (f_e)

When H_0 is true, differences between the observed and expected frequencies will be small. When H_0 is false, differences will be relatively large. To test the H_0 using χ^2, we first need to figure out the distribution that we would most often get just by chance if H_0 were true. The expected frequencies for this study are those that would occur by chance if no difference in the use of the center existed across year in school. According to H_0, then, because there are 100 subjects, and we expect the same amount of students by year in school, we would predict 25 students to be freshmen, 25 sophomores, 25 juniors, and 25 seniors.

Center Use	Freshman	Sophomore	Junior	Senior	Total
Observed *f*	20	31	28	21	100
Expected *f*	25	25	25	25	100

Of course, in any experiment we would expect the observed frequencies to be slightly different from the expected frequencies on the basis of chance, or random sampling variation, even when H_0 is true. But how much variation from the expected frequencies is reasonable to expect by chance? When do we start to think that use of the center really does differ by year in school? Here's where the χ^2 can help.

The χ^2 provides a test of the discrepancy between expected and obtained frequencies:

$$\chi^2 = \Sigma\left[\frac{(O_i - E_i)^2}{E_i}\right]$$

Where O_i is the observed frequency, and
E_i is the expected frequency

By looking at the formula, you can see a few things. First, the χ^2 will never be negative because we are squaring all differences between the expected and observed frequencies. Second, χ^2 will equal zero only when the observed frequencies are exactly the same as the predicted frequencies. And third, the larger the discrepancies, the larger the χ^2.

For our example:

$$\chi^2 = \Sigma\left[\frac{(O_i - E_i)^2}{E_i}\right] = \frac{(20 - 25)^2}{25} + \frac{(31 - 25)^2}{25} + \frac{(28 - 25)^2}{25} + \frac{(21 - 25)^2}{25}$$

$$= \frac{(-5)^2 + (6)^2 + (3)^2 + (-4)^2}{25} = 3.44$$

As has been the case with all our statistics, we must compare the calculated value of χ^2 with a critical value. To do so, enter Appendix E with the following degrees of freedom (*df*):

$$df = K - 1$$

Where: K is the number of categories

For our example, $df = K - 1 = 4 - 1 = 3$. You can see from the table that for $\alpha = 0.05$, with $df = 3$, the $\chi^2_{crit} = 7.81$. Since our observed value of χ^2 is less than the critical value, we do not reject the null hypothesis and conclude that use of the counseling center does not differ by year in school.

It is important to note then when the test of χ^2 is statistically significant, this outcome would not imply any sort of causal relationship: We cannot say that year in school "causes" the differences in counseling center behavior, any more than we could say that use of the counseling center "causes" people to be either freshman, sophomores, juniors, or seniors. Also, statistical significance does not guarantee magnitude of effect. Evaluation of magnitude of effect involves qualitative, as well as quantitative, considerations. Aren't you tired of having me say this?

Generally, studies utilizing χ^2 require a relatively large number of subjects. Many statisticians recommend a certain minimum expected frequency (f_e) per cell. A very conservative rule of thumb is that f_e must always be equal to or greater than 5. When you don't meet this requirement, the values of χ^2_{crit} in the table won't apply to your data, and so you won't know whether your χ^2_{obt} is significantly different from chance.

http://www.borg.com/~rjgtoons/edu.html

YATES' CORRECTION FOR CONTINUITY

We need to discuss one special case of the one-way test of χ^2 before we're done with the one-way χ^2. This is when you have a 2x1 table. In this situation, the χ^2 must be corrected, because the observed distribution of χ^2 tends not to be as smooth as it should be. When this happens, you must use Yates' correction for continuity:

$$\chi^2_Y = \Sigma\left[\frac{(|O_i - E_i| - 0.5)^2}{E_i}\right]$$

As you can see, the formula is basically the same, except for the minor adjustment made by subtracting 0.5 in the equation.

For example, suppose our researcher is now interested in whether men and women use the counseling center with the same frequency and that she has gathered the following data:

Center Use	Men	Women	Total
Observed *f*	15	35	50
Expected *f*	25	25	50

Our null hypothesis with a 2x1 table and χ^2_Y is the same as before:

H_0: The observed frequencies (f_0) equals the expected frequencies (f_e)

Using the data from our example, we get the following result:

$$\chi_Y^2 = \Sigma\left[\frac{(|O_i - E_i| - 0.5)^2}{E_i}\right] = \frac{(|15 - 25| - 0.5)^2}{25} + \frac{(|35 - 25| - 0.5)^2}{25}$$

$$= \frac{(9.5)^2 + (9.5)^2}{25} = 7.22$$

Now we must find the χ^2_{crit} in Appendix E. As you can see in this table, with $df = (K - 1) = 2 - 1 = 1$, the χ^2_{crit} is 3.84 with $\alpha = .05$. Because our χ^2_{obt} is larger than this critical value, we reject H_0. On the basis of this result, we conclude that women use the counseling center more than men do.

A BIT MORE

This chapter has only focused on the one-way test of χ^2. There are lots more nonparametric tests out there; this is just a teaser to whet your appetite! For example, you can also use χ^2 with two or more levels. For example, our researcher could examine whether men and women differed in their use of the counseling center by year in school. In general, it's safe to say that a nonparametric test exists, or can be cobbled to fit, virtually any research situation. In addition, nonparametric tests tend to have a relatively simple structure, to be based on less complex sets of principles and assumptions than their parametric brethren. For this reason, if you can't find a ready-made nonparametric test that fits your situation, a competent statistician can probably design one for you without much trouble.

At this point, you may be asking, "So why don't we always use nonparametrics? Why bother with parametric tests at all?" The answer is simple: Parametric tests are more powerful than nonparametric statistics. When the data allow, we prefer to use parametrics because they are less likely to invite a Type II error. Another way of saying this is that parametric tests let us claim significance more easily; they are less likely to miss significant relationships when such relationships are present. However, using a parametric test with data that don't meet parametric assumptions can cause even more problems—can result in a Type I error—and we can't even estimate the likelihood of a Type I error under these circumstances. That's when we need the nonparametric techniques. Not only are they, by and large, easier to compute, but they fill a much-needed spot in our statistical repertoire.

Problems

1. Senior education majors were asked about their plans for a job. Those who said they would like to teach the subject are represented below:

Teach in Junior College	Teach in a Teaching College	Teach in a Research University
22	19	9

a. What is H_0?
b. What are the *df*?
c. What is χ^2_{crit} with $\alpha = 0.05$?
d. What is the value of χ^2?
e. What conclusion do you make based on the results?

2. Assume you have the following data:

Teach in Junior College	Teach in a Research University
22	28

Using χ^2_Y,
a. What is H_0?
b. What are the *df*?
c. What is χ^2_{crit} with $\alpha = 0.01$?
d. What is the value of χ^2?
e. What conclusion do you make based on the results?

Answers to Problems

1. **a.** $f_O = f_e$ **b.** 2 **c.** 5.99
d. $\chi^2_{Obt} = 5.57$ **e.** do not reject H_0

2. **a.** $f_O = f_e$ **b.** 1 **c.** 6.64
d. $\chi^2_{Obt} = 0.50$ **e.** do not reject H_0

CHAPTER

14 How to Use SPSS

- **Starting SPSS**
- **Basic Steps in Data Analysis**
- **Finding Help in SPSS**

A mathematician, an applied mathematician, and a statistician all apply for the same job. At the interview, they are asked the question, "What is 1 + 1?" The mathematician replies, "I can prove that it exists but not that it is unique." The applied mathematician, after some thought, replies, "The answer is approximately 1.99, with an error in the region of 0.01." The statistician steps outside the room, mulls it over for several minutes, and eventually returns in desperation and inquires, "So what do you want it to be?"

Today's software programs make life much easier for students who are learning statistics. Most of the work in programs like SPSS is done by simply pointing and clicking. In SPSS, you can enter data, run analyses, and display your results in tables and graphs in a matter of minutes. Sound great? It is.

The purpose of this chapter is to introduce you to the basics of SPSS. All of the topics covered in this book can be done in SPSS. Please keep in mind that SPSS is a very powerful program. There are many things that can be done in SPSS that are beyond the scope of this book.

After reading this chapter, if you find you want more information on how to use SPSS, I encourage you to review the online tutorial that comes with the program. The tutorial is designed to familiarize readers with many of the features of SPSS. You may also want to obtain the SPSS *Brief Guide* as a supplement to the online guide. Green and Salkind's *Using SPSS for Windows and Macintosh: Analyzing and Understanding Data* is another helpful text for learning how to use SPSS.

STARTING SPSS

To start SPSS, click on the name of the program in the Start menu, just like you would for any other Windows program. After it starts, the first dialog box you are presented with in SPSS is shown in Figure 14-1.

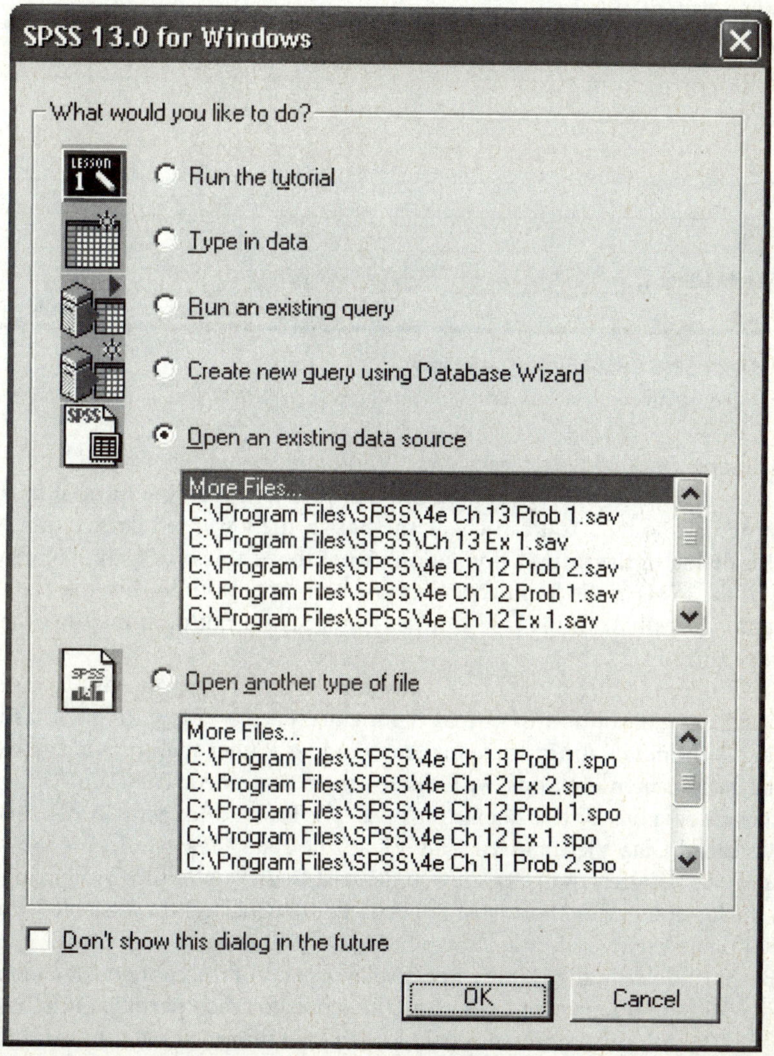

FIGURE 14-1 The SPSS opening dialog box.

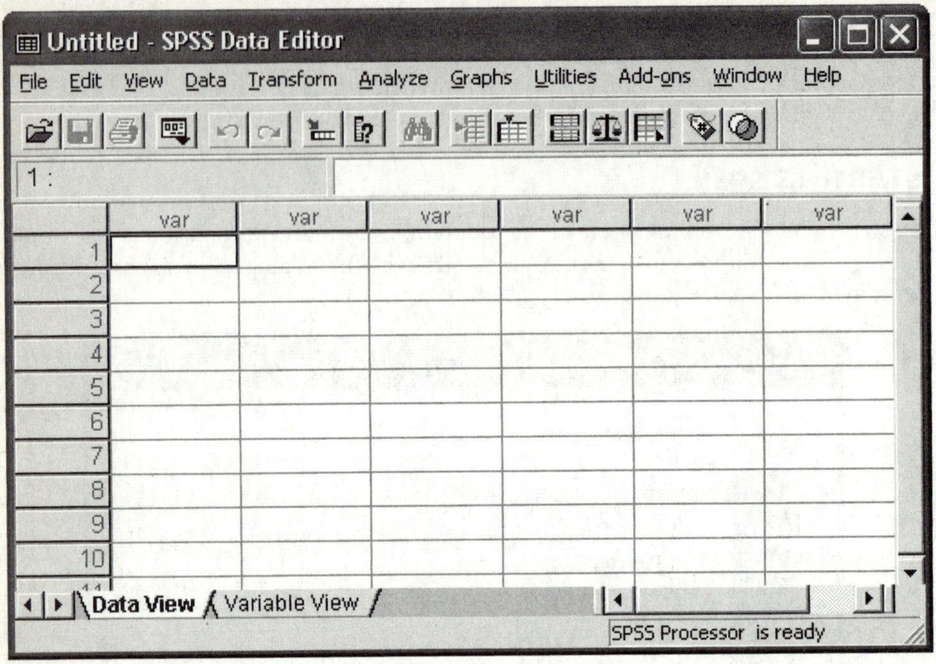

FIGURE 14-2 SPSS Data Editor (Data View).
Reprint courtesy of International Business Machines Corporation, © SPSS, Inc., an IBM Company.

The opening dialog box asks you, "What you would like to do?" and presents you with a number of choices, ranging from running the online tutorial to opening an existing data source. You can check the box in the lower left corner titled "Don't show this dialog in the future" if you don't want to see this box again. For now, click Cancel in the lower right-hand corner of the box. After you do this, the Data Editor opens automatically with the title Untitled—SPSS Data Editor at the top of the window (see Figure 14-2).

Just under the title is the menu bar. Most of the things you want to do in SPSS start by selecting an option in one of the menus. Each window in SPSS has its own menu bar with menus appropriate for that window. Rather than provide an overview of all the various menu options, we'll discuss them as needed. The Data Editor is used to create new data files or to edit existing ones. The Data Editor actually consists of two windows called Data View and Variable View. The Data View window is shown here. You can move between the Data View and Variable View windows by clicking on the tabs in the lower left-hand corner of the Data Editor. Click on the Variable View tab to see the Variable View window as shown in Figure 14-3.

Both windows in the Data Editor display aspects of the contents of a data file. In Data View, the rows represent cases (e.g., the scores for each participant in a research study) and the columns represent variables (i.e., the things we want to measure); and in Variable View, the rows represent variables and the columns represent the attributes of each variable. In other words, Data View contains the data that will be analyzed and Variable View contains information about the variables themselves.

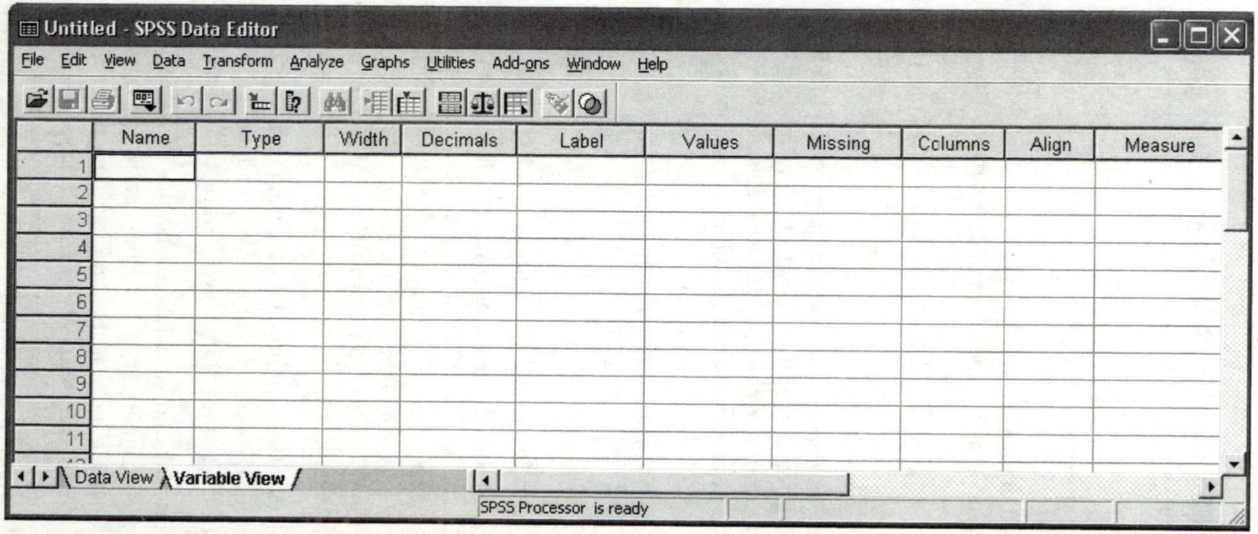

FIGURE 14-3 SPSS Data Editor (Variable View).

Reprint courtesy of International Business Machines Corporation, © SPSS, Inc., an IBM Company.

Now that you are familiar with the Data Editor, let's enter some data and run a simple analysis so that you have an overview of the main components of SPSS that we used throughout the book.

BASIC STEPS IN SPSS DATA ANALYSIS

Analyzing data in SPSS is very straightforward. Almost everything you need to do can be done in four basic steps:

1. ***Enter data.*** When you first open SPSS, the Data Editor is ready for data to be entered. You can get data into the Data Editor in several ways. You can enter it directly by typing it in or you can import data from another program (e.g., such as a spreadsheet). You can also open files that already have been entered into the Data Editor and saved in SPSS.
2. ***Select an analysis.*** After you have entered your data, you can select a procedure from one of the menus at the top of the Data Editor. We will be mainly using the Analyze and Graphs menus.
3. ***Select variables to analyze.*** After you select a procedure in SPSS, you are presented with a dialog box so that you can select the variables you want to analyze.
4. ***Run analysis and examine results.*** To run an analysis in SPSS, you simply point and click. After you have run an analysis, the Viewer window opens and displays the results.

That's it! Now let's walk through an example so this is clear.

Entering Data

Before you enter data into the Data Editor, you need to define the variables themselves. To do define variables, click the tab for Variable View at the bottom of the Data Editor window. In Data View, each row is a different variable. As an example, let's say you are interested in the relationship between reading comprehension and gender in school-aged children. For your study, you obtain the following information for a small group of children: age, gender, and score on a standardized test of reading comprehension. To define these variables in Variable View:

- In the first row of the Name column, type Age and press the Enter key.
- In the second row of the Name column, type Reading and press the Enter key.
- In the third row of the Name column, type Gender and press the Enter key.

You have just created and labeled your three variables. If you make a mistake, just backspace and retype the variable name. Variables can be given any name, provided that they have no more than eight characters. You may have noticed that each time you pressed the Enter key, SPSS automatically defined the variable type as Numeric. Numeric variables are variables with numbers only, such as age and reading test score. You can also enter non-numeric data, such as strings of text, into the Data Editor. Gender, in our example, is a non-numerical—or string—variable. To change the variable type for Gender, click on the cell for Gender in the third row of the Type column, as shown in Figure 14-4.

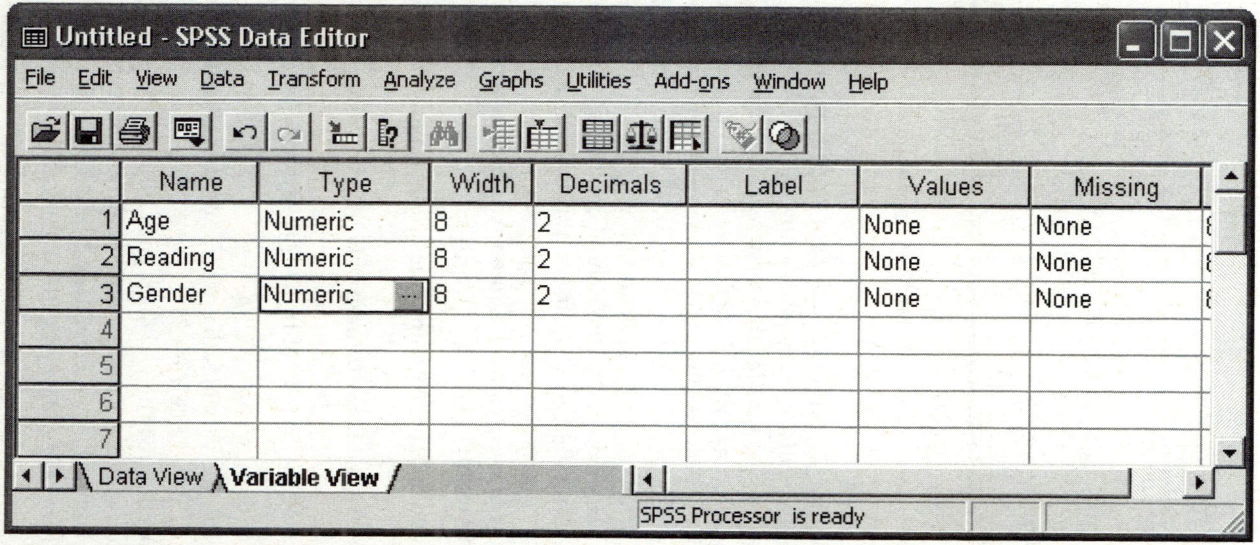

FIGURE 14-4 Defining variables in Variable View.

Reprint courtesy of International Business Machines Corporation, © SPSS, Inc., an IBM Company.

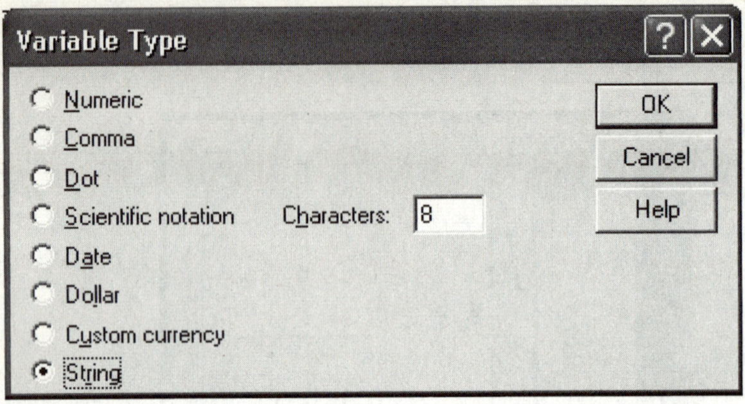

FIGURE 14-5 Variable Type dialog box.

Reprint courtesy of International Business Machines Corporation, © SPSS, Inc., an IBM Company.

After you click on the . . . button on the right side of the cell, you will be presented with the Variable Type dialog box shown in Figure 14-5.

To specify the appropriate type for this variable, select String and then click OK to save your changes and return to the Variable View window. If you want to change the number of decimals for your variable, click on the cell for the variable you want to change in the Decimals column and indicate the number of decimals desired by clicking on the up or down arrow, as shown in Figure 14-6.

For our example, let's work with whole numbers only, so select the number of decimals to be 0 for each variable. As you can see, this is the default setting for string variables.

You can also provide more information on variables in the Label column. To label the variables in our example:

- In the first row of the Label column, type Student Age in Years and press the Enter key.
- In the second row of the Label column, type Reading Test Score and press the Enter key.
- In the third row of the Label column, type Student Gender and press the Enter key.

Figure 14-7 displays the variables that we just defined. For now, let's not worry about the other columns in Variable View.

Now that we have defined the variables, click on the Data View tab to return to the Data View window to enter our example data. As you can see in Data View, the names of the variables that we created in the Variable View window appear in the first three columns. Let's begin entering data in the first row and the first column.

- In the Age column, type 6 and press the Tab key.
- In the Reading column, type 100 and press the Tab key.
- In the Gender column, type Male and press the Tab key.

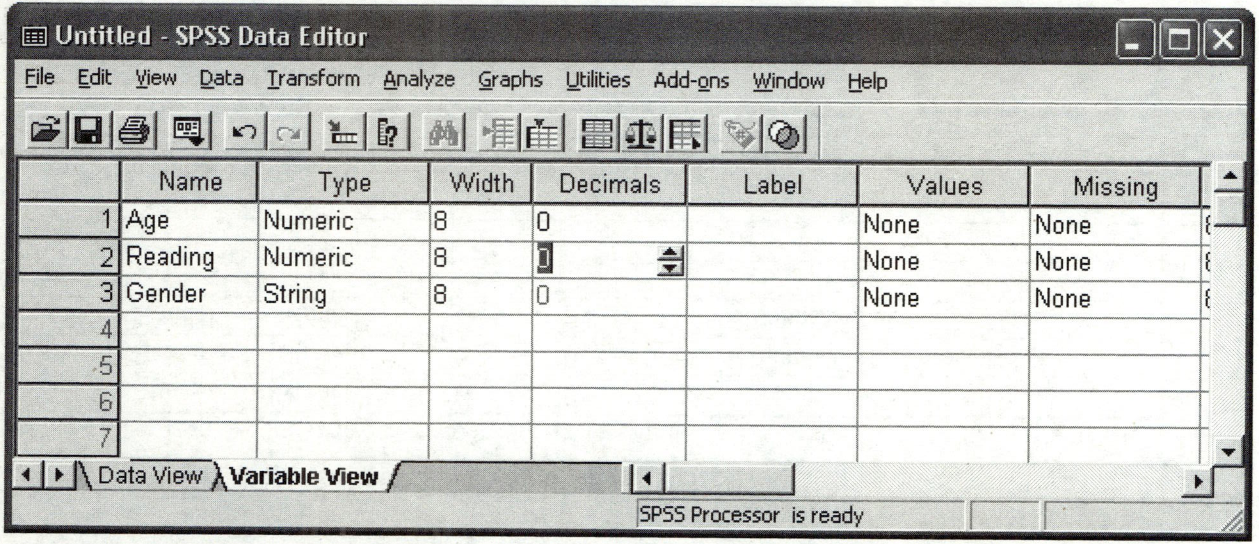

FIGURE 14-6 Selecting the number of decimals.

Reprint courtesy of International Business Machines Corporation, © SPSS, Inc., an IBM Company.

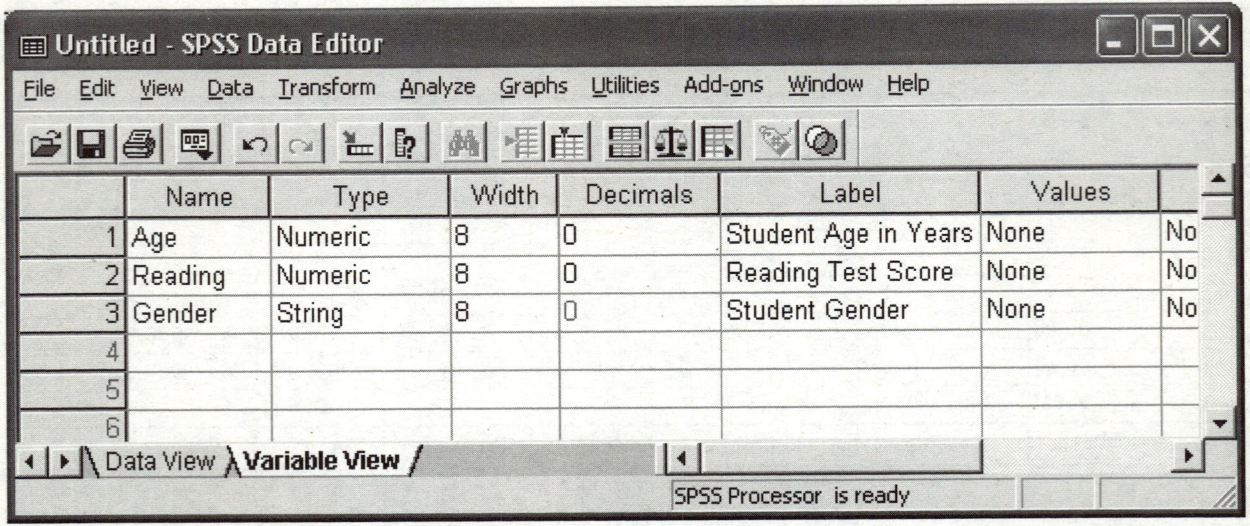

FIGURE 14-7 Variable View of example variables.

Reprint courtesy of International Business Machines Corporation, © SPSS, Inc., an IBM Company.

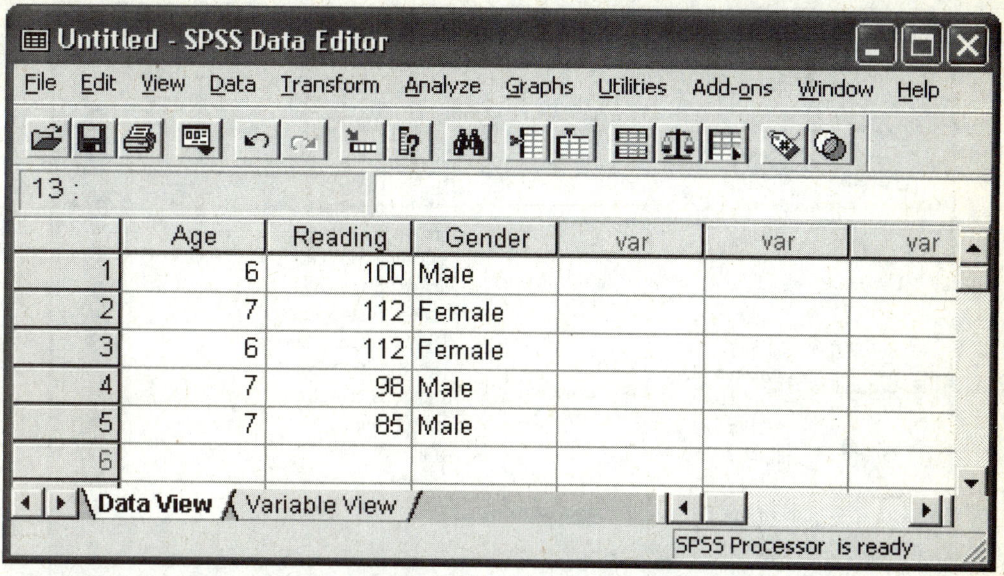

FIGURE 14-8 Example data in Data View.

We have now entered the data for one of the participants in the example study. According to our data, this is a 6-year-old boy who obtained a score of 100 on the reading test. Now enter the data for the other four cases to complete the set of data as shown in Figure 14-8.

Before we move on to the next step, let's save our data in SPSS. To save a file in SPSS, click on File in the menu bar at the top of the Data Editor and then on Save. When the dialog box appears, type in "Example Data" as show in Figure 14-9 and then click Save. This saves a copy of your dataset with the filename "Example Data."

Selecting an Analysis

After you have entered the example data and saved the data file, you are ready to select a procedure from the menus to conduct a statistical analysis or to create a chart. The Analyze menu in the Data Editor contains a list of all the analysis groups that can be conducted in SPSS, with several analyses within each grouping. Clicking on an item in a list will display the analyses that can be selected within each group.

For our example study, let's examine the frequency with which each score was obtained for each variable. To do this, move your mouse over the Descriptive Statistics item in the Analysis menu and click on Descriptive Frequencies. After you have done this, the Frequencies dialog box in Figure 14-10 will appear, displaying a list of the variables in our study.

Now you must select the variables you want to analyze. For our example, let's analyze all the variables. To do this, click on the first variable, Student Age in Years, then

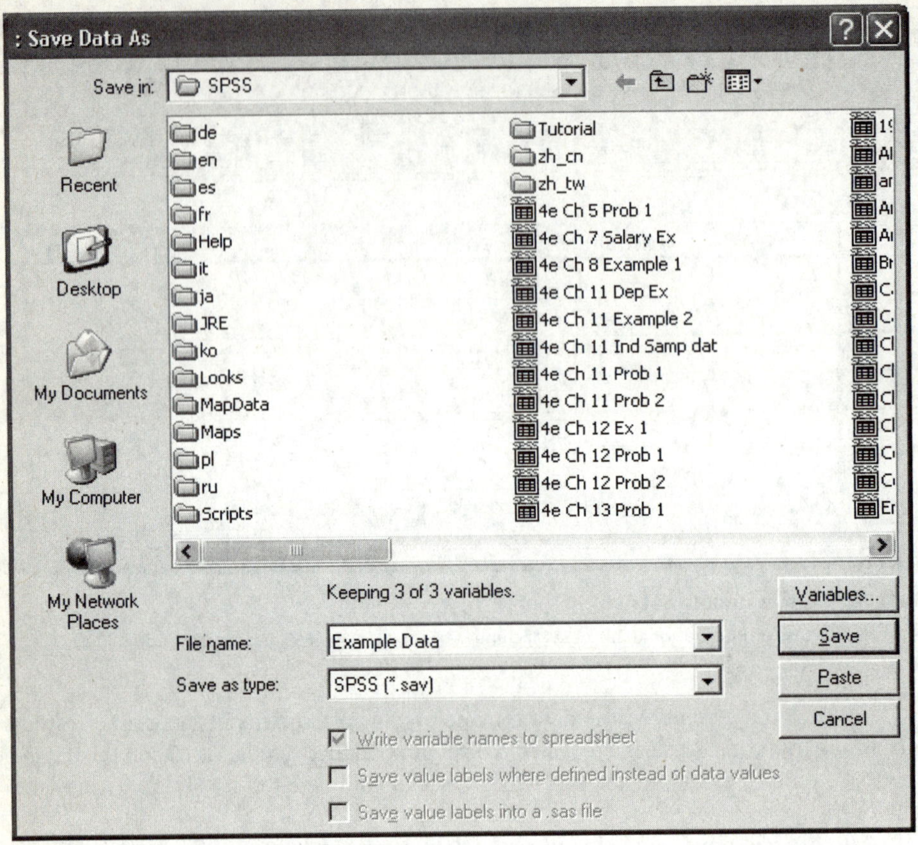

FIGURE 14-9 Save Data As dialog box.

Reprint courtesy of International Business Machines Corporation, © SPSS, Inc., an IBM Company.

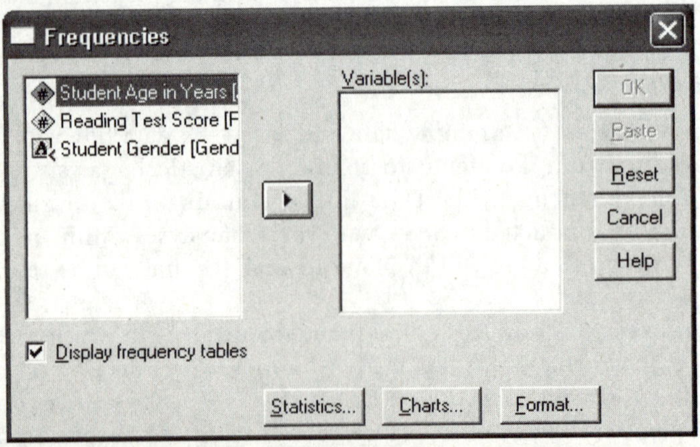

FIGURE 14-10 Frequencies dialog box.

Reprint courtesy of International Business Machines Corporation, © SPSS, Inc., an IBM Company.

click on the ▶ in the middle of the dialog box. As you can see, this moves the variable to the Variable(s) box. Now do the same thing for the other two variables.

Running an Analysis and Examining Results

After you have moved all the variables to the Variable(s) box, click OK in the dialog box to run the analysis. Results of statistical analyses and charts created in SPSS are displayed in the Viewer window. Results for our example are displayed in Figure 14-11.

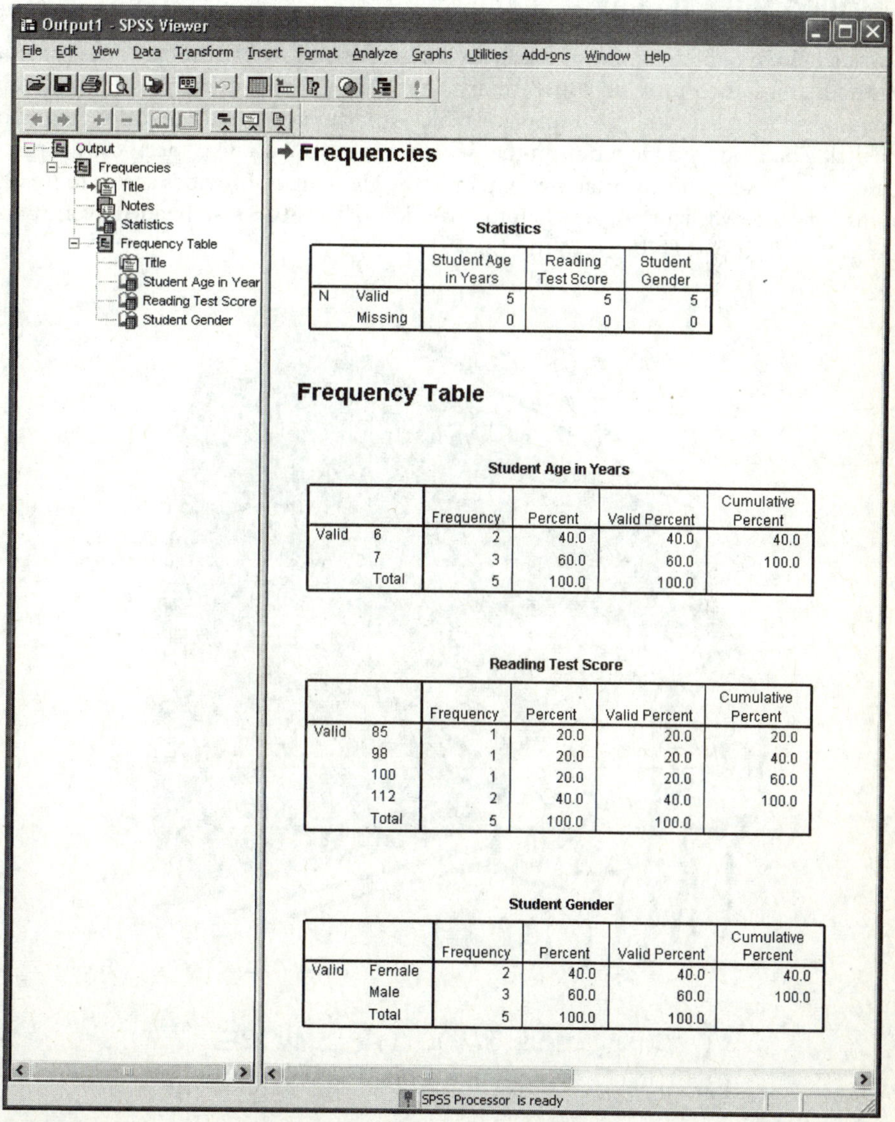

Frequencies

Statistics

		Student Age in Years	Reading Test Score	Student Gender
N	Valid	5	5	5
	Missing	0	0	0

Frequency Table

Student Age in Years

		Frequency	Percent	Valid Percent	Cumulative Percent
Valid	6	2	40.0	40.0	40.0
	7	3	60.0	60.0	100.0
	Total	5	100.0	100.0	

Reading Test Score

		Frequency	Percent	Valid Percent	Cumulative Percent
Valid	85	1	20.0	20.0	20.0
	98	1	20.0	20.0	40.0
	100	1	20.0	20.0	60.0
	112	2	40.0	40.0	100.0
	Total	5	100.0	100.0	

Student Gender

		Frequency	Percent	Valid Percent	Cumulative Percent
Valid	Female	2	40.0	40.0	40.0
	Male	3	60.0	60.0	100.0
	Total	5	100.0	100.0	

FIGURE 14-11 Viewer window displaying frequency results.

As you can see in this figure, the output for this analysis consists of the number and percentage of each score for each of our variables. You've now done your first statistical analysis in SPSS! Congratulations. To save the contents of the Viewer, click on File in the menu bar and then Save. You then provide a name for the output just like you did when saving the data file. The only difference between the two types of files is the output is saved with the .spo extension. To exit SPSS, click on File in the menu bar, then select Exit.

FINDING HELP IN SPSS

Getting help in SPSS is simple and easy to do. Every window in SPSS has a Help menu on the menu bar to provide you with assistance. The Topics menu item in the Help menu provides a list of all the topics for which you can get help. In addition, many of the dialog boxes have a Help button that will provide you with help specifically for that dialog box. Finally, the Tutorial menu item in the Help menu provides access to the introductory tutorial. This is a very helpful overview of the SPSS system and covers many things that we did not address in this book.

"I THINK YOU SHOULD BE MORE EXPLICIT HERE IN STEP TWO."

SidneyHarris/www.sciencecartoonsplus.com

CHAPTER 15 Postscript

Clem asks Abner, "Ain't statistics wonderful?" "How so?" says Abner. "Well, according to statistics, there's 42 million alligator eggs laid every year. Of those only about half get hatched. Of those that hatch, three-fourths of them get eaten by predators in the first thirty-six days. And of the rest, only 5 percent get to be a year old because of one thing or another. Ain't statistics wonderful?" Abner asks, "What's so wonderful about statistics?" "Why, if it wasn't for statistics, we'd be up to our asses in baby alligators!"

Well, you did it! You got all the way through this book! Whether you realize it or not, this means that you have covered a great deal of material, learned (probably) quite a bit more than you think you did, and are now able to do—or at least understand—most of the statistics that you will need for a large percentage of the research that you may become involved with. No small accomplishment!

In case you are inclined to discount what you've done, let's review it. This will not only give you further ammunition for self-congratulation, but it will also help to consolidate all the information you've been taking in.

Statistics, as a field of study, can be divided into two (not so equal) parts, descriptive and inferential. You've been introduced to both. First, the descriptive.

You've learned how to describe sets of data in terms of graphs (histograms, frequency polygons, cumulative frequency polygons), of central tendency (mean, median, mode), and of variability (range, variance, standard deviation). You've learned that a distribution—and even that word was probably somewhat unfamiliar when you began all this—can be symmetrical or skewed, and you've learned what happens to the measures of central tendency when you skew a distribution. You also learned a lot about the properties of the normal curve and how to find proportions of scores in different areas of it. And you've learned how to use and interpret *Z* scores, *T* scores, and percentiles, as well as other standard scores.

You've also learned a lot about how two distributions—two sets of data—can be related. You learned how to compute a correlation coefficient and what a correlation coefficient means. You learned what a scatterplot is and how the general shape of a scatterplot relates to the value of r_{xy}. And you also learned how to compute a correlation coefficient on data comprising ranks instead of measurements. You learned how to use a regression equation to predict a score on one variable, based on an individual's performance on a related variable, and to use something called the standard error of the estimate to tell you how much error to expect when making that prediction. That's a lot.

And then along came the inferential statistics: using a set of observable information to make inferences about larger groups that can't be observed. You started this section by absorbing a lot of general ideas and principles. You learned about probability and how it relates to sampling. You learned why it's important that a sample be unbiased and how to use random-sampling techniques to get an unbiased sample. You learned what a null hypothesis is, why we need to use a null hypothesis, and what kinds of error are associated with mistakenly rejecting or failing to reject the null hypothesis. You learned that it's a great big no-no to talk about "accepting" the null hypothesis, and why! You learned what it means for a result to be statistically significant, and you got acquainted with a friendly Greek named α, as well as something called "magnitude of effect."

Then you moved into actual inferential statistical tests themselves, starting with the *t* Test. Using the *t* Test, you now know how to decide whether two groups are significantly different from each other, and you know that correlated or matched groups have to be treated differently from independent groups.

As if looking at two groups weren't enough, you moved right in to explore comparisons among two or more groups. You learned about the workhorse of social science statistics, the analysis of variance (ANOVA). And you learned how to do a post hoc test, to look at the means of those two or more groups in even more detail.

You learned a fine, important-sounding new word: *nonparametric*. You learned that nonparametric tests let you examine frequencies and ranked data. You learned how to use and interpret the most widely used nonparametric statistic—called chi-squared. You now can work with data that don't fit the rules for the other techniques that you've learned.

Finally, you learned that most people use statistical software programs, such as SPSS, to conduct statistical analyses. You also learned that these programs are easy to learn and use.

You really have done a lot!

And we haven't even mentioned the single most important, and impressive, thing you've done. Imagine your reaction just a few months ago if someone had handed you the first paragraphs of this chapter and said, "Read this—this is what you will know at the end of this term." The very fact of your being able to think about statistics now without feeling frightened or overwhelmed or nauseous is much more significant than the facts and techniques that you've learned. Because your changed attitude means that you're able to actually use all this stuff, rather than just being intimidated by it. If you can't remember some statistical something now, you can go look it up, instead of giving up. If you can't find out where to look it up, you can ask somebody about it and have a reasonable expectation of understanding their answer.

Moreover, you're ready to move on to the next level: You've established for yourself a good, solid foundation that you can build on, just about as high as you want to go. There is more to statistics than we've been able to cover, of course. There are all the mathematical implications and "pre-plications" (well, what else do you call something that comes before and influences the thing you're interested in?) of the techniques you've learned. There are the fascinating nooks and crannies of those techniques—the sophisticated rules about when to use them, the exceptions to the rules, the suggestions for what to do instead. There are the extensions: applying the basic principles of correlation or regression or ANOVA to larger and more complex designs. And then there are the brand new techniques, things like analysis of covariance, factor analysis, and multiple regression, among many others, and lots and lots of clever nonparametric tricks. Why, you might even learn to enjoy this stuff!

But whether you learn to enjoy it or not, whether you go on to more advanced work or just stay with what you now know, whether you actively use your statistics or simply become an informed consumer—whatever you do with it, nobody can change or take away the fact that you did learn it, and you did survive. And it wasn't as bad as you thought it would be—truly now, was it?

APPENDIX A

Proportions of Area under the Standard Normal Curve

z	 0 z	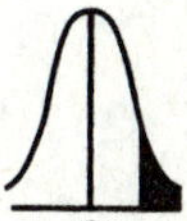 0 z	z	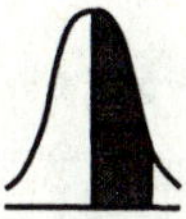 0 z	 0 z	z	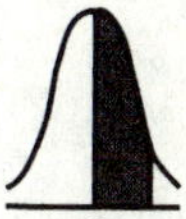 0 z	 0 z
0.00	.0000	.5000	0.17	.0675	.4325	0.34	.1331	.3669
0.01	.0040	.4960	0.18	.0714	.4286	0.35	.1368	.3632
0.02	.0080	.4920	0.19	.0753	.4247	0.36	.1406	.3594
0.03	.0120	.4880	0.20	.0793	.4207	0.37	.1443	.3557
0.04	.0160	.4840	0.21	.0832	.4168	0.38	.1480	.3520
0.05	.0199	.4801	0.22	.0871	.4129	0.39	.1517	.3483
0.06	.0239	.4761	0.23	.0910	.4090	0.40	.1554	.3446
0.07	.0279	.4721	0.24	.0948	.4052	0.41	.1591	.3409
0.08	.0319	.4681	0.25	.0987	.4013	0.42	.1628	.3372
0.09	.0359	.4641	0.26	.1026	.3974	0.43	.1664	.3336
0.10	.0398	.4602	0.27	.1064	.3936	0.44	.1700	.3300
0.11	.0438	.4562	0.28	.1103	.3897	0.45	.1736	.3264
0.12	.0478	.4522	0.29	.1141	.3859	0.46	.1772	.3228
0.13	.0517	.4483	0.30	.1179	.3821	0.47	.1808	.3192
0.14	.0557	.4443	0.31	.1217	.3783	0.48	.1844	.3156
0.15	.0596	.4404	0.32	.1255	.3745	0.49	.1879	.3121
0.16	.0636	.4364	0.33	.1293	.3707	0.50	.1915	.3085

Source: Runyon and Haber, *Fundamentals of Behavioral Statistics,* 2nd ed., 1971, Addison-Wesley, Reading, Mass.

APPENDIX A (continued)

z	 0 z	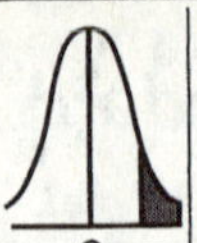 0 z	z	 0 z	 0 z	z	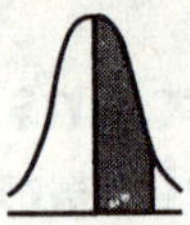 0 z	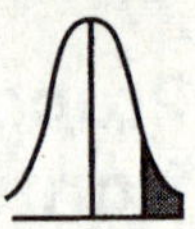 0 z
0.51	.1950	.3050	0.89	.3133	.1867	1.27	.3980	.1020
0.52	.1985	.3015	0.90	.3159	.1841	1.28	.3997	.1003
0.53	.2019	.2981	0.91	.3186	.1814	1.29	.4015	.0985
0.54	.2054	.2946	0.92	.3212	.1788	1.30	.4032	.0968
0.55	.2088	.2912	0.93	.3238	.1762	1.31	.4049	.0951
0.56	.2123	.2877	0.94	.3264	.1736	1.32	.4066	.0934
0.57	.2157	.2843	0.95	.3289	.1711	1.33	.4082	.0918
0.58	.2190	.2810	0.96	.3315	.1685	1.34	.4099	.0901
0.59	.2224	.2776	0.97	.3340	.1660	1.35	.4115	.0885
0.60	.2257	.2743	0.98	.3365	.1635	1.36	.4131	.0869
0.61	.2291	.2709	0.99	.3389	.1611	1.37	.4147	.0853
0.62	.2324	.2676	1.00	.3413	.1587	1.38	.4162	.0838
0.63	.2357	.2643	1.01	.3438	.1562	1.39	.4177	.0823
0.64	.2389	.2611	1.02	.3461	.1539	1.40	.4192	.0808
0.65	.2422	.2578	1.03	.3485	.1515	1.41	.4207	.0793
0.66	.2454	.2546	1.04	.3508	.1492	1.42	.4222	.0778
0.67	.2486	.2514	1.05	.3531	.1469	1.43	.4236	.0764
0.68	.2517	.2483	1.06	.3554	.1446	1.44	.4251	.0749
0.69	.2549	.2451	1.07	.3577	.1423	1.45	.4265	.0735
0.70	.2580	.2420	1.08	.3599	.1401	1.46	.4279	.0721
0.71	.2611	.2389	1.09	.3621	.1379	1.47	.4292	.0708
0.72	.2642	.2358	1.10	.3643	.1357	1.48	.4306	.0694
0.73	.2673	.2327	1.11	.3665	.1335	1.49	.4319	.0681
0.74	.2704	.2296	1.12	.3686	.1314	1.50	.4332	.0668
0.75	.2734	.2266	1.13	.3708	.1292	1.51	.4345	.0655
0.76	.2764	.2236	1.14	.3729	.1271	1.52	.4357	.0643
0.77	.2794	.2206	1.15	.3749	.1251	1.53	.4370	.0630
0.78	.2823	.2177	1.16	.3770	.1230	1.54	.4382	.0618
0.79	.2852	.2148	1.17	.3790	.1210	1.55	.4394	.0606
0.80	.2881	.2119	1.18	.3810	.1190	1.56	.4406	.0594
0.81	.2910	.2090	1.19	.3830	.1170	1.57	.4418	.0582
0.82	.2939	.2061	1.20	.3849	.1151	1.58	.4429	.0571
0.83	.2967	.2033	1.21	.3869	.1131	1.59	.4441	.0559
0.84	.2995	.2005	1.22	.3888	.1112	1.60	.4452	.0548
0.85	.3023	.1977	1.23	.3907	.1093	1.61	.4463	.0537
0.86	.3051	.1949	1.24	.3925	.1075	1.62	.4474	.0526
0.87	.3078	.1922	1.25	.3944	.1056	1.63	.4484	.0516
0.88	.3106	.1894	1.26	.3962	.1038	1.64	.4495	.0505

APPENDIX A (continued)

z	0 z	0 z	z	0 z	0 z	z	0 z	0 z
1.65	.4505	.0495	2.03	.4788	.0212	2.41	.4920	.0080
1.66	.4515	.0485	2.04	.4793	.0207	2.42	.4922	.0078
1.67	.4525	.0475	2.05	.4798	.0202	2.43	.4925	.0075
1.68	.4535	.0465	2.06	.4803	.0197	2.44	.4927	.0073
1.69	.4545	.0455	2.07	.4808	.0192	2.45	.4929	.0071
1.70	.4554	.0446	2.08	.4812	.0188	2.46	.4931	.0069
1.71	.4564	.0436	2.09	.4817	.0183	2.47	.4932	.0068
1.72	.4573	.0427	2.10	.4821	.0179	2.48	.4934	.0066
1.73	.4582	.0418	2.11	.4826	.0174	2.49	.4936	.0064
1.74	.4591	.0409	2.12	.4830	.0170	2.50	.4938	.0062
1.75	.4599	.0401	2.13	.4834	.0166	2.51	.4940	.0060
1.76	.4608	.0392	2.14	.4838	.0162	2.52	.4941	.0059
1.77	.4616	.0384	2.15	.4842	.0158	2.53	.4943	.0057
1.78	.4625	.0375	2.16	.4846	.0154	2.54	.4945	.0055
1.79	.4633	.0367	2.17	.4850	.0150	2.55	.4946	.0054
1.80	.4641	.0359	2.18	.4854	.0146	2.56	.4948	.0052
1.81	.4649	.0351	2.19	.4857	.0143	2.57	.4949	.0051
1.82	.4656	.0344	2.20	.4861	.0139	2.58	.4951	.0049
1.83	.4664	.0336	2.21	.4864	.0136	2.59	.4952	.0048
1.84	.4671	.0329	2.22	.4868	.0132	2.60	.4953	.0047
1.85	.4678	.0322	2.23	.4871	.0129	2.61	.4955	.0045
1.86	.4686	.0314	2.24	.4875	.0125	2.62	.4956	.0044
1.87	.4693	.0307	2.25	.4878	.0122	2.63	.4957	.0043
1.88	.4699	.0301	2.26	.4881	.0119	2.64	.4959	.0041
1.89	.4706	.0294	2.27	.4884	.0116	2.65	.4960	.0040
1.90	.4713	.0287	2.28	.4887	.0113	2.66	.4961	.0039
1.91	.4719	.0281	2.29	.4890	.0110	2.67	.4962	.0038
1.92	.4726	.0274	2.30	.4893	.0107	2.68	.4963	.0037
1.93	.4732	.0268	2.31	.4896	.0104	2.69	.4964	.0036
1.94	.4738	.0262	2.32	.4898	.0102	2.70	.4965	.0035
1.95	.4744	.0256	2.33	.4901	.0099	2.71	.4966	.0034
1.96	.4750	.0250	2.34	.4904	.0096	2.72	.4967	.0033
1.97	.4756	.0244	2.35	.4906	.0094	2.73	.4968	.0032
1.98	.4761	.0239	2.36	.4909	.0091	2.74	.4969	.0031
1.99	.4767	.0233	2.37	.4911	.0089	2.75	.4970	.0030
2.00	.4772	.0228	2.38	.4913	.0087	2.76	.4971	.0029
2.01	.4778	.0222	2.39	.4916	.0084	2.77	.4972	.0028
2.02	.4783	.0217	2.40	.4918	.0082	2.78	.4973	.0027

(*continued*)

APPENDIX A (continued)

z	 0 z	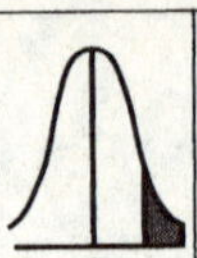 0 z	z	 0 z	 0 z	z	 0 z	 0 z
2.79	.4974	.0026	2.98	.4986	.0014	3.17	.4992	.0008
2.80	.4974	.0026	2.99	.4986	.0014	3.18	.4993	.0007
2.81	.4975	.0025	3.00	.4987	.0013	3.19	.4993	.0007
2.82	.4976	.0024	3.01	.4987	.0013	3.20	.4993	.0007
2.83	.4977	.0023	3.02	.4987	.0013	3.21	.4993	.0007
2.84	.4977	.0023	3.03	.4988	.0012	3.22	.4994	.0006
2.85	.4978	.0022	3.04	.4988	.0012	3.23	.4994	.0006
2.86	.4979	.0021	3.05	.4989	.0011	3.24	.4994	.0006
2.87	.4979	.0021	3.06	.4989	.0011	3.25	.4994	.0006
2.88	.4980	.0020	3.07	.4989	.0011	3.30	.4995	.0005
2.89	.4981	.0019	3.08	.4990	.0010	3.35	.4996	.0004
2.90	.4981	.0019	3.09	.4990	.0010	3.40	.4997	.0003
2.91	.4982	.0018	3.10	.4990	.0010	3.45	.4997	.0003
2.92	.4982	.0018	3.11	.4991	.0009	3.50	.4998	.0002
2.93	.4983	.0017	3.12	.4991	.0009	3.60	.4998	.0002
2.94	.4984	.0016	3.13	.4991	.0009	3.70	.4999	.0001
2.95	.4984	.0016	3.14	.4992	.0008	3.80	.4999	.0001
2.96	.4985	.0015	3.15	.4992	.0008	3.90	.49995	.00005
2.97	.4985	.0015	3.16	.4992	.0008	4.00	.49997	.00003

APPENDIX B

Table of Random Numbers

USING THE RANDOM-NUMBER TABLE TO DRAW A SAMPLE

Step 1. Define your population—for example, all the fifth-grade students in the six elementary schools in Kokomo, Indiana.

Step 2. List all the members of the population. In our example, you would have to go to the individual schools or to the Board of Education and get this information. (This is the hardest step.)

Step 3. Assign a number to each member of the population: 1, 2, 3, 4, 5, and on out through the last student on your list.

Step 4. Decide on the size of your sample. This will depend on all sorts of things: the kind of experiment you plan to do, the consequences of drawing a wrong conclusion (the likelihood of error goes down as the sample size goes up), the amount of money available. Let's say you decide to draw a sample of 50.

Step 5. The numbers in the random-number table are grouped into five-digit sets. These groupings are merely for your convenience, to help you keep your place. Select a column of as many adjacent numbers as the number of digits in your sample size. Since your sample has 50, you'll need to use two-digit columns. For a sample of 200, you would use sets of three adjacent columns. Your columns of digits can come from any grouping, from anywhere in that grouping, or can even span across groupings if you wish. Decide where you want to enter your set of columns by closing your eyes and putting your finger on the column.

Step 6. The first number you find, if it is 50 or less, is the number of the first child in your sample. Find the child with that number, and record his or her name. The next number identifies the next child. Keep on identifying sample members this way until you have 50 of them, discarding any numbers that are repeated or that are above 50.

RANDOMLY ASSIGNING SUBJECTS TO TREATMENT GROUPS

Suppose that you have 30 subjects and that you want to assign 10 subjects to each of three treatment groups:

Step 1. In the table of random numbers, make a blind selection of a two-digit column (because your total N, 30, has two digits).

Step 2. List the first 30 numbers from that column on a piece of paper (or on your word processor).

Step 3. Write or type the names of your 30 subjects in a second list, pairing each name with one of the numbers from Step 2.

Step 4. Rearrange the names on the list so that they are in numerical order according to the numbers assigned to them.

Step 5. Put the first 10 names into treatment Group 1, the next 10 into Group 2, and the last 10 into Group 3.

APPENDIX B (continued)

00	54463	22662	65905	70639	79365	67382	29085	69831	47058	08186
01	15389	85205	18850	39226	42249	90669	96325	23248	60933	26927
02	85941	40756	82414	02015	13858	78030	16269	65978	01385	15345
03	61149	69440	11286	88218	58925	03638	52862	62733	33451	77455
04	05219	81619	10651	67079	92511	59888	84502	72095	83463	75577
05	41417	98326	87719	92294	46614	50948	64886	20002	97365	30976
06	28357	94070	20652	35774	16249	75019	21145	05217	47286	76305
07	17783	00015	10806	83091	91530	36466	39981	62481	49177	75779
08	40950	84820	29881	85966	62800	70326	84740	62660	77379	90279
09	82995	64157	66164	41180	10089	41757	78258	96488	88629	37231
10	96754	17676	55659	44105	47361	34833	86679	23930	53249	27083
11	34357	88040	53364	71726	45690	66334	60332	22554	90600	71113
12	06318	37403	49927	57715	50423	67372	63116	48888	21505	80182
13	62111	52820	07243	79931	89292	84767	85693	73947	22278	11551
14	47534	09243	67879	00544	23410	12740	02540	54440	32949	13491
15	98614	75993	84460	62846	59844	14922	48730	73443	48167	34770
16	24856	03648	44898	09351	98795	18644	39765	71058	90368	44104
17	96887	12479	80621	66223	86085	78285	02432	53342	42846	94771
18	90801	21472	42815	77408	37390	76766	52615	32141	30268	18106
19	55165	77312	83666	36028	28420	70219	81369	41943	47366	41067
20	75884	12952	84318	95108	72305	64620	91318	89872	45375	85436
21	16777	37116	58550	42958	21460	43910	01175	87894	81378	10620
22	46230	43877	80207	88877	89380	32992	91380	03164	98656	59337
23	42902	66892	46134	01432	94710	23474	20423	60137	60609	13119
24	81007	00333	39693	28039	10154	95425	39220	19774	31782	49037
25	68089	01122	51111	72373	06902	74373	96199	97017	41273	21546
26	20411	67081	89950	16944	93054	87687	96693	87236	77054	33848
27	58212	13160	06468	15718	82627	76999	05999	58680	96739	63700
28	70577	42866	24969	61210	76046	67699	42054	12696	93758	03283
29	94522	74358	71659	62038	79643	79169	44741	05437	39038	13163
30	42626	86819	85651	88678	17401	03252	99547	32404	17918	62880
31	16051	33763	57194	16752	54450	19031	58580	47629	54132	60631
32	08244	27647	33851	44705	94211	46716	11738	55784	95374	72655
33	59497	04392	09419	89964	51211	04894	72882	17805	21896	83864
34	97155	13428	40293	09985	58434	01412	69124	82171	59058	82859
35	98409	66162	95763	47420	20792	61527	20441	39435	11859	41567
36	45476	84882	65109	96597	25930	66790	65706	61203	53634	22557
37	89300	69700	50741	30329	11658	23166	05400	66669	48708	03887
38	50051	95137	91631	66315	91428	12275	24816	68091	71710	33258
39	31753	85178	31310	89642	98364	02306	24617	09609	83942	22716
40	79152	53829	77250	20190	56535	18760	69942	77448	33278	48805
41	44560	38750	83635	56540	64900	42912	13953	79149	18710	68618
42	68328	83378	63369	71381	39564	05615	42451	64559	97501	65747
43	46939	38689	58625	08342	30459	85863	20781	09284	26333	91777
44	83544	86141	15707	96256	23068	13782	08467	89469	93842	55349
45	91621	00881	04900	54224	46177	55309	17852	27491	89415	23466
46	91896	67126	04151	03795	59077	11848	12630	98375	52068	60142
47	55751	62515	21108	80830	02263	29303	37204	96926	30506	09808
48	85156	87689	95493	88842	00664	55017	55539	17771	69448	87530
49	07521	56898	12236	60277	39102	62315	12239	07105	11844	01117

Source: Adapted from *Statistical Methods,* 6th ed., by G. W. Snedecor and W. G. Cochran.

APPENDIX B (continued)

00	59391	58030	52098	82718	87024	82848	04190	96574	90464	29065
01	99567	76364	77204	04615	27062	96621	43918	01896	83991	51141
02	10363	97518	51400	25670	98342	61891	27101	37855	06235	33316
03	86859	19558	64432	16706	99612	59798	32803	67708	15297	28612
04	11258	24591	36863	55368	31721	94335	34936	02566	80972	08188
05	95068	88628	35911	14530	33020	80428	39936	31855	34334	64865
06	54463	47237	73800	91017	36239	71824	83671	39892	60518	37092
07	16874	62677	57412	13215	31389	62233	80827	73917	82802	84420
08	92494	63157	76593	91316	03505	72389	96363	52887	01087	66091
09	15669	56689	35682	40844	53256	81872	35213	09840	34471	74441
10	99116	75486	84989	23476	52967	67104	39495	39100	17217	74073
11	15696	10703	65178	90637	63110	17622	53988	71087	84148	11670
12	97720	15369	51269	69620	03388	13699	33423	67453	43269	56720
13	11666	13841	71681	98000	35979	39719	81899	07449	47985	46967
14	71628	73130	78783	75691	41632	09847	61547	18707	85489	69944
15	40501	51089	99943	91843	41995	88931	73631	69361	05375	15417
16	22518	55576	98215	82068	10798	86211	36584	67466	69373	40054
17	75112	30485	62173	02132	14878	92879	22281	16783	86352	00077
18	80327	02671	98191	84342	90813	49268	95441	15496	20168	09271
19	60251	45548	02146	05597	48228	81366	34598	72856	66762	17002
20	57430	82270	10421	05540	43648	75888	66049	21511	47676	33444
21	73528	39559	34434	88596	54086	71693	43132	14414	79949	85193
22	25991	65959	70769	64721	86413	33475	42740	06175	82758	66248
23	78388	16638	09134	59880	63806	48472	39318	35434	24057	74739
24	12477	09965	96657	57994	59439	76330	24596	77515	09577	91871
25	83266	32883	42451	15579	38155	29793	40914	65990	16255	17777
26	76970	80876	10237	39515	79152	74798	39357	09054	73579	92359
27	37074	65198	44785	68624	98336	84481	97610	78735	46703	98265
28	83712	06514	30101	78295	54656	85417	43189	60048	72781	72606
29	20287	56862	69727	94443	64936	08366	27227	05158	50326	59566
30	74261	32592	86538	27041	65172	85532	07571	80609	39285	65340
31	64081	49863	08478	96001	18888	14810	70545	89755	59064	07210
32	05617	75818	47750	67814	29575	10526	66192	44464	27058	40467
33	26793	74951	95466	74307	13330	42664	85515	20632	05497	33625
34	65988	72850	48737	54719	52056	01596	03845	35067	03134	70322
35	27366	42271	44300	73399	21105	03280	73457	43093	05192	48657
36	56760	10909	98147	34736	33863	95256	12731	66598	50771	83665
37	72880	43338	93643	58904	59543	23943	11231	83268	65938	81581
38	77888	38100	03062	58103	47961	83841	25878	23746	55903	44115
39	28440	07819	21580	51459	47971	29882	13990	29226	23608	15873
40	63525	94441	77033	12147	51054	49955	58312	76923	96071	05813
41	47606	93410	16359	89033	89696	47231	64498	31776	05383	39902
42	52669	45030	96279	14709	52372	87832	02735	50803	72744	88208
43	16738	60159	07425	62369	07515	82721	37875	71153	21315	00132
44	59348	11695	45751	15865	74739	05572	32688	20271	65128	14551
45	12900	71775	29845	60774	94924	21810	38636	33717	67598	82521
46	75086	23537	49939	33595	13484	97588	28617	17979	70749	35234
47	99495	51434	29181	09993	38190	42553	68922	52125	91077	40197
48	26075	31671	45386	36583	93459	48599	52022	41330	60651	91321
49	13636	93596	23377	51133	95126	61496	42474	45141	46660	42338

(*continued*)

APPENDIX B (continued)

50	64249	63664	39652	40646	97306	31741	07294	84149	46797	82487
51	26538	44249	04050	48174	65570	44072	40192	51153	11397	58212
52	05845	00512	78630	55328	18116	69296	91705	86224	29503	57071
53	74897	68373	67359	51014	33510	83048	17056	72506	82949	54600
54	20872	54570	35017	88132	25730	22626	86723	91691	13191	77212
55	31432	96156	89177	75541	81355	24480	77243	76690	42507	84362
56	66890	61505	01240	00660	05873	13568	76082	79172	57913	93448
57	48194	57790	79970	33106	86904	48119	52503	24130	72824	21627
58	11303	87118	81471	52936	08555	28420	49416	44448	04269	27029
59	54374	57325	16947	45356	78371	10563	97191	53798	12693	27928
60	64852	34421	61046	90849	13966	39810	42699	21753	76192	10508
61	16309	20384	09491	91588	97720	89846	30376	76970	23063	35894
62	42587	37065	24526	72602	57589	98131	37292	05967	26002	51945
63	40177	98590	97161	41682	84533	67588	62036	49967	01990	72308
64	82309	76128	93965	26743	24141	04838	40254	26065	07938	76236
65	79788	68243	59732	04257	27084	14743	17520	95401	55811	76099
66	40538	79000	89559	25026	42274	23489	34502	75508	06059	86682
67	64016	73598	18609	73150	62463	33102	45205	87440	96767	67042
68	49767	12691	17903	93871	99721	79109	09425	26904	07419	76013
69	76974	55108	29795	08404	82684	00497	51126	79935	57450	55671
70	23854	08480	85983	96025	50117	64610	99425	62291	86943	21541
71	68973	70551	25098	78033	98573	79848	31778	29555	61446	23037
72	36444	93600	65350	14971	25325	00427	52073	64280	18847	24768
73	03003	87800	07391	11594	21196	00781	32550	57158	58887	73041
74	17540	26188	36647	78386	04558	61463	57842	90382	77019	24210
75	38916	55809	47982	41968	69760	79422	80154	91486	19180	15100
76	64288	19843	69122	42502	48508	28820	59933	72998	99942	10515
77	86809	51564	38040	39418	49915	19000	58050	16899	79952	57849
78	99800	99566	14742	05028	30033	94889	53381	23656	75787	59223
79	92345	31890	95712	08279	91794	94068	49337	88674	35355	12267
80	90363	65162	32245	82279	79256	80834	06088	99462	56705	06118
81	64437	32242	48431	04835	39070	59702	31508	60935	22390	52246
82	91714	53662	28373	34333	55791	74758	51144	18827	10704	76803
83	20902	17646	31391	31459	33315	03444	55743	74701	58851	27427
84	12217	86007	70371	52281	14510	76094	96579	54853	78339	20839
85	45177	02863	42307	53571	22532	74921	17735	42201	80540	54721
86	28325	90814	08804	52746	47913	54577	47525	77705	95330	21866
87	29019	28776	56116	54791	64604	08815	46049	71186	34650	14994
88	84979	81353	56219	67062	26146	82567	33122	14124	46240	92973
89	50371	26347	48513	63915	11158	25563	91915	18431	92978	11591
90	53422	06825	69711	67950	64716	18003	49581	45378	99878	61130
91	67453	35651	89316	41620	32048	70225	47597	33137	31443	51445
92	07294	85353	74819	23445	68237	07202	99515	62282	53809	26685
93	79544	00302	45338	16015	66613	88968	14595	63836	77716	79596
94	64144	85442	82060	46471	24162	39500	87351	36637	42833	71875
95	90919	11883	58318	00042	52402	28210	34075	33272	00840	73268
96	06670	57353	86275	92276	77591	46924	60839	55437	03183	13191
97	36634	93976	52062	83678	41256	60948	18685	48992	19462	96062
98	75101	72891	85745	67106	26010	62107	60885	37503	55461	71213
99	05112	71222	72654	51583	05228	62056	57390	42746	39272	96659

APPENDIX B (continued)

50	32847	31282	03345	89593	69214	70381	78285	20054	91018	16742
51	16916	00041	30236	55023	14253	76582	12092	86533	92426	37655
52	66176	34047	21005	27137	03191	48970	64625	22394	39622	79085
53	46299	13335	12180	16861	38043	59292	62675	63631	37020	78195
54	22847	47839	45385	23289	47526	54098	45683	55849	51575	64689
55	41851	54160	92320	69936	34803	92479	33399	71160	64777	83378
56	28444	59497	91586	95917	68553	28639	06455	34174	11130	91994
57	47520	62378	98855	83174	13088	16561	68559	26679	06238	51254
58	34978	63271	13142	82681	05271	08822	06490	44984	49307	62717
59	37404	80416	69035	92980	49486	74378	75610	74976	70056	15478
60	32400	65482	52099	53676	74648	94148	65095	69597	52771	71551
61	89262	86332	51718	70663	11623	29834	79820	73002	84886	03591
62	86866	09127	98021	03871	27789	58444	44832	36505	40672	30180
63	90814	14833	08759	74645	05046	94056	99094	65091	32663	73040
64	19192	82756	20553	58446	55376	88914	75096	26119	83898	43816
65	77585	52593	56612	95766	10019	29531	73064	20953	53523	58136
66	23757	16364	05096	03192	62386	45389	85332	18877	55710	96459
67	45989	96257	23850	26216	23309	21526	07425	50254	19455	29315
68	92970	94243	07316	41467	64837	52406	25225	51553	31220	14032
69	74346	59596	40088	98176	17896	86900	20249	77753	19099	48885
70	87646	41309	27636	45153	29988	94770	07255	70908	05340	99751
71	50099	71038	45146	06146	55211	99429	43169	66259	97786	59180
72	10127	46900	64984	75348	04115	33624	68774	60013	35515	62556
73	67995	81977	18984	64091	02785	27762	42529	97144	80407	64524
74	26304	80217	84934	82657	69291	35397	98714	35104	08187	48109
75	81994	41070	56642	64091	31229	02595	13513	45148	78722	30144
76	59537	34662	79631	89403	65212	09975	06118	86197	58208	16162
77	51228	10937	62396	81460	47331	91403	95007	06047	16846	64809
78	31089	37995	29577	07828	42272	54016	21950	86192	99046	84864
79	38207	97938	93459	75174	79460	55436	57206	87644	21296	43395
80	88666	31142	09474	89712	63153	62333	42212	06140	42594	43671
81	53365	56134	67582	92557	89520	33452	05134	70628	27612	33738
82	89807	74530	38004	90102	11693	90257	05500	79920	62700	43325
83	18682	81038	85662	90915	91631	22223	91588	80774	07716	12548
84	63571	32579	63942	25371	09234	94592	98475	76884	37635	33608
85	68927	56492	67799	95398	77642	54913	91853	08424	81450	76229
86	56401	63186	39389	88798	31356	89235	97036	32341	33292	73757
87	24333	95603	02359	72942	46287	95382	08452	62862	97869	71775
88	17025	84202	95199	62272	06366	16175	97577	99304	41587	03686
89	02804	08253	52133	20224	68034	50865	57868	22343	55111	03607
90	08298	03879	20995	19850	73090	13191	18963	82244	78479	99121
91	59883	01785	82403	96062	03785	03488	12970	64896	38336	30030
92	46982	06682	62864	91837	74021	89094	39952	64158	79614	78235
93	31121	47266	07661	02051	67599	24471	69843	83696	71402	76287
94	97867	56641	63416	17577	30161	87320	37752	73276	48969	41915
95	57364	86746	08415	14621	49430	22311	15836	72492	49372	44103
96	09559	26263	69511	28064	75999	44540	13337	10918	79846	54809
97	53873	55571	00608	42661	91332	63956	74087	59008	47493	99581
98	35531	19162	86406	05299	77511	24311	57257	22826	77555	05941
99	28229	88629	25695	94932	30721	16197	78742	34974	97528	45447

APPENDIX C

Critical Values of *t*

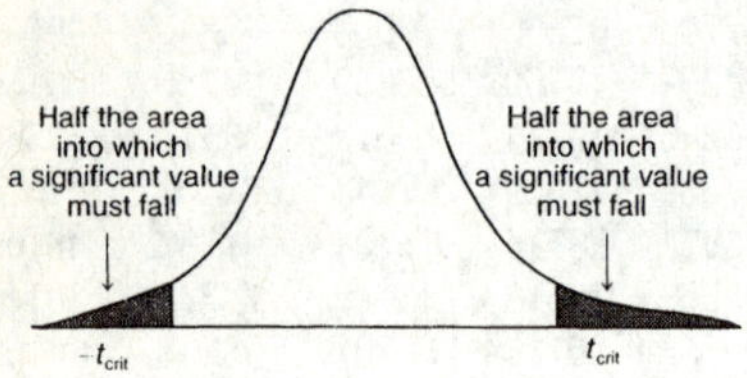

Two-Tailed or Nondirectional Test

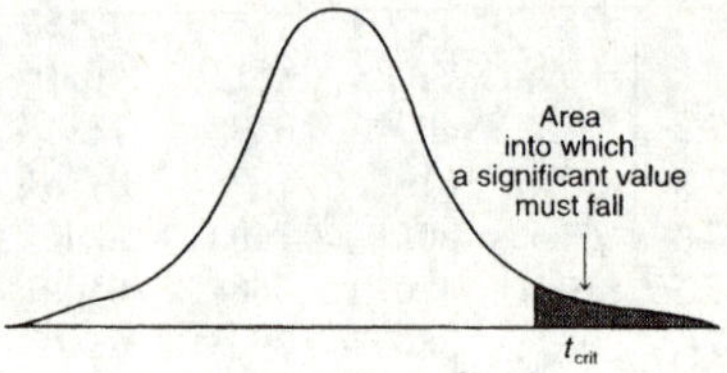

One-Tailed or Directional Test

Level of Significance (Two-Tailed)				Level of Significance (One-Tailed)			
df	**.05***	**.01****	**.001*****	**df**	**.05***	**.01****	**.001*****
1	12.706	63.657	636.62	1	6.314	31.821	318.31
2	4.606	9.925	31.598	2	2.920	6.955	22.326
3	3.182	5.841	12.924	3	2.353	4.541	10.213
4	2.776	4.604	8.610	4	2.132	3.747	7.173
5	2.571	4.032	6.869	5	2.015	3.365	5.893
6	2.447	3.707	5.959	6	1.943	3.143	5.208
7	2.365	3.499	5.408	7	1.895	2.998	4.785
8	2.306	3.355	5.041	8	1.860	2.896	4.501
9	2.262	3.250	4.781	9	1.833	2.821	4.297
10	2.228	3.169	4.587	10	1.812	2.764	4.144
11	2.201	3.106	4.437	11	1.796	2.718	4.025
12	2.179	3.055	4.318	12	1.782	2.681	3.930
13	2.160	3.012	4.221	13	1.771	2.650	3.852
14	2.145	2.977	4.140	14	1.761	2.624	3.787
15	2.131	2.947	4.073	15	1.753	2.602	3.733
16	2.120	2.921	4.015	16	1.746	2.583	3.686
17	2.110	2.898	3.965	17	1.740	2.567	3.646

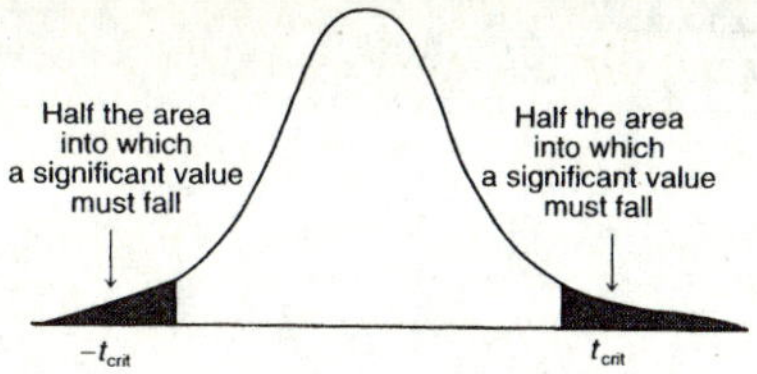

Two-Tailed or Nondirectional Test

	Level of Significance		
df	**.05***	**.01****	**.001*****
18	2.101	2.878	3.922
19	2.093	2.861	3.883
20	2.086	2.845	3.850
21	2.080	2.831	3.819
22	2.074	2.819	3.792
23	2.069	2.807	3.767
24	2.064	2.797	3.745
25	2.060	2.787	3.725
26	2.056	2.779	3.707
27	2.052	2.771	3.690
28	2.048	2.763	3.674
29	2.045	2.756	3.659
30	2.042	2.750	3.646
40	2.021	2.704	3.551
60	2.000	2.660	3.460
120	1.980	2.617	3.373
∞	1.960	2.576	3.291

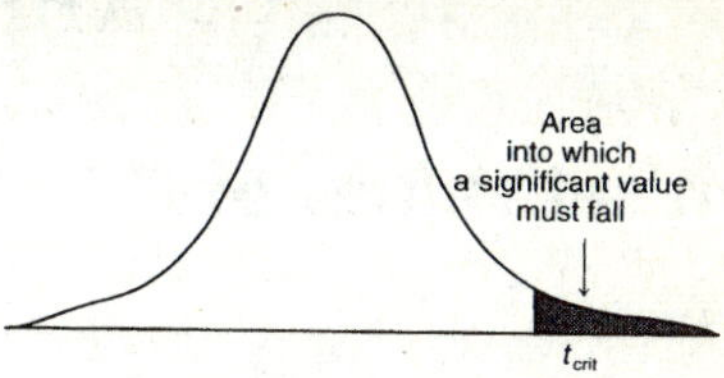

One-Tailed or Directional Test

	Level of Significance		
df	**.05***	**.01****	**.001*****
18	1.734	2.552	3.610
19	1.729	2.539	3.579
20	1.725	2.528	3.552
21	1.721	2.518	3.527
22	1.717	2.508	3.505
23	1.714	2.500	3.485
24	1.711	2.492	3.467
25	1.708	2.485	3.450
26	1.706	2.479	3.435
27	1.703	2.473	3.421
28	1.701	2.467	3.408
29	1.699	2.462	3.396
30	1.697	2.457	3.385
40	1.684	2.423	3.307
60	1.671	2.390	3.232
120	1.658	2.358	3.160
∞	1.645	2.326	3.090

USING THIS TABLE

For a two-tailed test of significance (i.e., when you have not predicted ahead of time which group will have higher scores or measurements than the other), use the values on the left side of the table. For a one-tailed test (when you know beforehand which group ought to score higher), use the values on the right side.

If the two groups are independent of each other, $df = N_1 + N_2 - 2$; if the two groups are not independent (correlated), $df = N - 1$, where N is the number of pairs of scores.

APPENDIX D

Critical Values of *F*

Within-group df	Between-group df 1	2	3	4	5	6	7	8	9	10	11	12	14	16	20	24	30	40	50	75	100	200	500	∞	
1	161 **4,052**	200 **4,999**	216 **5,403**	225 **5,625**	230 **5,764**	234 **5,859**	237 **5,928**	239 **5,981**	241 **6,022**	242 **6,056**	243 **6,082**	244 **6,106**	245 **6,142**	246 **6,169**	248 **6,208**	249 **6,234**	250 **6,258**	251 **6,286**	252 **6,302**	253 **6,323**	253 **6,334**	254 **6,352**	254 **6,361**	254 **6,366**	1
2	18.51 **98.49**	19.00 **99.00**	19.16 **99.17**	19.25 **99.25**	19.30 **99.30**	19.33 **99.33**	19.36 **99.34**	19.37 **99.36**	19.38 **99.38**	19.39 **99.40**	19.40 **99.41**	19.41 **99.42**	19.42 **99.43**	19.43 **99.44**	19.44 **99.45**	19.45 **99.46**	19.46 **99.47**	19.47 **99.48**	19.47 **99.48**	19.48 **99.49**	19.49 **99.49**	19.49 **99.49**	19.50 **99.50**	19.50 **99.50**	2
3	10.13 **34.12**	9.55 **30.82**	9.28 **29.46**	9.12 **28.71**	9.01 **28.24**	8.94 **27.91**	8.88 **27.67**	8.84 **27.49**	8.81 **27.34**	8.78 **27.23**	8.76 **27.13**	8.74 **27.05**	8.71 **26.92**	8.69 **26.83**	8.66 **26.69**	8.64 **26.60**	8.62 **26.50**	8.60 **26.41**	8.58 **26.35**	8.57 **26.27**	8.56 **26.23**	8.54 **26.18**	8.54 **26.14**	8.53 **26.12**	3
4	7.71 **21.20**	6.94 **18.00**	6.59 **16.69**	6.39 **15.98**	6.26 **15.52**	6.16 **15.21**	6.09 **14.98**	6.04 **14.80**	6.00 **14.66**	5.96 **14.54**	5.93 **14.45**	5.91 **14.37**	5.87 **14.24**	5.84 **14.15**	5.80 **14.02**	5.77 **13.93**	5.74 **13.83**	5.71 **13.74**	5.70 **13.69**	5.68 **13.61**	5.66 **13.57**	5.65 **13.52**	5.64 **13.48**	5.63 **13.46**	4
5	6.61 **16.26**	5.79 **13.27**	5.41 **12.06**	5.19 **11.39**	5.05 **10.97**	4.95 **10.67**	4.88 **10.45**	4.82 **10.27**	4.78 **10.15**	4.74 **10.05**	4.70 **9.96**	4.68 **9.89**	4.64 **9.77**	4.60 **9.68**	4.56 **9.55**	4.53 **9.47**	4.50 **9.38**	4.46 **9.29**	4.44 **9.24**	4.42 **9.17**	4.40 **9.13**	4.38 **9.07**	4.37 **9.04**	4.36 **9.02**	5
6	5.99 **13.74**	5.14 **10.92**	4.76 **9.78**	4.53 **9.15**	4.39 **8.75**	4.28 **8.47**	4.21 **8.26**	4.15 **8.10**	4.10 **7.98**	4.06 **7.87**	4.03 **7.79**	4.00 **7.72**	3.96 **7.60**	3.92 **7.52**	3.87 **7.39**	3.84 **7.31**	3.81 **7.23**	3.77 **7.14**	3.75 **7.09**	3.72 **7.02**	3.71 **6.99**	3.69 **6.94**	3.68 **6.90**	3.67 **6.88**	6
7	5.59 **12.25**	4.74 **9.55**	4.35 **8.45**	4.12 **7.85**	3.97 **7.46**	3.87 **7.19**	3.79 **7.00**	3.73 **6.84**	3.68 **6.71**	3.63 **6.62**	3.60 **6.54**	3.57 **6.47**	3.52 **6.35**	3.49 **6.27**	3.44 **6.15**	3.41 **6.07**	3.38 **5.98**	3.34 **5.90**	3.32 **5.85**	3.29 **5.78**	3.28 **5.75**	3.25 **5.70**	3.24 **5.67**	3.23 **5.65**	7
8	5.32 **11.26**	4.46 **8.65**	4.07 **7.59**	3.84 **7.01**	3.69 **6.63**	3.58 **6.37**	3.50 **6.19**	3.44 **6.03**	3.39 **5.91**	3.34 **5.82**	3.31 **5.74**	3.28 **5.67**	3.23 **5.56**	3.20 **5.48**	3.15 **5.36**	3.12 **5.28**	3.08 **5.20**	3.05 **5.11**	3.03 **5.06**	3.00 **5.00**	2.98 **4.96**	2.96 **4.91**	2.94 **4.88**	2.93 **4.86**	8
9	5.12 **10.56**	4.26 **8.02**	3.86 **6.99**	3.63 **6.42**	3.48 **6.06**	3.37 **5.80**	3.29 **5.62**	3.23 **5.47**	3.18 **5.35**	3.13 **5.26**	3.10 **5.18**	3.07 **5.11**	3.02 **5.00**	2.98 **4.92**	2.93 **4.80**	2.90 **4.73**	2.86 **4.64**	2.82 **4.56**	2.80 **4.51**	2.77 **4.45**	2.76 **4.41**	2.73 **4.36**	2.72 **4.33**	2.71 **4.31**	9
10	4.96 **10.04**	4.10 **7.56**	3.71 **6.55**	3.48 **5.99**	3.33 **5.64**	3.22 **5.39**	3.14 **5.21**	3.07 **5.06**	3.02 **4.95**	2.97 **4.85**	2.94 **4.78**	2.91 **4.71**	2.86 **4.60**	2.82 **4.52**	2.77 **4.41**	2.74 **4.33**	2.70 **4.25**	2.67 **4.17**	2.64 **4.12**	2.61 **4.05**	2.59 **4.01**	2.56 **3.96**	2.55 **3.93**	2.54 **3.91**	10
11	4.84 **9.65**	3.98 **7.20**	3.59 **6.22**	3.36 **5.67**	3.20 **5.32**	3.09 **5.07**	3.01 **4.88**	2.95 **4.74**	2.90 **4.63**	2.86 **4.54**	2.82 **4.46**	2.79 **4.40**	2.74 **4.29**	2.70 **4.21**	2.65 **4.10**	2.61 **4.02**	2.57 **3.94**	2.53 **3.86**	2.50 **3.80**	2.47 **3.74**	2.45 **3.70**	2.42 **3.66**	2.41 **3.62**	2.40 **3.60**	11
12	4.75 **9.33**	3.88 **6.93**	3.49 **5.95**	3.26 **5.41**	3.11 **5.06**	3.00 **4.82**	2.92 **4.65**	2.85 **4.50**	2.80 **4.39**	2.76 **4.30**	2.72 **4.22**	2.69 **4.16**	2.64 **4.05**	2.60 **3.98**	2.54 **3.86**	2.50 **3.78**	2.46 **3.70**	2.42 **3.61**	2.40 **3.56**	2.36 **3.49**	2.35 **3.46**	2.32 **3.41**	2.31 **3.38**	2.30 **3.36**	12
13	4.67 **9.07**	3.80 **6.70**	3.41 **5.74**	3.18 **5.20**	3.02 **4.86**	2.92 **4.62**	2.84 **4.44**	2.77 **4.30**	2.72 **4.19**	2.67 **4.10**	2.63 **4.02**	2.60 **3.96**	2.55 **3.85**	2.51 **3.78**	2.46 **3.67**	2.42 **3.59**	2.38 **3.51**	2.34 **3.42**	2.32 **3.37**	2.28 **3.30**	2.26 **3.27**	2.24 **3.21**	2.22 **3.18**	2.21 **3.16**	13
14	4.60 **8.86**	3.74 **6.51**	3.34 **5.56**	3.11 **5.03**	2.96 **4.69**	2.85 **4.46**	2.77 **4.28**	2.70 **4.14**	2.65 **4.03**	2.60 **3.94**	2.56 **3.86**	2.53 **3.80**	2.48 **3.70**	2.44 **3.62**	2.39 **3.51**	2.35 **3.43**	2.31 **3.34**	2.27 **3.26**	2.24 **3.21**	2.21 **3.14**	2.19 **3.11**	2.16 **3.06**	2.14 **3.02**	2.13 **3.00**	14
15	4.54 **8.68**	3.68 **6.36**	3.29 **5.42**	3.06 **4.89**	2.90 **4.56**	2.79 **4.32**	2.70 **4.14**	2.64 **4.00**	2.59 **3.89**	2.55 **3.80**	2.51 **3.73**	2.48 **3.67**	2.43 **3.56**	2.39 **3.48**	2.33 **3.36**	2.29 **3.29**	2.25 **3.20**	2.21 **3.12**	2.18 **3.07**	2.15 **3.00**	2.12 **2.97**	2.10 **2.92**	2.08 **2.89**	2.07 **2.87**	15
16	4.49 **8.53**	3.63 **6.23**	3.24 **5.29**	3.01 **4.77**	2.85 **4.44**	2.74 **4.20**	2.66 **4.03**	2.59 **3.89**	2.54 **3.78**	2.49 **3.69**	2.45 **3.61**	2.42 **3.55**	2.37 **3.45**	2.33 **3.37**	2.28 **3.25**	2.24 **3.18**	2.20 **3.10**	2.16 **3.01**	2.13 **2.96**	2.09 **2.89**	2.07 **2.86**	2.04 **2.80**	2.02 **2.77**	2.01 **2.75**	16

Source: Adapted from *Statistical Methods,* 6th ed., by G. W. Snedecor and W. G. Cochran. Copyright © 1967 by Iowa State University Press, Ames, Iowa. Reprinted by permission.

Within-group df	1	2	3	4	5	6	7	8	9	10	11	12	14	16	20	24	30	40	50	75	100	200	500	∞	
	Between-group df (Continued)																								
17	4.45 **8.40**	3.59 **6.11**	3.20 **5.18**	2.96 **4.67**	2.81 **4.34**	2.70 **4.10**	2.62 **3.93**	2.55 **3.79**	2.50 **3.68**	2.45 **3.59**	2.41 **3.52**	2.38 **3.45**	2.33 **3.35**	2.29 **3.27**	2.23 **3.16**	2.19 **3.08**	2.15 **3.00**	2.11 **2.92**	2.08 **2.86**	2.04 **2.79**	2.02 **2.76**	1.99 **2.70**	1.97 **2.67**	1.96 **2.65**	17
18	4.41 **8.28**	3.55 **6.01**	3.16 **5.09**	2.93 **4.58**	2.77 **4.25**	2.66 **4.01**	2.58 **3.85**	2.51 **3.71**	2.46 **3.60**	2.41 **3.51**	2.37 **3.44**	2.34 **3.37**	2.29 **3.27**	2.25 **3.19**	2.19 **3.07**	2.15 **3.00**	2.11 **2.91**	2.07 **2.83**	2.04 **2.78**	2.00 **2.71**	1.98 **2.68**	1.95 **2.62**	1.93 **2.59**	1.92 **2.57**	18
19	4.38 **8.18**	3.52 **5.93**	3.13 **5.01**	2.90 **4.50**	2.74 **4.17**	2.63 **3.94**	2.55 **3.77**	2.48 **3.63**	2.43 **3.52**	2.38 **3.43**	2.34 **3.36**	2.31 **3.30**	2.26 **3.19**	2.21 **3.12**	2.15 **3.00**	2.11 **2.92**	2.07 **2.84**	2.02 **2.76**	2.00 **2.70**	1.96 **2.63**	1.94 **2.60**	1.91 **2.54**	1.90 **2.51**	1.88 **2.49**	19
20	4.35 **8.10**	3.49 **5.85**	3.10 **4.94**	2.87 **4.43**	2.71 **4.10**	2.60 **3.87**	2.52 **3.71**	2.45 **3.56**	2.40 **3.45**	2.35 **3.37**	2.31 **3.30**	2.28 **3.23**	2.23 **3.13**	2.18 **3.05**	2.12 **2.94**	2.08 **2.86**	2.04 **2.77**	1.99 **2.69**	1.96 **2.63**	1.92 **2.56**	1.90 **2.53**	1.87 **2.47**	1.85 **2.44**	1.84 **2.42**	20
21	4.32 **8.02**	3.47 **5.78**	3.07 **4.87**	2.84 **4.37**	2.68 **4.04**	2.57 **3.81**	2.49 **3.65**	2.42 **3.51**	2.37 **3.40**	2.32 **3.31**	2.28 **3.24**	2.25 **3.17**	2.20 **3.07**	2.15 **2.99**	2.09 **2.88**	2.05 **2.80**	2.00 **2.72**	1.96 **2.63**	1.93 **2.58**	1.89 **2.51**	1.87 **2.47**	1.84 **2.42**	1.82 **2.38**	1.81 **2.36**	21
22	4.30 **7.94**	3.44 **5.72**	3.05 **4.82**	2.82 **4.31**	2.66 **3.99**	2.55 **3.76**	2.47 **3.59**	2.40 **3.45**	2.35 **3.35**	2.30 **3.26**	2.26 **3.18**	2.23 **3.12**	2.18 **3.02**	2.13 **2.94**	2.07 **2.83**	2.03 **2.75**	1.98 **2.67**	1.93 **2.58**	1.91 **2.53**	1.87 **2.46**	1.84 **2.42**	1.81 **2.37**	1.80 **2.33**	1.78 **2.31**	22
23	4.28 **7.88**	3.42 **5.66**	3.03 **4.76**	2.80 **4.26**	2.64 **3.94**	2.53 **3.71**	2.45 **3.54**	2.38 **3.41**	2.32 **3.30**	2.28 **3.21**	2.24 **3.14**	2.20 **3.07**	2.14 **2.97**	2.10 **2.89**	2.04 **2.78**	2.00 **2.70**	1.96 **2.62**	1.91 **2.53**	1.88 **2.48**	1.84 **2.41**	1.82 **2.37**	1.79 **2.32**	1.77 **2.28**	1.76 **2.26**	23
24	4.26 **7.82**	3.40 **5.61**	3.01 **4.72**	2.78 **4.22**	2.62 **3.90**	2.51 **3.67**	2.43 **3.50**	2.36 **3.36**	2.30 **3.25**	2.26 **3.17**	2.22 **3.09**	2.18 **3.03**	2.13 **2.93**	2.09 **2.85**	2.02 **2.74**	1.98 **2.66**	1.94 **2.58**	1.89 **2.49**	1.86 **2.44**	1.82 **2.36**	1.80 **2.33**	1.76 **2.27**	1.74 **2.23**	1.73 **2.21**	24
25	4.24 **7.77**	3.38 **5.57**	2.99 **4.68**	2.76 **4.18**	2.60 **3.86**	2.49 **3.63**	2.41 **3.46**	2.34 **3.32**	2.28 **3.21**	2.24 **3.13**	2.20 **3.05**	2.16 **2.99**	2.11 **2.89**	2.06 **2.81**	2.00 **2.70**	1.96 **2.62**	1.92 **2.54**	1.87 **2.45**	1.84 **2.40**	1.80 **2.32**	1.77 **2.29**	1.74 **2.23**	1.72 **2.19**	1.71 **2.17**	25
26	4.22 **7.72**	3.37 **5.53**	2.98 **4.64**	2.74 **4.14**	2.59 **3.82**	2.47 **3.59**	2.39 **3.42**	2.32 **3.29**	2.27 **3.17**	2.22 **3.09**	2.18 **3.02**	2.15 **2.96**	2.10 **2.86**	2.05 **2.77**	1.99 **2.66**	1.95 **2.58**	1.90 **2.50**	1.85 **2.41**	1.82 **2.36**	1.78 **2.28**	1.76 **2.25**	1.72 **2.19**	1.70 **2.15**	1.69 **2.13**	26
27	4.21 **7.68**	3.35 **5.49**	2.96 **4.60**	2.73 **4.11**	2.57 **3.79**	2.46 **3.56**	2.37 **3.39**	2.30 **3.26**	2.25 **3.14**	2.20 **3.06**	2.16 **2.98**	2.13 **2.93**	2.08 **2.83**	2.03 **2.74**	1.97 **2.63**	1.93 **2.55**	1.88 **2.47**	1.84 **2.38**	1.80 **2.33**	1.76 **2.25**	1.74 **2.21**	1.71 **2.16**	1.68 **2.12**	1.67 **2.10**	27
28	4.20 **7.64**	3.34 **5.45**	2.95 **4.57**	2.71 **4.07**	2.56 **3.76**	2.44 **3.53**	2.36 **3.36**	2.29 **3.23**	2.24 **3.11**	2.19 **3.03**	2.15 **2.95**	2.12 **2.90**	2.06 **2.80**	2.02 **2.71**	1.96 **2.60**	1.91 **2.52**	1.87 **2.44**	1.81 **2.35**	1.78 **2.30**	1.75 **2.22**	1.72 **2.18**	1.69 **2.13**	1.67 **2.09**	1.65 **2.06**	28
29	4.18 **7.60**	3.33 **5.42**	2.93 **4.54**	2.70 **4.04**	2.54 **3.73**	2.43 **3.50**	2.35 **3.33**	2.28 **3.20**	2.22 **3.08**	2.18 **3.00**	2.14 **2.92**	2.10 **2.87**	2.05 **2.77**	2.00 **2.68**	1.94 **2.57**	1.90 **2.49**	1.85 **2.41**	1.80 **2.32**	1.77 **2.27**	1.73 **2.19**	1.71 **2.15**	1.68 **2.10**	1.65 **2.06**	1.64 **2.03**	29
30	4.17 **7.56**	3.32 **5.39**	2.92 **4.51**	2.69 **4.02**	2.53 **3.70**	2.42 **3.47**	2.34 **3.30**	2.27 **3.17**	2.21 **3.06**	2.16 **2.98**	2.12 **2.90**	2.09 **2.84**	2.04 **2.74**	1.99 **2.66**	1.93 **2.55**	1.89 **2.47**	1.84 **2.38**	1.79 **2.29**	1.76 **2.24**	1.72 **2.16**	1.69 **2.13**	1.66 **2.07**	1.64 **2.03**	1.62 **2.01**	30
32	4.15 **7.50**	3.30 **5.34**	2.90 **4.46**	2.67 **3.97**	2.51 **3.66**	2.40 **3.42**	2.32 **3.25**	2.25 **3.12**	2.19 **3.01**	2.14 **2.94**	2.10 **2.86**	2.07 **2.80**	2.02 **2.70**	1.97 **2.62**	1.91 **2.51**	1.86 **2.42**	1.82 **2.34**	1.76 **2.25**	1.74 **2.20**	1.69 **2.12**	1.67 **2.08**	1.64 **2.02**	1.61 **1.98**	1.59 **1.96**	32
34	4.13 **7.44**	3.28 **5.29**	2.88 **4.42**	2.65 **3.93**	2.49 **3.61**	2.38 **3.38**	2.30 **3.21**	2.23 **3.08**	2.17 **2.97**	2.12 **2.89**	2.08 **2.82**	2.05 **2.76**	2.00 **2.66**	1.95 **2.58**	1.89 **2.47**	1.84 **2.38**	1.80 **2.30**	1.74 **2.21**	1.71 **2.15**	1.67 **2.08**	1.64 **2.04**	1.61 **1.98**	1.59 **1.94**	1.57 **1.91**	34
36	4.11 **7.39**	3.26 **5.25**	2.86 **4.38**	2.63 **3.89**	2.48 **3.58**	2.36 **3.35**	2.28 **3.18**	2.21 **3.04**	2.15 **2.94**	2.10 **2.86**	2.06 **2.78**	2.03 **2.72**	1.98 **2.62**	1.93 **2.54**	1.87 **2.43**	1.82 **2.35**	1.78 **2.26**	1.72 **2.17**	1.69 **2.12**	1.65 **2.04**	1.62 **2.00**	1.59 **1.94**	1.56 **1.90**	1.55 **1.87**	36
38	4.10 **7.35**	3.25 **5.21**	2.85 **4.34**	2.62 **3.86**	2.46 **3.54**	2.35 **3.32**	2.26 **3.15**	2.19 **3.02**	2.14 **2.91**	2.09 **2.82**	2.05 **2.75**	2.02 **2.69**	1.96 **2.59**	1.92 **2.51**	1.85 **2.40**	1.80 **2.32**	1.76 **2.22**	1.71 **2.14**	1.67 **2.08**	1.63 **2.00**	1.60 **1.97**	1.57 **1.90**	1.54 **1.86**	1.53 **1.84**	38
40	4.08 **7.31**	3.23 **5.18**	2.84 **4.31**	2.61 **3.83**	2.45 **3.51**	2.34 **3.29**	2.25 **3.12**	2.18 **2.99**	2.12 **2.88**	2.07 **2.80**	2.04 **2.73**	2.00 **2.66**	1.95 **2.56**	1.90 **2.49**	1.84 **2.37**	1.79 **2.29**	1.74 **2.20**	1.69 **2.11**	1.66 **2.05**	1.61 **1.97**	1.59 **1.94**	1.55 **1.88**	1.53 **1.84**	1.51 **1.81**	40

Between-group df (Continued)

Within-group df	1	2	3	4	5	6	7	8	9	10	11	12	14	16	20	24	30	40	50	75	100	200	500	∞	
42	4.07 **7.27**	3.22 **5.15**	2.83 **4.29**	2.59 **3.80**	2.44 **3.49**	2.32 **3.26**	2.24 **3.10**	2.17 **2.96**	2.11 **2.86**	2.06 **2.77**	2.02 **2.70**	1.99 **2.64**	1.94 **2.54**	1.89 **2.46**	1.82 **2.35**	1.78 **2.26**	1.73 **2.17**	1.68 **2.08**	1.64 **2.02**	1.60 **1.94**	1.57 **1.91**	1.54 **1.85**	1.51 **1.80**	1.49 **1.78**	42
44	4.06 **7.24**	3.21 **5.12**	2.82 **4.26**	2.58 **3.78**	2.43 **3.46**	2.31 **3.24**	2.23 **3.07**	2.16 **2.94**	2.10 **2.84**	2.05 **2.75**	2.01 **2.68**	1.98 **2.62**	1.92 **2.52**	1.88 **2.44**	1.81 **2.32**	1.76 **2.24**	1.72 **2.15**	1.66 **2.06**	1.63 **2.00**	1.58 **1.92**	1.56 **1.88**	1.52 **1.82**	1.50 **1.78**	1.48 **1.75**	44
46	4.05 **7.21**	3.20 **5.10**	2.81 **4.24**	2.57 **3.76**	2.42 **3.44**	2.30 **3.22**	2.22 **3.05**	2.14 **2.92**	2.09 **2.82**	2.04 **2.73**	2.00 **2.66**	1.97 **2.60**	1.91 **2.50**	1.87 **2.42**	1.80 **2.30**	1.75 **2.22**	1.71 **2.13**	1.65 **2.04**	1.62 **1.98**	1.57 **1.90**	1.54 **1.86**	1.51 **1.80**	1.48 **1.76**	1.46 **1.72**	46
48	4.04 **7.19**	3.19 **5.08**	2.80 **4.22**	2.56 **3.74**	2.41 **3.42**	2.30 **3.20**	2.21 **3.04**	2.14 **2.90**	2.08 **2.80**	2.03 **2.71**	1.99 **2.64**	1.96 **2.58**	1.90 **2.48**	1.86 **2.40**	1.79 **2.28**	1.74 **2.20**	1.70 **2.11**	1.64 **2.02**	1.61 **1.96**	1.56 **1.88**	1.53 **1.84**	1.50 **1.78**	1.47 **1.73**	1.45 **1.70**	48
50	4.03 **7.17**	3.18 **5.06**	2.79 **4.20**	2.56 **3.72**	2.40 **3.41**	2.29 **3.18**	2.20 **3.02**	2.13 **2.88**	2.07 **2.78**	2.02 **2.70**	1.98 **2.62**	1.95 **2.56**	1.90 **2.46**	1.85 **2.39**	1.78 **2.26**	1.74 **2.18**	1.69 **2.10**	1.63 **2.00**	1.60 **1.94**	1.55 **1.86**	1.52 **1.82**	1.48 **1.76**	1.46 **1.71**	1.44 **1.68**	50
55	4.02 **7.12**	3.17 **5.01**	2.78 **4.16**	2.54 **3.68**	2.38 **3.37**	2.27 **3.15**	2.18 **2.98**	2.11 **2.85**	2.05 **2.75**	2.00 **2.66**	1.97 **2.59**	1.93 **2.53**	1.88 **2.43**	1.83 **2.35**	1.76 **2.23**	1.72 **2.15**	1.67 **2.06**	1.61 **1.96**	1.58 **1.90**	1.52 **1.82**	1.50 **1.78**	1.46 **1.71**	1.43 **1.66**	1.41 **1.64**	55
60	4.00 **7.08**	3.15 **4.98**	2.76 **4.13**	2.52 **3.65**	2.37 **3.34**	2.25 **3.12**	2.17 **2.95**	2.10 **2.82**	2.04 **2.72**	1.99 **2.63**	1.95 **2.56**	1.92 **2.50**	1.86 **2.40**	1.81 **2.32**	1.75 **2.20**	1.70 **2.12**	1.65 **2.03**	1.59 **1.93**	1.56 **1.87**	1.50 **1.79**	1.48 **1.74**	1.44 **1.68**	1.41 **1.63**	1.39 **1.60**	60
65	3.99 **7.04**	3.14 **4.95**	2.75 **4.10**	2.51 **3.62**	2.36 **3.31**	2.24 **3.09**	2.15 **2.93**	2.08 **2.79**	2.02 **2.70**	1.98 **2.61**	1.94 **2.54**	1.90 **2.47**	1.85 **2.37**	1.80 **2.30**	1.73 **2.18**	1.68 **2.09**	1.63 **2.00**	1.57 **1.90**	1.54 **1.84**	1.49 **1.76**	1.46 **1.71**	1.42 **1.64**	1.39 **1.60**	1.37 **1.56**	65
70	3.98 **7.01**	3.13 **4.92**	2.74 **4.08**	2.50 **3.60**	2.35 **3.29**	2.23 **3.07**	2.14 **2.91**	2.07 **2.77**	2.01 **2.67**	1.97 **2.59**	1.93 **2.51**	1.89 **2.45**	1.84 **2.35**	1.79 **2.28**	1.72 **2.15**	1.67 **2.07**	1.62 **1.98**	1.56 **1.88**	1.53 **1.82**	1.47 **1.74**	1.45 **1.69**	1.40 **1.62**	1.37 **1.56**	1.35 **1.53**	70
80	3.96 **6.96**	3.11 **4.88**	2.72 **4.04**	2.48 **3.56**	2.33 **3.25**	2.21 **3.04**	2.12 **2.87**	2.05 **2.74**	1.99 **2.64**	1.95 **2.55**	1.91 **2.48**	1.88 **2.41**	1.82 **2.32**	1.77 **2.24**	1.70 **2.11**	1.65 **2.03**	1.60 **1.94**	1.54 **1.84**	1.51 **1.78**	1.45 **1.70**	1.42 **1.65**	1.38 **1.57**	1.35 **1.52**	1.32 **1.49**	80
100	3.94 **6.90**	3.09 **4.82**	2.70 **3.98**	2.46 **3.51**	2.30 **3.20**	2.19 **2.99**	2.10 **2.82**	2.03 **2.69**	1.97 **2.59**	1.92 **2.51**	1.88 **2.43**	1.85 **2.36**	1.79 **2.26**	1.75 **2.19**	1.68 **2.06**	1.63 **1.98**	1.57 **1.89**	1.51 **1.79**	1.48 **1.73**	1.42 **1.64**	1.39 **1.59**	1.34 **1.51**	1.30 **1.46**	1.28 **1.43**	100
125	3.92 **6.84**	3.07 **4.78**	2.68 **3.94**	2.44 **3.47**	2.29 **3.17**	2.17 **2.95**	2.08 **2.79**	2.01 **2.65**	1.95 **2.56**	1.90 **2.47**	1.86 **2.40**	1.83 **2.33**	1.77 **2.23**	1.72 **2.15**	1.65 **2.03**	1.60 **1.94**	1.55 **1.85**	1.49 **1.75**	1.45 **1.68**	1.39 **1.59**	1.36 **1.54**	1.31 **1.46**	1.27 **1.40**	1.25 **1.37**	125
150	3.91 **6.81**	3.06 **4.75**	2.67 **3.91**	2.43 **3.44**	2.27 **3.14**	2.16 **2.92**	2.07 **2.76**	2.00 **2.62**	1.94 **2.53**	1.89 **2.44**	1.85 **2.37**	1.82 **2.30**	1.76 **2.20**	1.71 **2.12**	1.64 **2.00**	1.59 **1.91**	1.54 **1.83**	1.47 **1.72**	1.44 **1.66**	1.37 **1.56**	1.34 **1.51**	1.29 **1.43**	1.25 **1.37**	1.22 **1.33**	150
200	3.89 **6.76**	3.04 **4.71**	2.65 **3.88**	2.41 **3.41**	2.26 **3.11**	2.14 **2.90**	2.05 **2.73**	1.98 **2.60**	1.92 **2.50**	1.87 **2.41**	1.83 **2.34**	1.80 **2.28**	1.74 **2.17**	1.69 **2.09**	1.62 **1.97**	1.57 **1.88**	1.52 **1.79**	1.45 **1.69**	1.42 **1.62**	1.35 **1.53**	1.32 **1.48**	1.26 **1.39**	1.22 **1.33**	1.19 **1.28**	200
400	3.86 **6.70**	3.02 **4.66**	2.62 **3.83**	2.39 **3.36**	2.23 **3.06**	2.12 **2.85**	2.03 **2.69**	1.96 **2.55**	1.90 **2.46**	1.85 **2.37**	1.81 **2.29**	1.78 **2.23**	1.72 **2.12**	1.67 **2.04**	1.60 **1.92**	1.54 **1.84**	1.49 **1.74**	1.42 **1.64**	1.38 **1.57**	1.32 **1.47**	1.28 **1.42**	1.22 **1.32**	1.16 **1.24**	1.13 **1.19**	400
1000	3.85 **6.66**	3.00 **4.62**	2.61 **3.80**	2.38 **3.34**	2.22 **3.04**	2.10 **2.82**	2.02 **2.66**	1.95 **2.53**	1.89 **2.43**	1.84 **2.34**	1.80 **2.26**	1.76 **2.20**	1.70 **2.09**	1.65 **2.01**	1.58 **1.89**	1.53 **1.81**	1.47 **1.71**	1.41 **1.61**	1.36 **1.54**	1.30 **1.44**	1.26 **1.38**	1.19 **1.28**	1.13 **1.19**	1.08 **1.11**	1000
∞	3.84 **6.64**	2.99 **4.60**	2.60 **3.78**	2.37 **3.32**	2.21 **3.02**	2.09 **2.80**	2.01 **2.64**	1.94 **2.51**	1.88 **2.41**	1.83 **2.32**	1.79 **2.24**	1.75 **2.18**	1.69 **2.07**	1.64 **1.99**	1.57 **1.87**	1.52 **1.79**	1.46 **1.69**	1.40 **1.59**	1.35 **1.52**	1.28 **1.41**	1.24 **1.36**	1.17 **1.25**	1.11 **1.15**	1.00 **1.00**	∞

APPENDIX E

Critical Values of Chi-Square

df	.01	.05	.10
1	6.64	3.84	2.71
2	9.21	5.99	4.60
3	11.34	7.82	6.25
4	13.28	9.49	7.78
5	15.09	11.07	9.24
6	16.81	12.59	10.64
7	18.48	14.07	12.02
8	20.09	15.51	13.36
9	21.67	16.92	14.68
10	23.21	18.31	15.99
11	24.72	19.68	17.28
12	26.22	21.03	18.55
13	27.69	22.36	19.81
14	29.14	23.68	21.06
15	30.58	25.00	22.31
16	32.00	26.97	23.54
17	33.41	27.59	24.77

Source: Abridged from Table IV of Fisher and Yates, *Statistical Tables for Biological, Agricultural, and Medical Research,* published by Oliver and Boyd Ltd., Edinburgh, and by permission of the authors and publishers.

(The significance level for each value is given at the top of the column.)

APPENDIX E (continued)

df	.01	.05	.10
18	34.80	28.87	25.99
19	36.19	30.14	27.20
20	37.57	31.41	28.41
21	38.93	32.67	29.62
22	40.29	33.92	30.81
23	41.64	35.17	32.01
24	42.98	36.42	33.20
25	44.31	37.65	34.38
26	45.64	38.88	35.56
27	46.96	40.11	36.74
28	48.28	41.34	37.92
29	49.59	42.56	39.09
30	50.89	43.77	40.26

APPENDIX F

Glossary of Formulas

- Chi-Square
- Pearson Product-Moment Correlation
- *F* test
- Linear Regression Equation
- Mean
- Median
- Omega Squared
- Range
- Scheffé Method of Post hoc Analysis
- Spearman Rank Correlation
- Standard Deviation
- *t* Test
- Variance
- Yates' Correction for Continuity
- *Z* Score

CHI-SQUARE

$$\chi^2 = \sum\left[\frac{(O_i - E_i)^2}{E_i}\right]$$

Where: O_i = the observed frequency

E_i = the expected frequency

F TEST

$$F_{obt} = \frac{MS_B}{MS_W}$$

Where: $MS_W = \frac{SS_W}{df_W}$

$MS_B = \frac{SS_B}{df_B}$

LINEAR REGRESSION EQUATION

$$\hat{Y} = \overline{Y} + b(X - \overline{X})$$

Where: $\hat{Y}$ = predicted value of Y

X = score on variable X

$\overline{X}, \overline{Y}$ = means of variables X and Y

$$b = r_{xy}\left(\frac{SD_y}{SD_x}\right)$$

MEAN

$$\overline{X} = \frac{\Sigma X}{N}$$

Where: Σ = "the sum of"

X = each obtained score

N = total number of scores

OMEGA-SQUARED

$$\hat{\omega}^2 = \frac{SS_B - (K - 1)MS_W}{SS_T + MS_W}$$

Where: $MS_W = \frac{SS_W}{df_W}$

$MS_B = \frac{SS_B}{df_B}$

$SS_T = SS_W + SS_B$

K = Number of groups

PEARSON PRODUCT-MOMENT CORRELATION COEFFICIENT

$$r_{xy} = \frac{Cov_{xy}}{SD_x SD_y}$$

Where: $Cov_{xy} = \frac{\Sigma(X - \overline{X})(Y - \overline{Y})}{N - 1}$ or $\frac{\Sigma xy}{N - 1}$

$x = (X - \overline{X})$, the deviation scores for X

$y = (Y - \overline{Y})$, the deviation scores for Y

Σxy = the sum of the products of the paired deviation scores

N = number of pairs of scores

SD_x = standard deviation of X

SD_y = standard deviation of Y

RANGE

$$Range = H - L$$

Where: H = the highest score

L = the lowest score

SCHEFFÉ METHOD OF POST HOC ANALYSIS

$$C_{obt} = \frac{\overline{X}_1 - \overline{X}_2}{\sqrt{MS_W\left(\frac{1}{N_1} + \frac{1}{N_2}\right)}}$$

Where: $\overline{X}_1, \overline{X}_2$ are the means of two groups being compared

N_1, N_2 are the Ns of those two groups

MS_W is the within-group mean square from your ANOVA

SPEARMAN RANK CORRELATION COEFFICIENT

$$r_s = \frac{Cov_{xy}}{SD_x SD_y}$$

Where: X, Y = ranks

STANDARD DEVIATION (SD)

$$SD^2 = \sqrt{\frac{\Sigma(X - \overline{X})^2}{N-1}}$$

Where: Σ = "the sum of," X refers to each obtained score

$\overline{X}$ = the mean of X

N = to the total number of scores

STANDARD ERROR OF ESTIMATE

$$\sigma_{est} = SD_y\sqrt{(1 - r_{xy}^2)}$$

Where: SD_Y = the standard deviation of variable Y

r_{xy} = the correlation between variables X and Y

t TEST OF DEPENDENT (MATCHED) SAMPLES

$$t_{obt} = \frac{\overline{X}_1 - \overline{X}_2}{\sqrt{S_{\overline{x}_1}^2 + S_{\overline{x}_1}^2 - 2r_{12}S_{\overline{x}_1}S_{\overline{x}_2}}}$$

Where: $\overline{X}_1, \overline{X}_2$ = the means of the two measurement

$S_{\bar{x}1}\, S_{\bar{x}2}$ = the standard error of the means $\left(\frac{S}{\sqrt{N}}\right)$

r_{12} = the correlation between the two measurements

t TEST OF INDEPENDENT SAMPLES

$$t_{obt} = \frac{\overline{X}_1 - \overline{X}_2}{\sqrt{\left[\frac{(n_1 - 1)SD_1^2 + (n_2 - 1)SD_2^2}{n_1 + n_2 - 2}\right]\left(\frac{1}{n_1} + \frac{1}{n_2}\right)}}$$

Where: t_{obt} = the value of *t* obtained through your data

n_1, n_2 = the number of participants in Group 1 (n_1) and Group 2 (n_2)

SD_1^2, SD_2^2 = the estimates of the variances of the two populations

$\overline{X}_1, \overline{X}_2$ = the means of the two groups

VARIANCE (SD^2)

$$SD^2 = \frac{\sum(X - \overline{X})^2}{N - 1}$$

Where: $\sum$ = "the sum of," *X* refers to each obtained score

$\overline{X}$ = the mean of *X*

N = to the total number of scores

YATES' CORRECTION FOR CONTINUITY

$$\chi_Y^2 = \sum\left[\frac{(|O_i - E_i| - .5)^2}{E_i}\right]$$

Where: O_i = the observed frequency

E_i = the expected frequency

Z SCORE

$$Z = \frac{X - \overline{X}}{SD_x}$$

Where: *X* = an individual's raw score

$\overline{X}$ = the mean raw score

SD_x = the standard deviation

INDEX